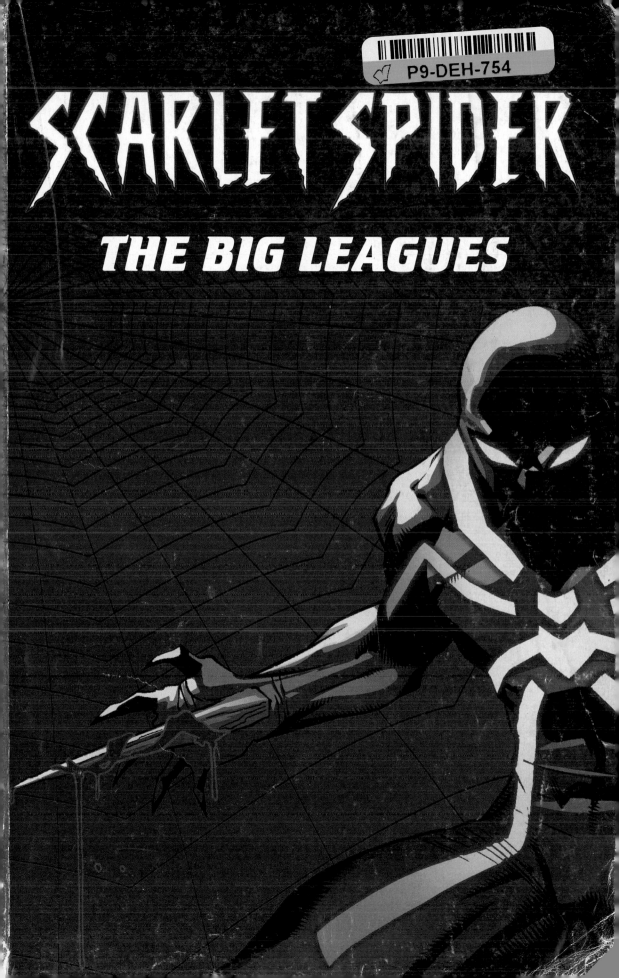

SCARLET SPIDER

THE BIG LEAGUES

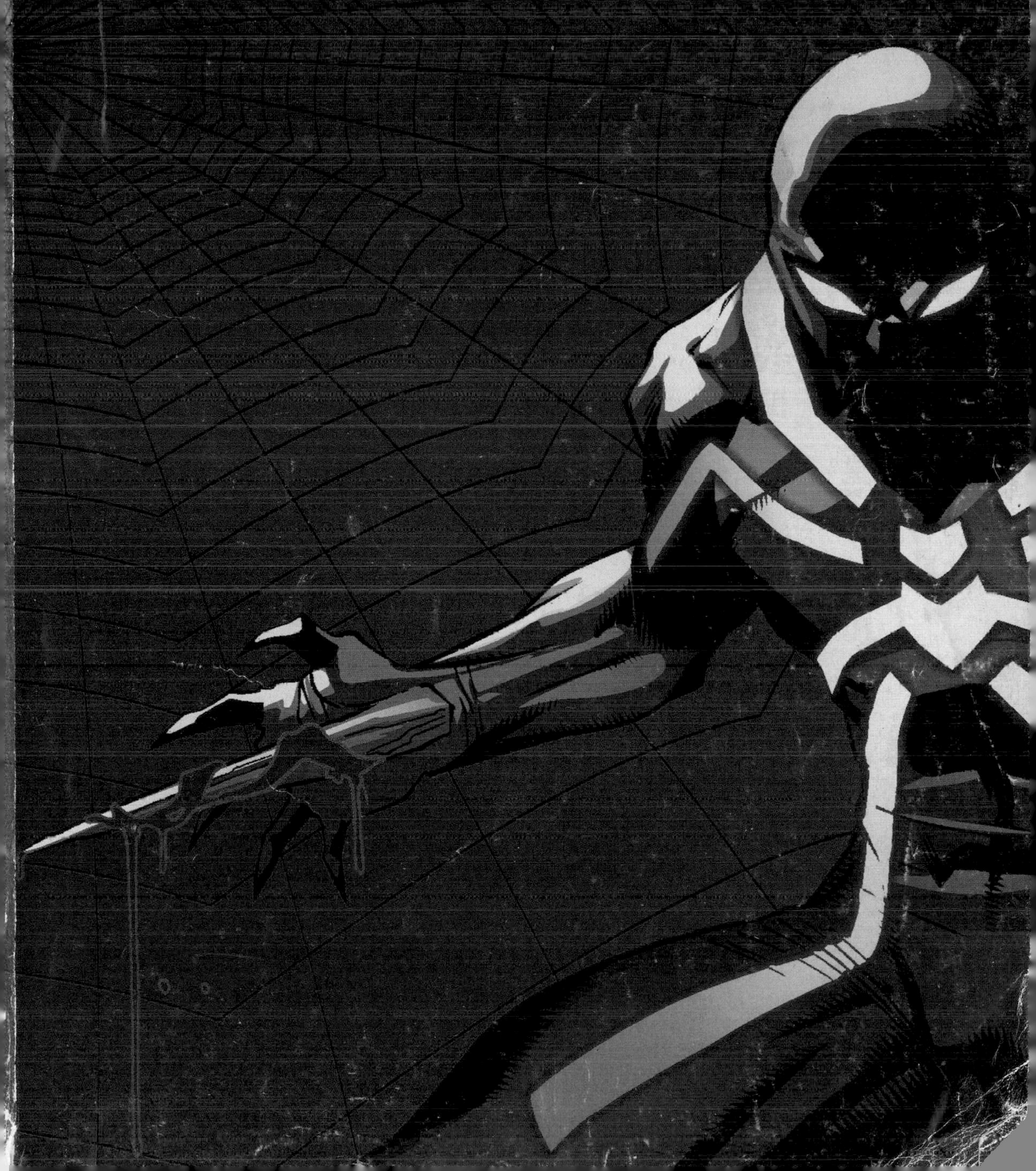

SCARLET SPIDER

THE BIG LEAGUES

SCARLET SPIDER #16

WRITER: **CHRIS YOST**
PENCILER: **KHOI PHAM**
INKERS: **TERRY PALLOT** & **VICTOR OLAZABA**
COLORIST: **ANTONIO FABELA**

SCARLET SPIDER #17-19

WRITER: **CHRIS YOST** WITH **ERIK BURNHAM** (#19)
PENCILER: **CARLO BARBERI** WITH **ALÉ GARZA** (#18)
INKER: **WALDEN WONG** WITH **TERRY PALLOT** & **BIT** (#19)
ADDITIONAL ART (#19): **HORACIO DOMINGUES**
COLORIST: **REX LOKUS** WITH **ANTONIO FABELA** & **CHRIS SOTOMAYOR** (#19)

SCARLET SPIDER #20

WRITERS: **CHRIS YOST** & **ERIK BURNHAM**
ARTIST: **K-STUDIO'S IN-HYUK LEE**
DREAM SEQUENCE PENCILER: **PAT OLLIFFE**
DREAM SEQUENCE INKER: **BIT**
DREAM SEQUENCE COLORIST: **LEE LOUGHRIDGE**
EPILOGUE PENCILER: **PACO MEDINA**
EPILOGUE INKER: **JUAN VLASCO**
EPILOGUE COLORIST: **LEE LOUGHRIDGE**

LETTERER: **VC'S JOE CARAMAGNA**
COVER ARTISTS: **RYAN STEGMAN** & **EDGAR DELGADO** (#16-18 & #20) WITH **JORDIE BELLAIRE** (#19)
EDITOR: **TOM BRENNAN**
SENIOR EDITOR: **STEPHEN WACKER**

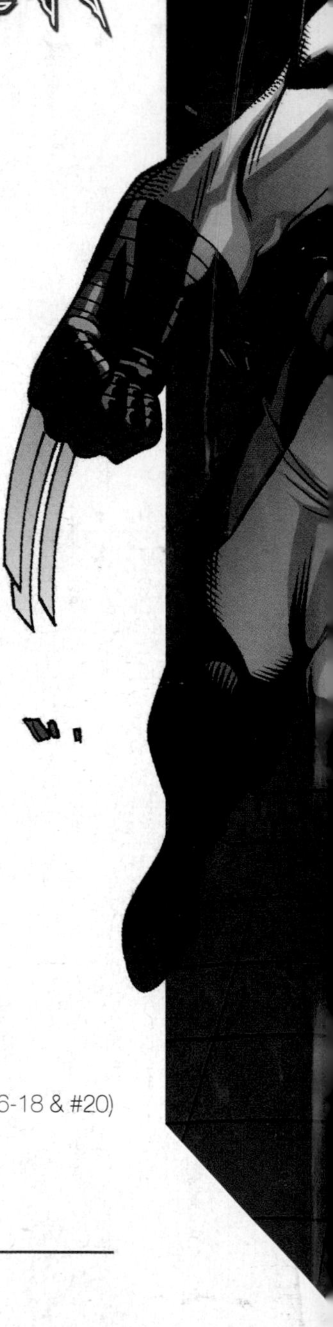

SUPERIOR SPIDER-MAN TEAM-UP #2

WRITER: **CHRIS YOST**
ARTIST: **MARCO CHECCHETTO**
COLOR ARTIST: **RACHELLE ROSENBERG**
LETTERER: **VC'S JOE CARAMAGNA**
COVER ARTISTS: **PAOLO RIVERA** & **JOE RIVERA**
ASSOCIATE EDITOR: **TOM BRENNAN**
EDITOR: **SANA AMANAT**
SENIOR EDITOR: **STEPHEN WACKER**

COLLECTION EDITOR & DESIGN: CORY LEVINE
ASSISTANT EDITORS: ALEX STARBUCK & NELSON RIBEIRO
EDITORS, SPECIAL PROJECTS: JENNIFER GRÜNWALD & MARK D. BEAZLEY
SENIOR EDITOR, SPECIAL PROJECTS: JEFF YOUNGQUIST
SVP OF PRINT & DIGITAL PUBLISHING SALES: DAVID GABRIEL

EDITOR IN CHIEF: AXEL ALONSO
CHIEF CREATIVE OFFICER: JOE QUESADA
PUBLISHER: DAN BUCKLEY
EXECUTIVE PRODUCER: ALAN FINE

SCARLET SPIDER VOL. 3: THE BIG LEAGUES. Contains material originally published in magazine form as SCARLET SPIDER #16-20 and SUPERIOR SPIDER-MAN TEAM-UP #2. First printing 2013. ISBN# 978-0-7851-6649-8. Published by MARVEL WORLDWIDE, INC., a subsidiary of MARVEL ENTERTAINMENT, LLC. OFFICE OF PUBLICATION: 135 West 50th Street, New York, NY 10020. Copyright © 2013 Marvel Characters, Inc. All rights reserved. All characters featured in this issue and the distinctive names and likenesses thereof, and all related indicia are trademarks of Marvel Characters, Inc. No similarity between any of the names, characters, persons, and/or institutions in this magazine with those of any living or dead person or institution is intended, and any such similarity which may exist is purely coincidental. **Printed in the U.S.A.** ALAN FINE, EVP - Office of the President, Marvel Worldwide, Inc. and EVP & CMO Marvel Characters B.V.; DAN BUCKLEY, Publisher & President - Print, Animation & Digital Divisions; JOE QUESADA, Chief Creative Officer; TOM BREVOORT, SVP of Publishing; DAVID BOGART, SVP of Operations & Procurement, Publishing; C.B. CEBULSKI, SVP of Creator & Content Development; DAVID GABRIEL, SVP of Print & Digital Publishing Sales; JIM O'KEEFE, VP of Operations & Logistics; DAN CARR, Executive Director of Publishing Technology; SUSAN CRESPI, Editorial Operations Manager; ALEX MORALES, Publishing Operations Manager; STAN LEE, Chairman Emeritus. For information regarding advertising in Marvel Comics or on Marvel.com, please contact Niza Disla, Director of Marvel Partnerships, at ndisla@marvel.com. For Marvel subscription inquiries, please call 800-217-9158. **Manufactured between 9/6/2013 and 10/14/2013 by QUAD/GRAPHICS, VERSAILLES, KY, USA.**

10 9 8 7 6 5 4 3 2 1

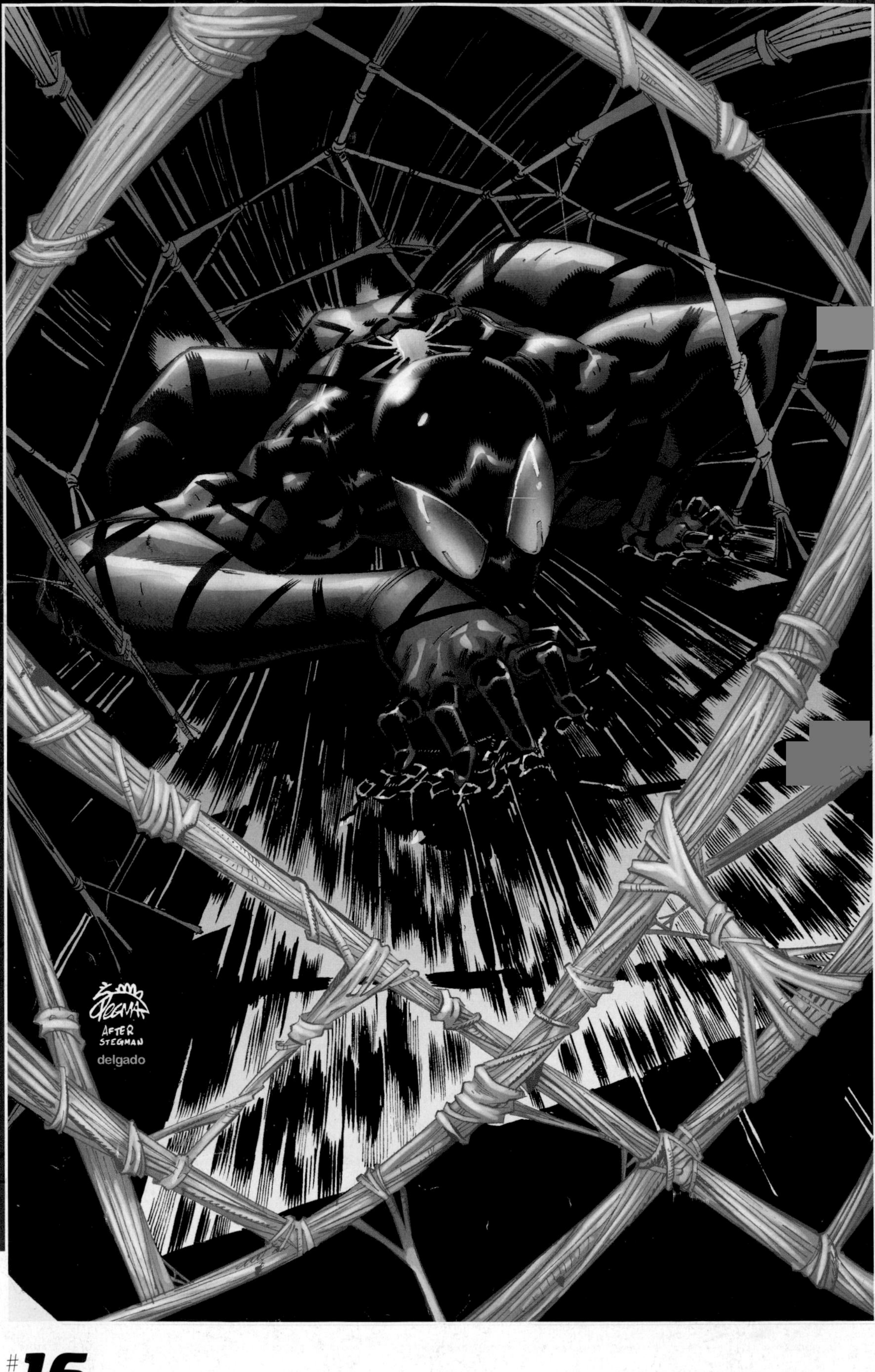
STEGMAN
AFTER
STEGMAN
delgado

#16

"A GOOD, OL' FASHIONED RODEO"

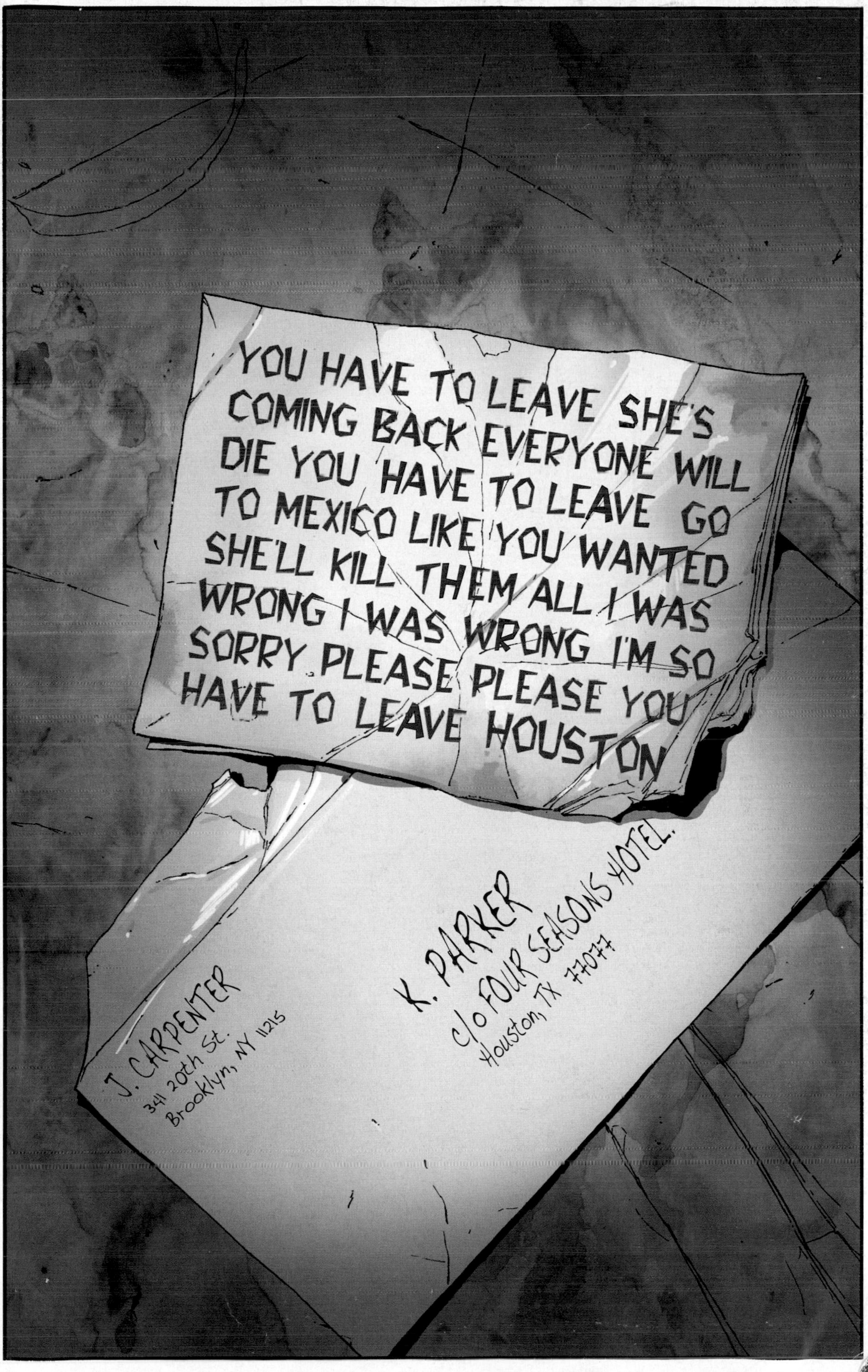

YOU HAVE TO LEAVE SHE'S COMING BACK EVERYONE WILL DIE YOU HAVE TO LEAVE GO TO MEXICO LIKE YOU WANTED SHE'LL KILL THEM ALL I WAS WRONG I WAS WRONG I'M SO SORRY PLEASE PLEASE YOU HAVE TO LEAVE HOUSTON
J. CARPENTER
341 20th St.
Brooklyn, NY 11215
K. PARKER
c/o FOUR SEASONS HOTEL.
Houston, TX 77077

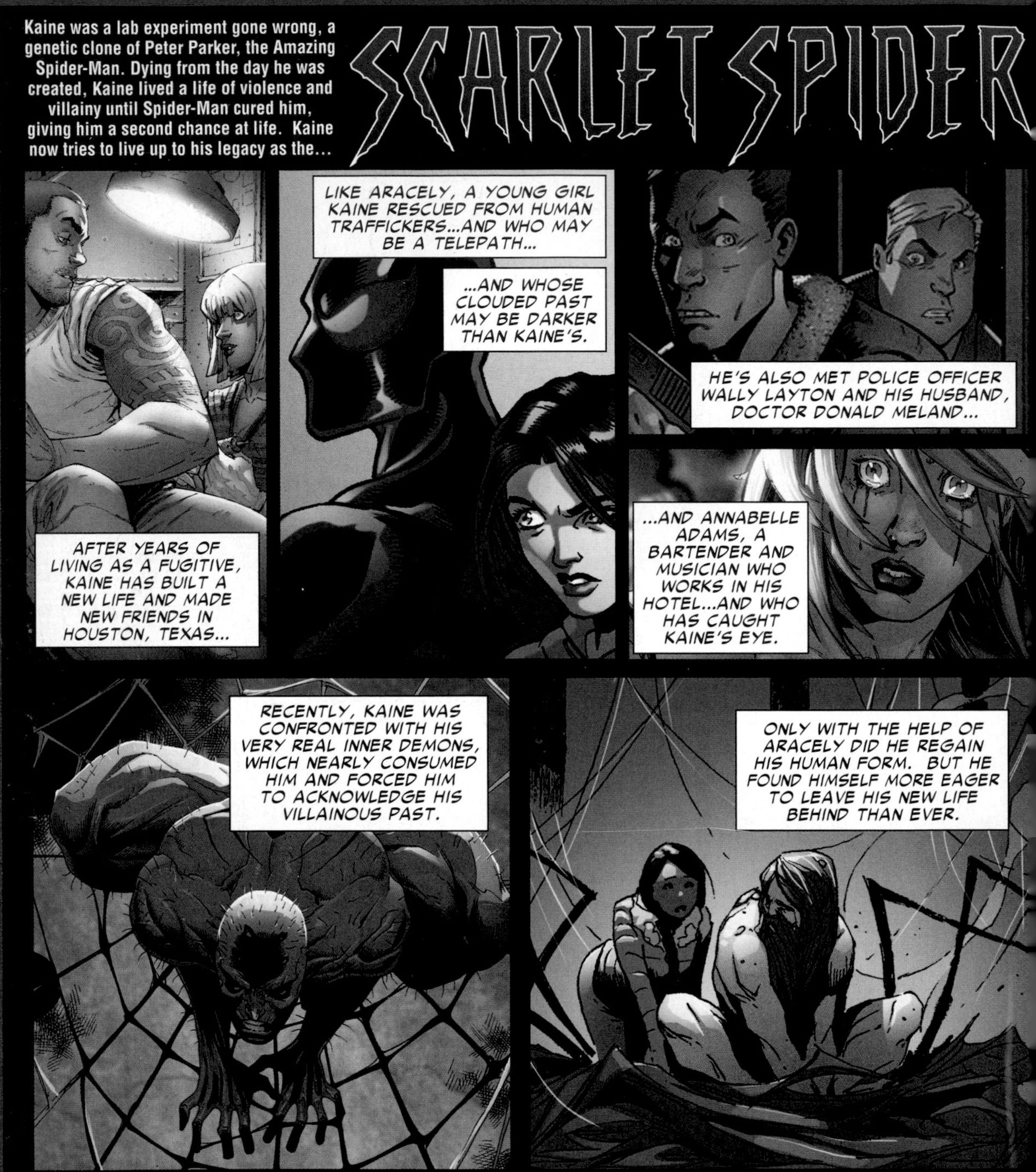
Kaine was a lab experiment gone wrong, a genetic clone of Peter Parker, the Amazing Spider-Man. Dying from the day he was created, Kaine lived a life of violence and villainy until Spider-Man cured him, giving him a second chance at life. Kaine now tries to live up to his legacy as the...
SCARLET SPIDER
AFTER YEARS OF LIVING AS A FUGITIVE, KAINE HAS BUILT A NEW LIFE AND MADE NEW FRIENDS IN HOUSTON, TEXAS...
LIKE ARACELY, A YOUNG GIRL KAINE RESCUED FROM HUMAN TRAFFICKERS...AND WHO MAY BE A TELEPATH...
...AND WHOSE CLOUDED PAST MAY BE DARKER THAN KAINE'S.
HE'S ALSO MET POLICE OFFICER WALLY LAYTON AND HIS HUSBAND, DOCTOR DONALD MELAND...
...AND ANNABELLE ADAMS, A BARTENDER AND MUSICIAN WHO WORKS IN HIS HOTEL...AND WHO HAS CAUGHT KAINE'S EYE.
RECENTLY, KAINE WAS CONFRONTED WITH HIS VERY REAL INNER DEMONS, WHICH NEARLY CONSUMED HIM AND FORCED HIM TO ACKNOWLEDGE HIS VILLAINOUS PAST.
ONLY WITH THE HELP OF ARACELY DID HE REGAIN HIS HUMAN FORM. BUT HE FOUND HIMSELF MORE EAGER TO LEAVE HIS NEW LIFE BEHIND THAN EVER.

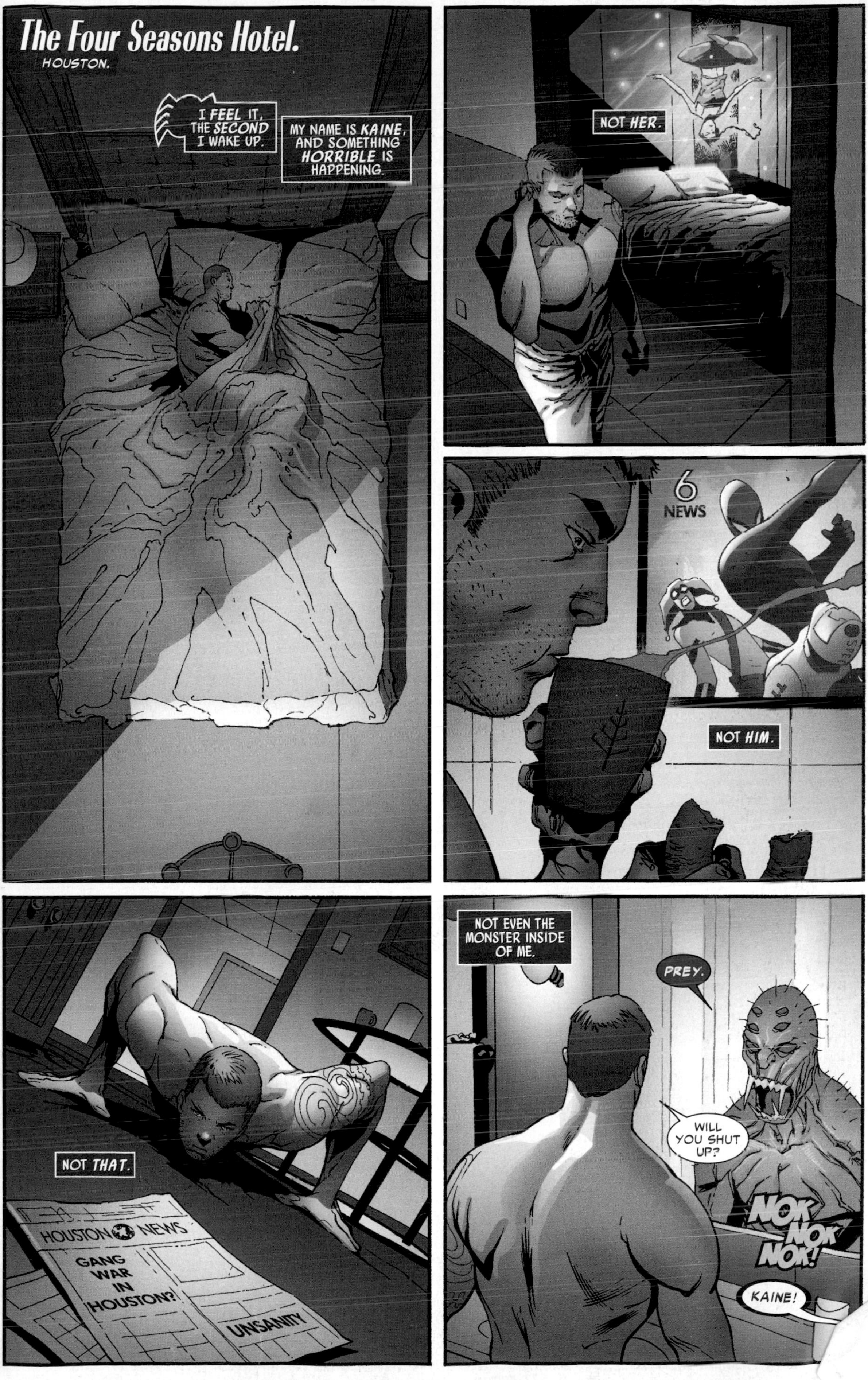

The Four Seasons Hotel.
HOUSTON.
I FEEL IT, THE SECOND I WAKE UP.
MY NAME IS KAINE, AND SOMETHING HORRIBLE IS HAPPENING.
NOT HER.
6 NEWS
NOT HIM.
NOT THAT.
HOUSTON NEWS
GANG WAR IN HOUSTON?
UNSANITY
NOT EVEN THE MONSTER INSIDE OF ME.
PREY.
WILL YOU SHUT UP?
NOK NOK NOK!
KAINE!

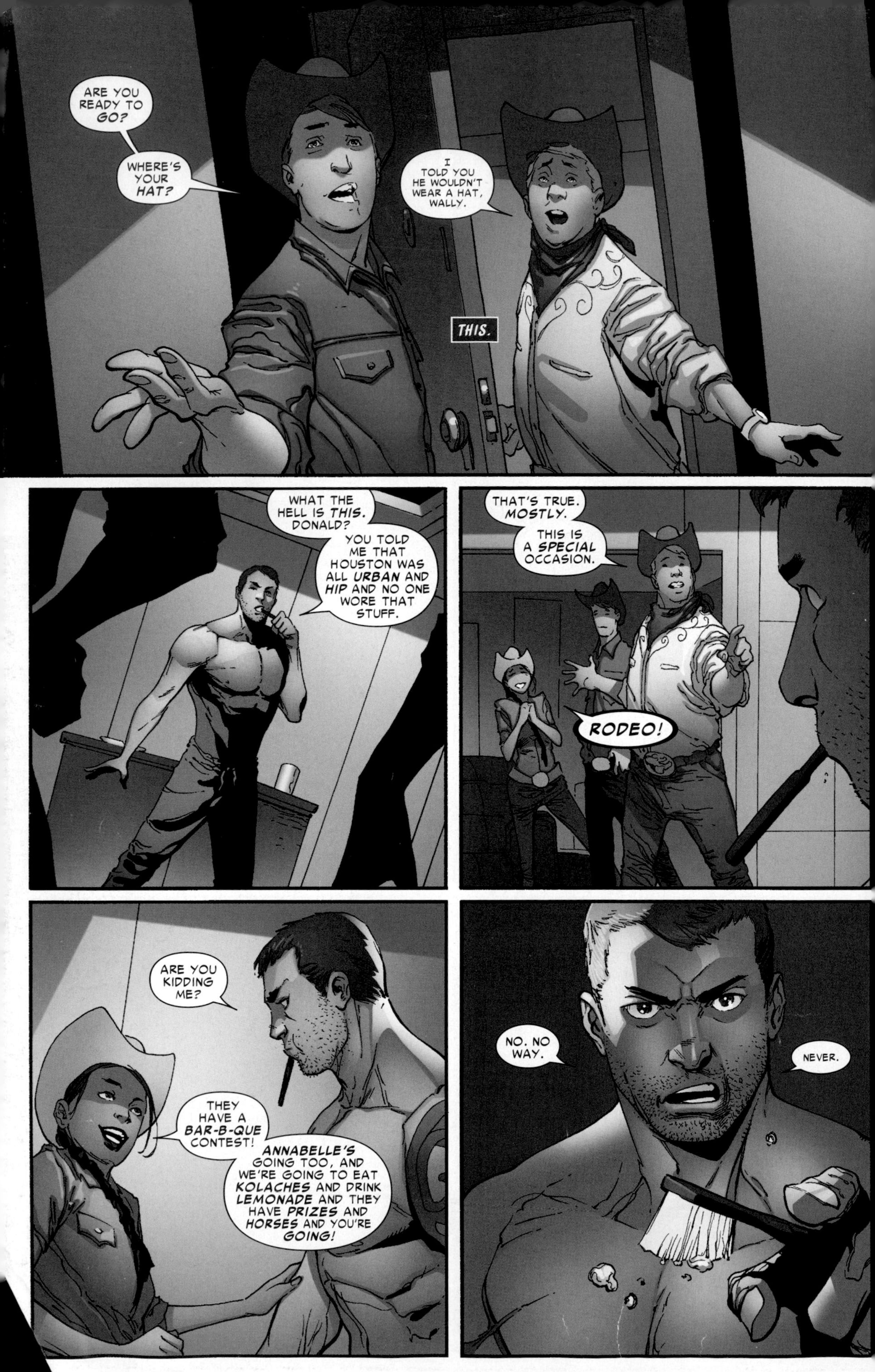
ARE YOU READY TO GO?
WHERE'S YOUR HAT?
I TOLD YOU HE WOULDN'T WEAR A HAT, WALLY.
THIS.
WHAT THE HELL IS THIS. DONALD?
YOU TOLD ME THAT HOUSTON WAS ALL URBAN AND HIP AND NO ONE WORE THAT STUFF.
THAT'S TRUE. MOSTLY.
THIS IS A SPECIAL OCCASION.
RODEO!
ARE YOU KIDDING ME?
THEY HAVE A BAR-B-QUE CONTEST!
ANNABELLE'S GOING TOO, AND WE'RE GOING TO EAT KOLACHES AND DRINK LEMONADE AND THEY HAVE PRIZES AND HORSES AND YOU'RE GOING!
NO. NO WAY.
NEVER.

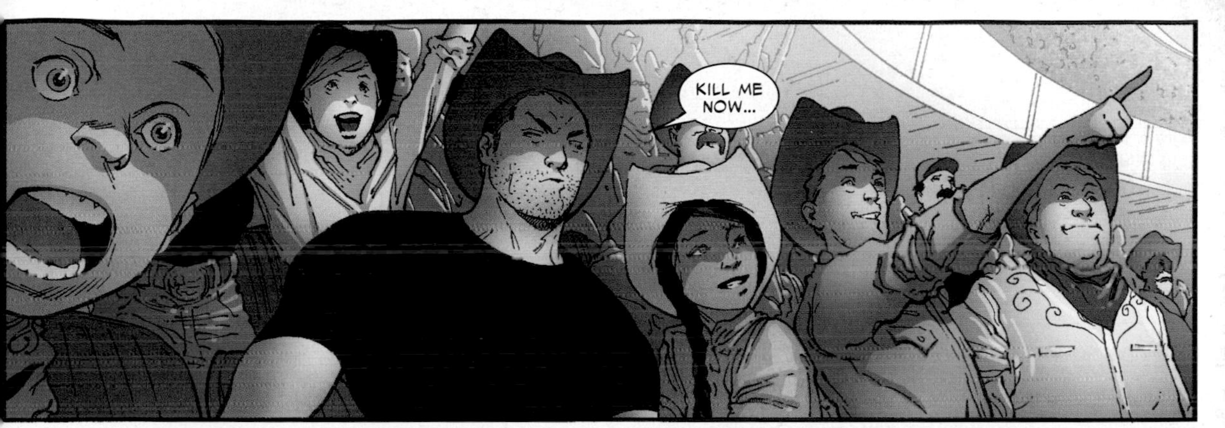
KILL ME NOW...

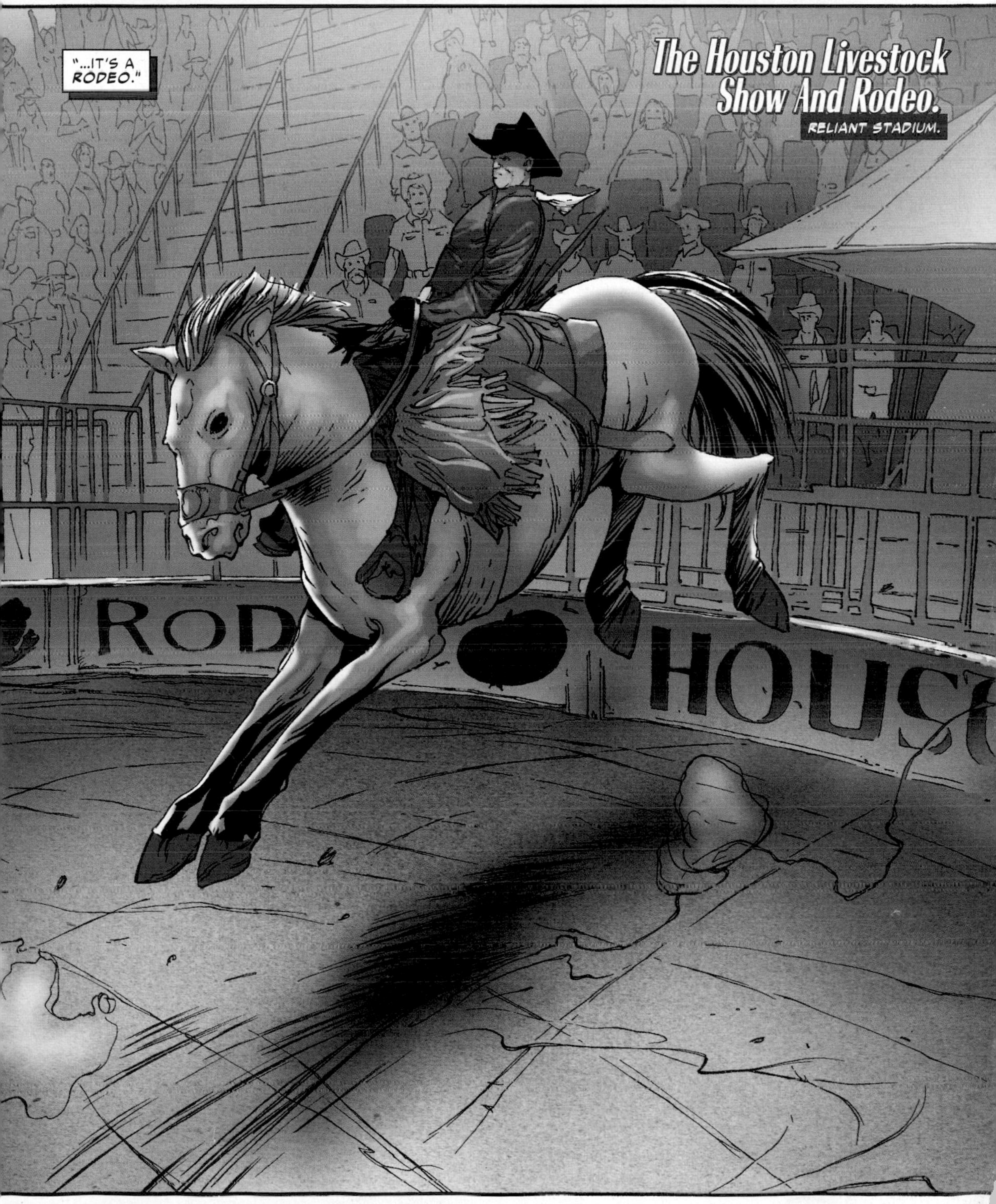
"...IT'S A RODEO."
The Houston Livestock Show And Rodeo.
RELIANT STADIUM.
RODE
HOUS

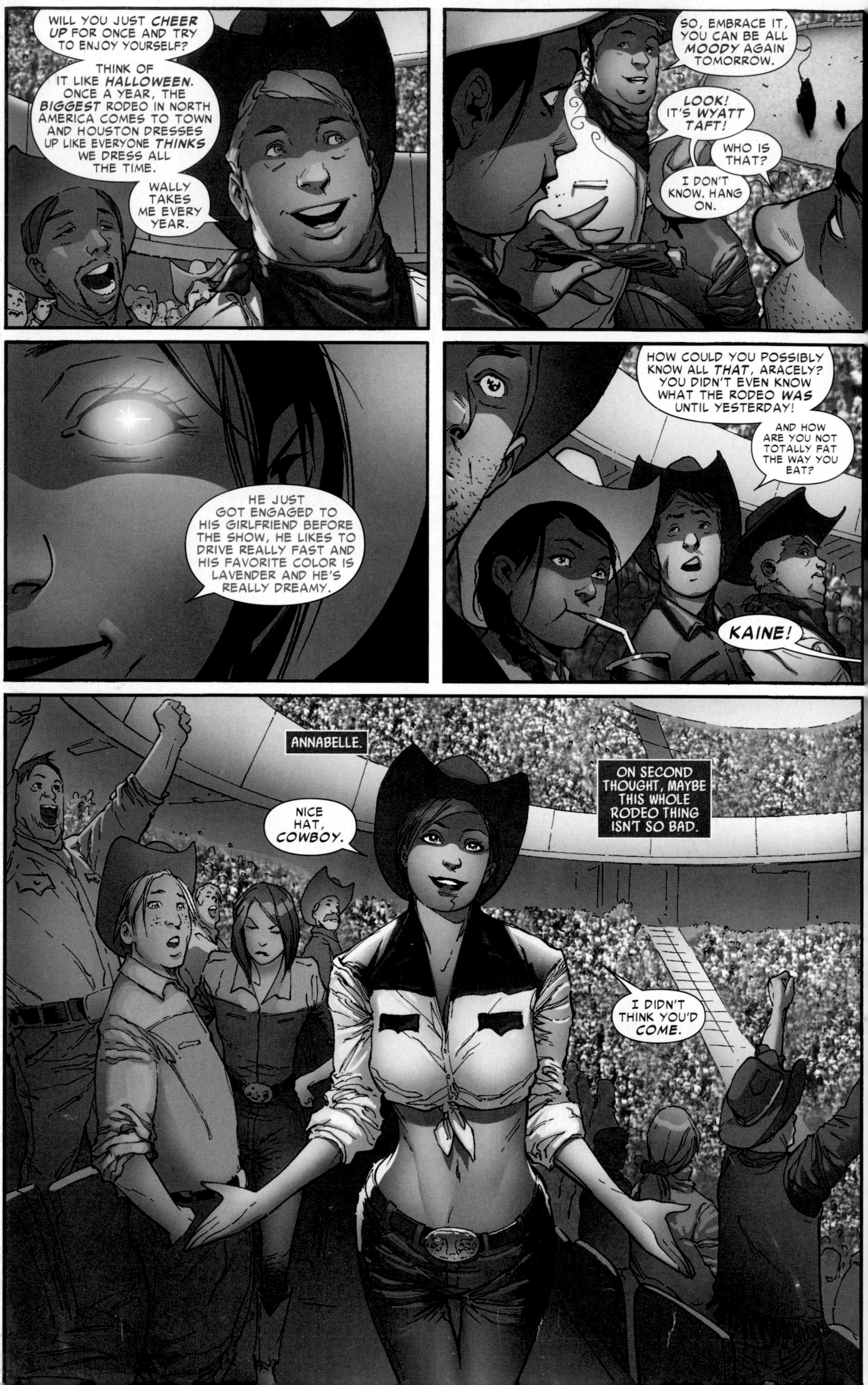
WILL YOU JUST CHEER UP FOR ONCE AND TRY TO ENJOY YOURSELF?
THINK OF IT LIKE HALLOWEEN. ONCE A YEAR, THE BIGGEST RODEO IN NORTH AMERICA COMES TO TOWN AND HOUSTON DRESSES UP LIKE EVERYONE THINKS WE DRESS ALL THE TIME.
WALLY TAKES ME EVERY YEAR.
SO, EMBRACE IT, YOU CAN BE ALL MOODY AGAIN TOMORROW.
LOOK! IT'S WYATT TAFT!
WHO IS THAT?
I DON'T KNOW. HANG ON.
HE JUST GOT ENGAGED TO HIS GIRLFRIEND BEFORE THE SHOW, HE LIKES TO DRIVE REALLY FAST AND HIS FAVORITE COLOR IS LAVENDER AND HE'S REALLY DREAMY.
HOW COULD YOU POSSIBLY KNOW ALL THAT, ARACELY? YOU DIDN'T EVEN KNOW WHAT THE RODEO WAS UNTIL YESTERDAY!
AND HOW ARE YOU NOT TOTALLY FAT THE WAY YOU EAT?
KAINE!
ANNABELLE.
NICE HAT, COWBOY.
ON SECOND THOUGHT, MAYBE THIS WHOLE RODEO THING ISN'T SO BAD.
I DIDN'T THINK YOU'D COME.

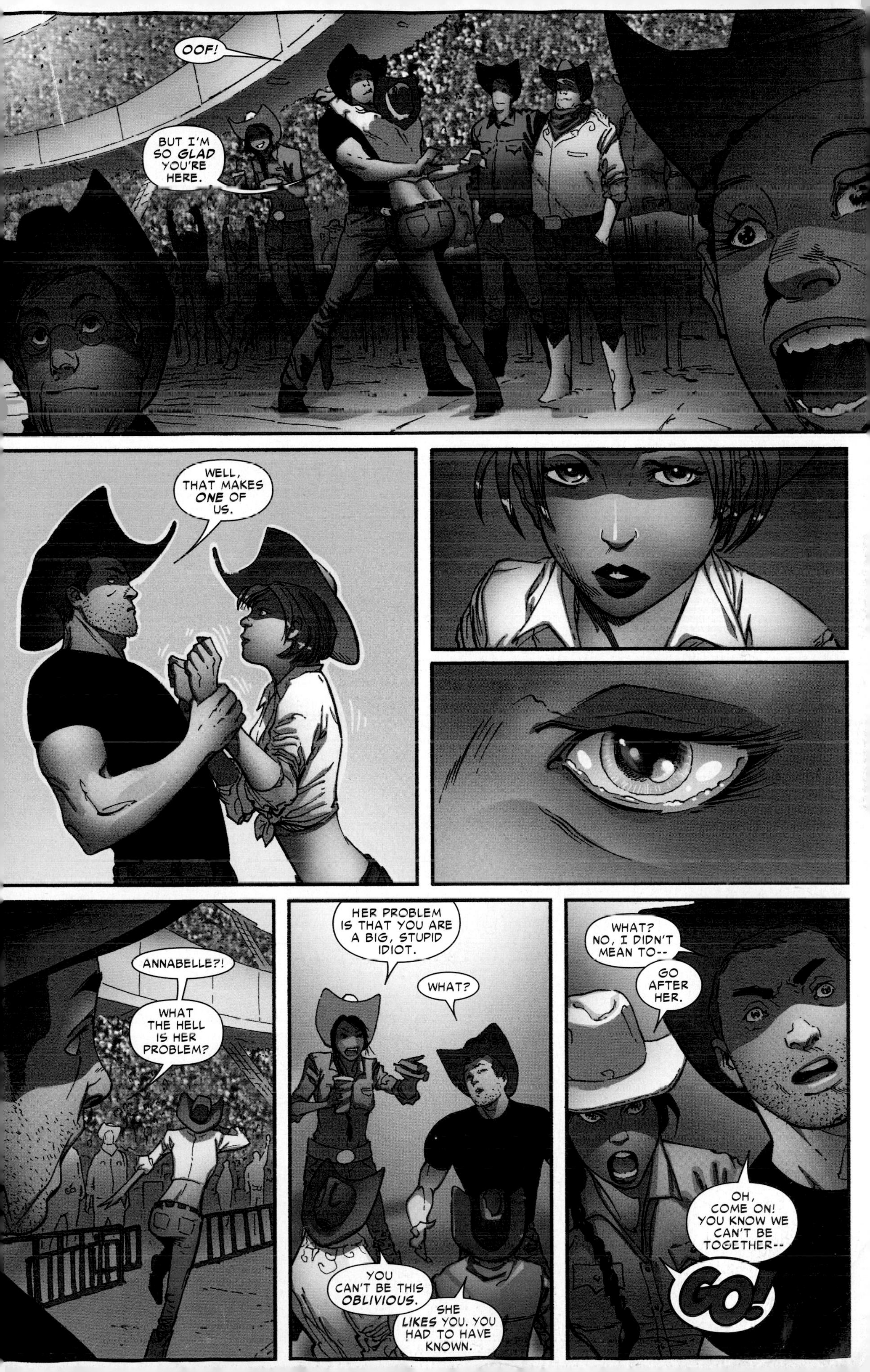
OOF!
BUT I'M SO GLAD YOU'RE HERE.
WELL, THAT MAKES ONE OF US.
ANNABELLE?!
WHAT THE HELL IS HER PROBLEM?
HER PROBLEM IS THAT YOU ARE A BIG, STUPID IDIOT.
WHAT?
YOU CAN'T BE THIS OBLIVIOUS.
SHE LIKES YOU. YOU HAD TO HAVE KNOWN.
WHAT? NO, I DIDN'T MEAN TO--
GO AFTER HER.
OH, COME ON! YOU KNOW WE CAN'T BE TOGETHER--
GO!

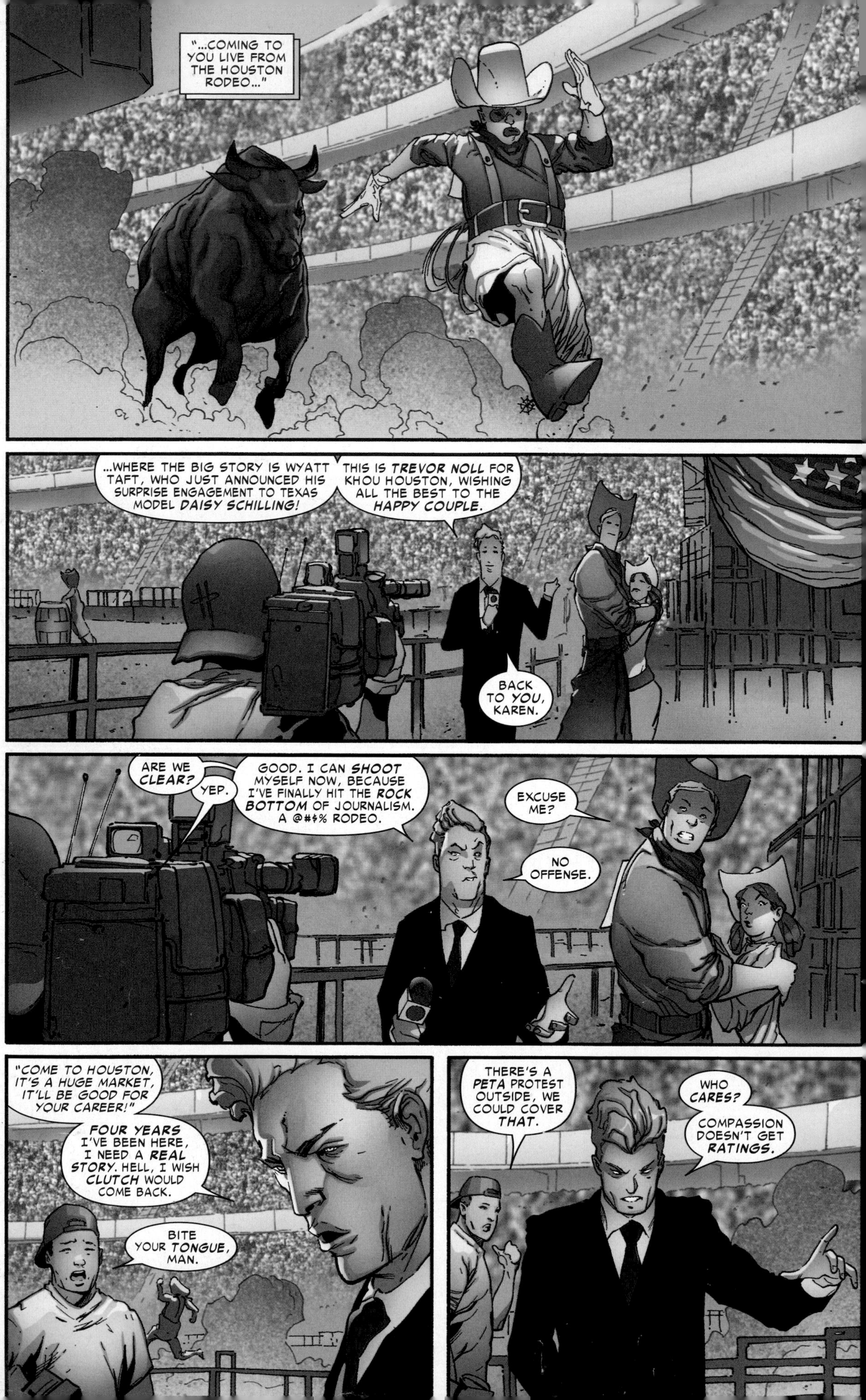
"...COMING TO YOU LIVE FROM THE HOUSTON RODEO..."
...WHERE THE BIG STORY IS WYATT TAFT, WHO JUST ANNOUNCED HIS SURPRISE ENGAGEMENT TO TEXAS MODEL DAISY SCHILLING!
THIS IS TREVOR NOLL FOR KHOU HOUSTON, WISHING ALL THE BEST TO THE HAPPY COUPLE.
BACK TO YOU, KAREN.
ARE WE CLEAR?
YEP.
GOOD. I CAN SHOOT MYSELF NOW, BECAUSE I'VE FINALLY HIT THE ROCK BOTTOM OF JOURNALISM. A @#$% RODEO.
EXCUSE ME?
NO OFFENSE.
"COME TO HOUSTON, IT'S A HUGE MARKET, IT'LL BE GOOD FOR YOUR CAREER!"
FOUR YEARS I'VE BEEN HERE, I NEED A REAL STORY. HELL, I WISH CLUTCH WOULD COME BACK.
BITE YOUR TONGUE, MAN.
THERE'S A PETA PROTEST OUTSIDE, WE COULD COVER THAT.
WHO CARES?
COMPASSION DOESN'T GET RATINGS.

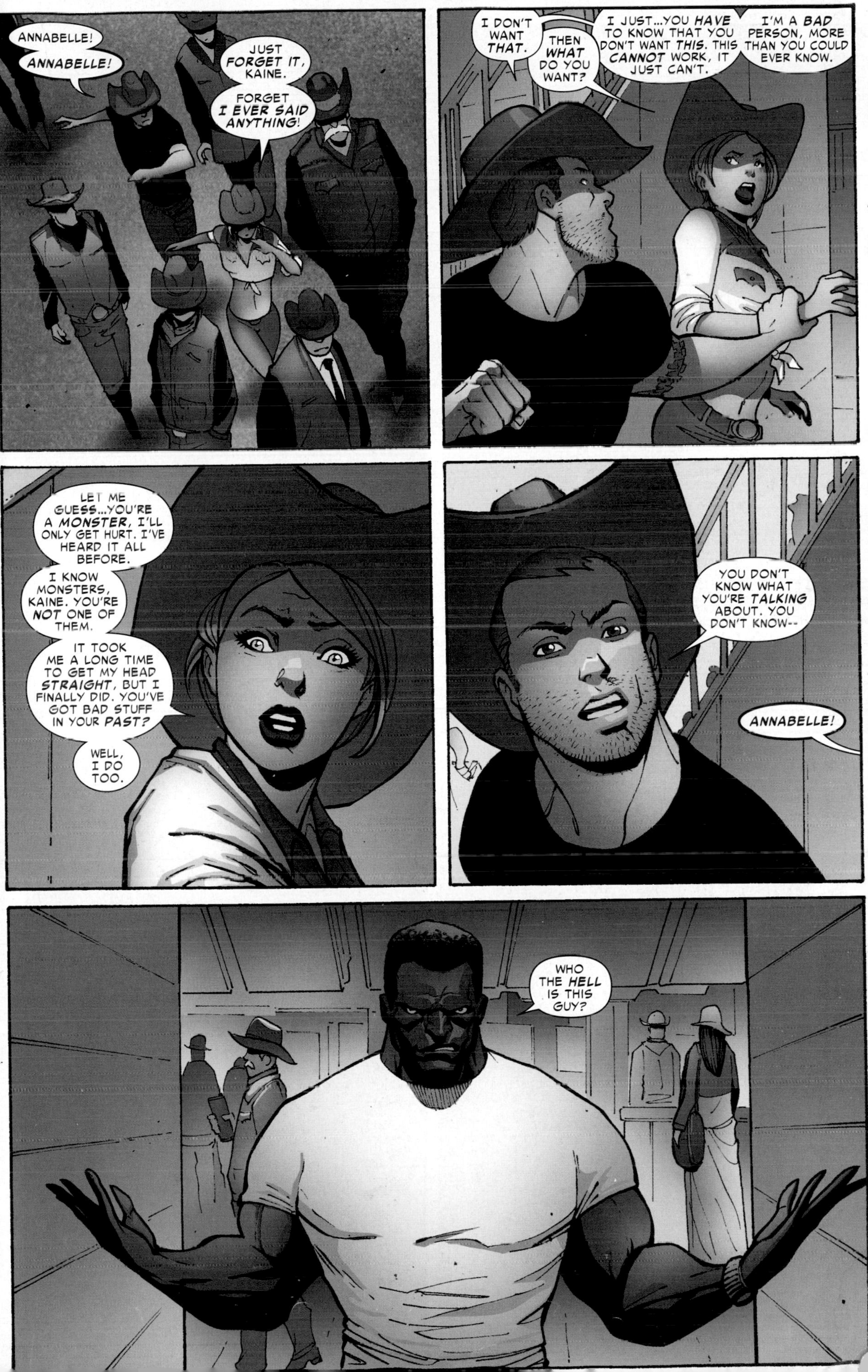
ANNABELLE!
ANNABELLE!
JUST FORGET IT, KAINE.
FORGET I EVER SAID ANYTHING!
I DON'T WANT THAT.
THEN WHAT DO YOU WANT?
I JUST...YOU HAVE TO KNOW THAT YOU DON'T WANT THIS. THIS CANNOT WORK, IT JUST CAN'T.
I'M A BAD PERSON, MORE THAN YOU COULD EVER KNOW.
LET ME GUESS...YOU'RE A MONSTER, I'LL ONLY GET HURT. I'VE HEARD IT ALL BEFORE.
I KNOW MONSTERS, KAINE. YOU'RE NOT ONE OF THEM.
IT TOOK ME A LONG TIME TO GET MY HEAD STRAIGHT, BUT I FINALLY DID. YOU'VE GOT BAD STUFF IN YOUR PAST?
WELL, I DO TOO.
YOU DON'T KNOW WHAT YOU'RE TALKING ABOUT. YOU DON'T KNOW--
ANNABELLE!
WHO THE HELL IS THIS GUY?

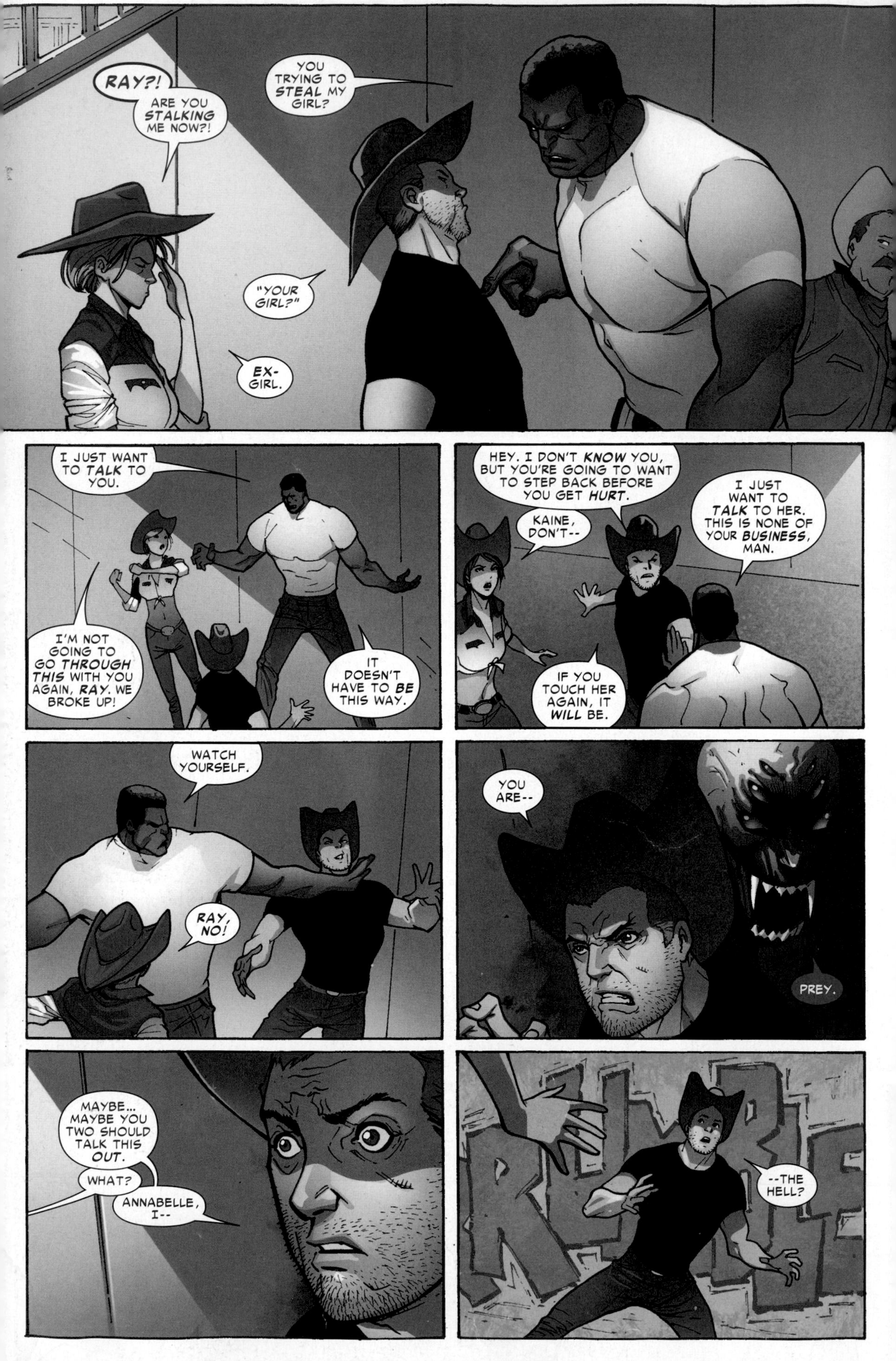
RAY?! ARE YOU STALKING ME NOW?!
YOU TRYING TO STEAL MY GIRL?
"YOUR GIRL?"
EX-GIRL.
I JUST WANT TO TALK TO YOU.
I'M NOT GOING TO GO THROUGH THIS WITH YOU AGAIN, RAY. WE BROKE UP!
IT DOESN'T HAVE TO BE THIS WAY.
HEY. I DON'T KNOW YOU, BUT YOU'RE GOING TO WANT TO STEP BACK BEFORE YOU GET HURT.
KAINE, DON'T--
I JUST WANT TO TALK TO HER. THIS IS NONE OF YOUR BUSINESS, MAN.
IF YOU TOUCH HER AGAIN, IT WILL BE.
WATCH YOURSELF.
RAY, NO!
YOU ARE--
PREY.
MAYBE... MAYBE YOU TWO SHOULD TALK THIS OUT.
WHAT?
ANNABELLE, I--
--THE HELL?

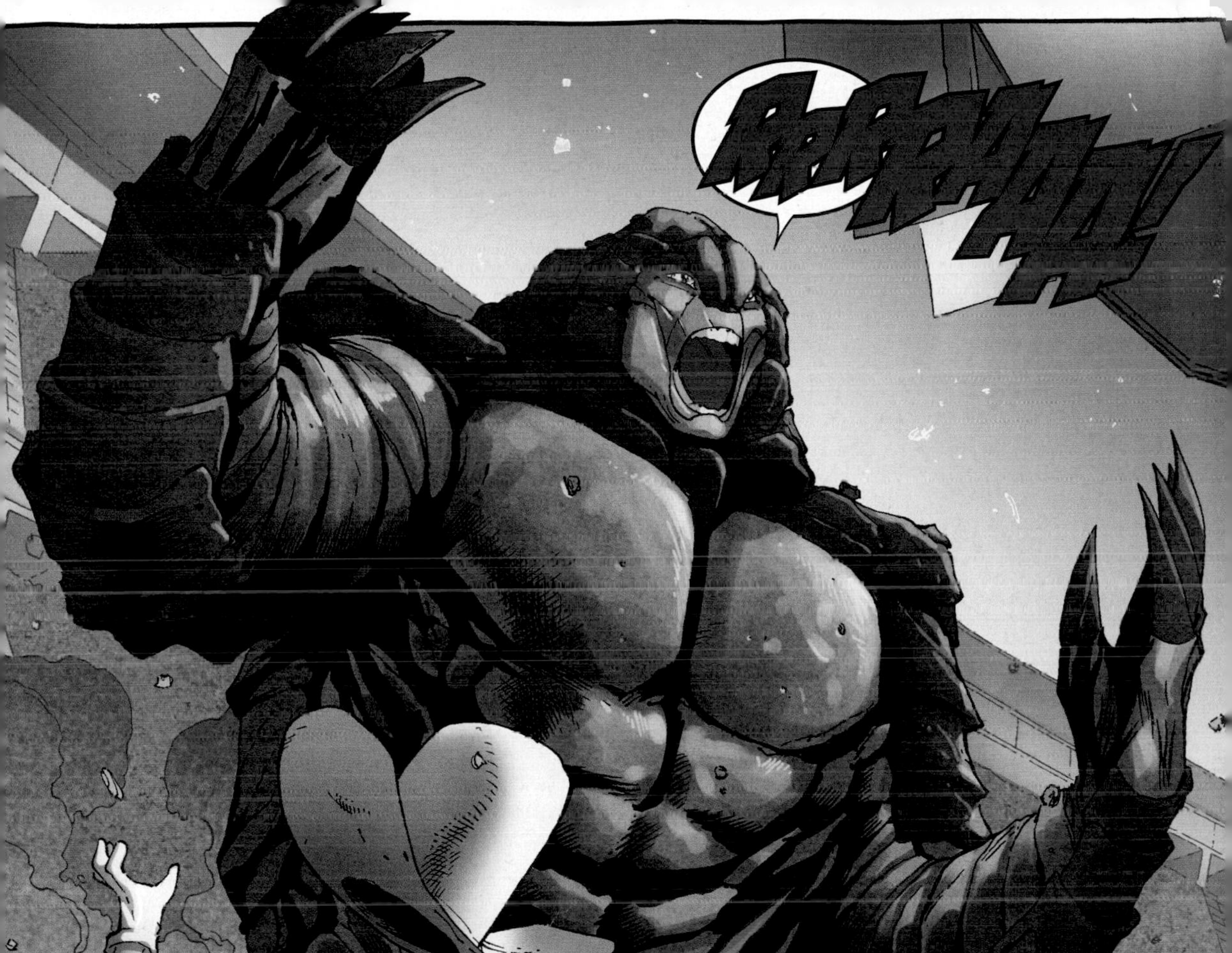
RRRAAAH!

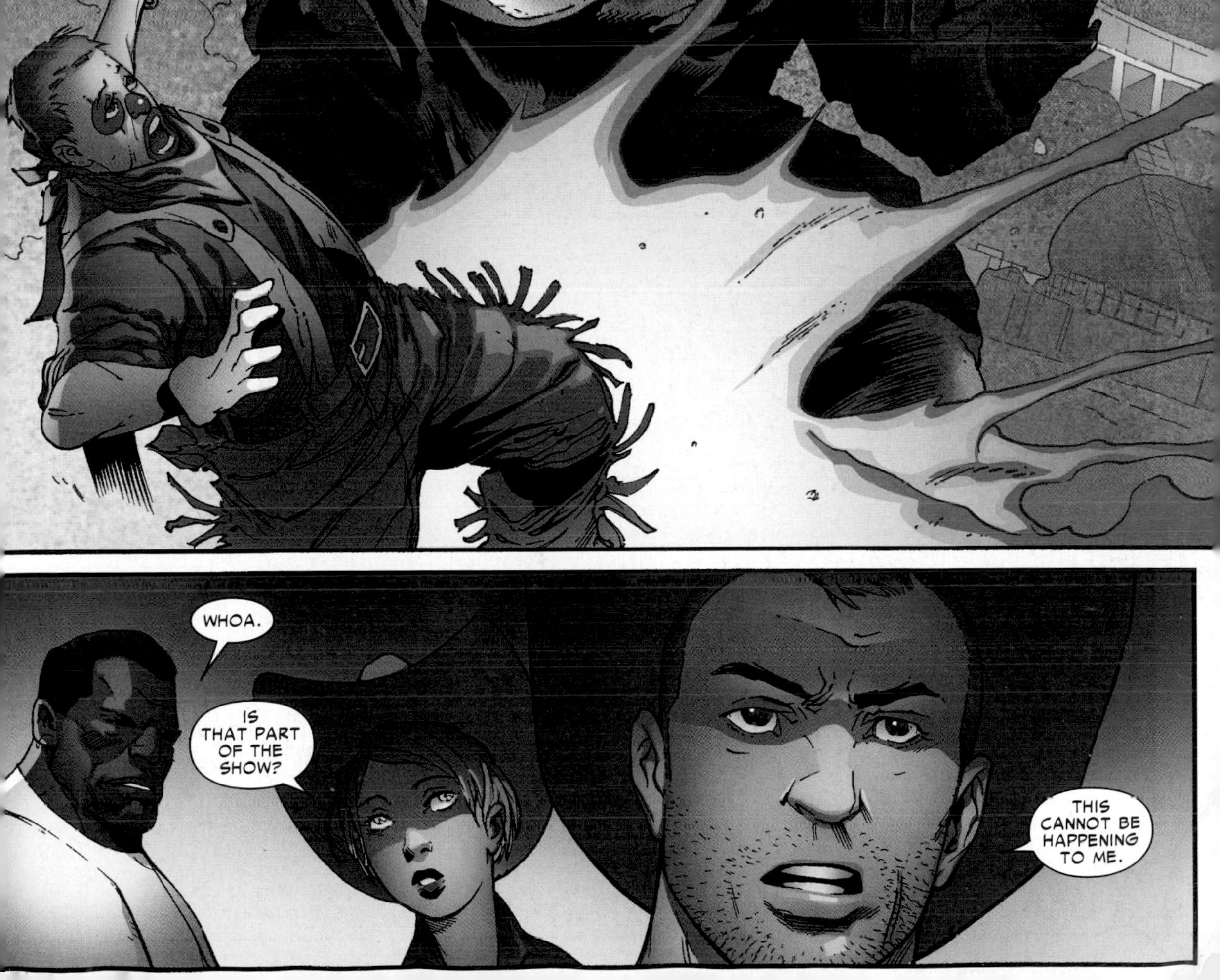
WHOA.
IS THAT PART OF THE SHOW?
THIS CANNOT BE HAPPENING TO ME.

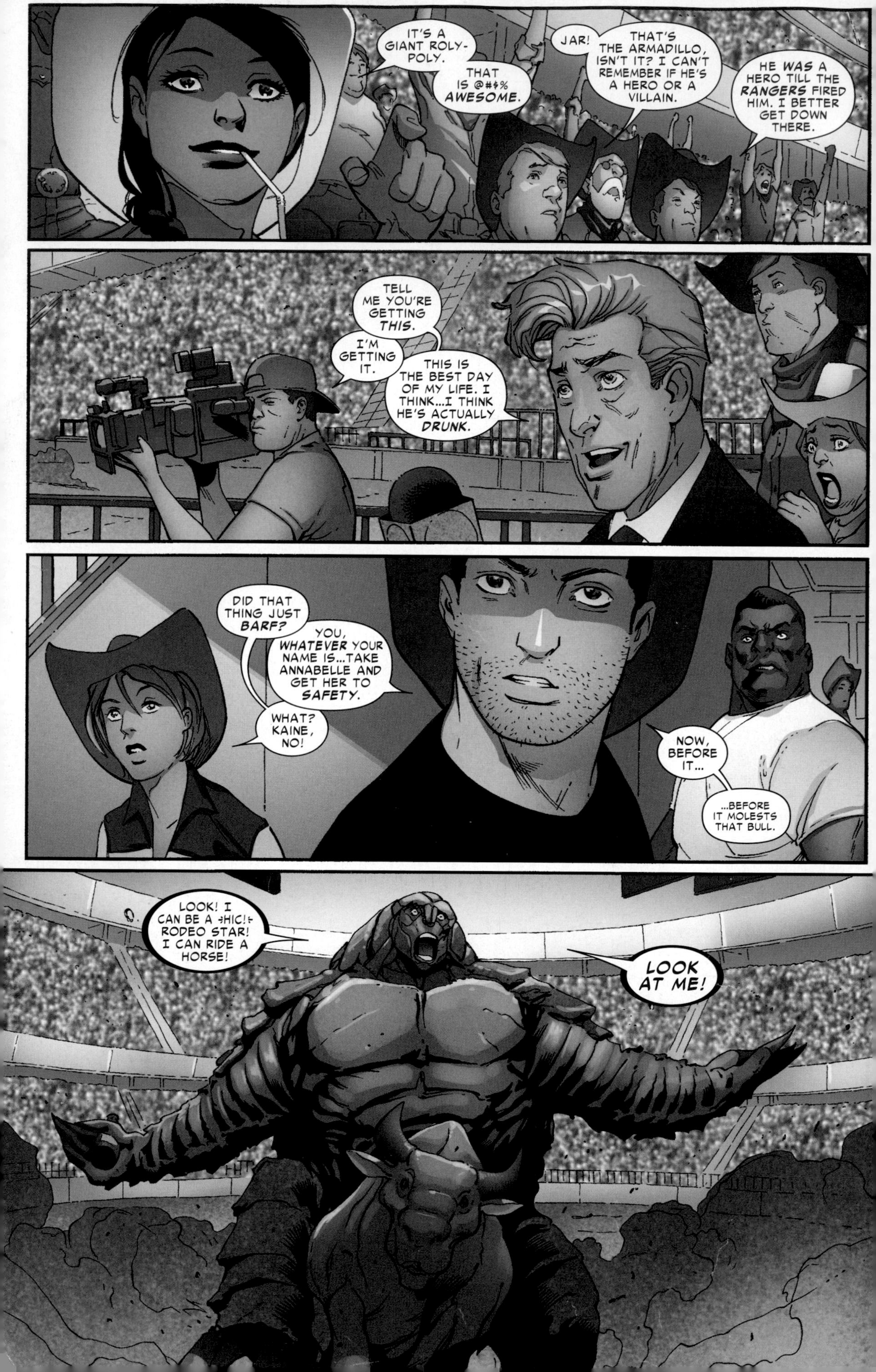
IT'S A GIANT ROLY-POLY.
THAT IS @#$% AWESOME.
JAR!
THAT'S THE ARMADILLO, ISN'T IT? I CAN'T REMEMBER IF HE'S A HERO OR A VILLAIN.
HE WAS A HERO TILL THE RANGERS FIRED HIM. I BETTER GET DOWN THERE.
TELL ME YOU'RE GETTING THIS.
I'M GETTING IT.
THIS IS THE BEST DAY OF MY LIFE. I THINK...I THINK HE'S ACTUALLY DRUNK.
DID THAT THING JUST BARF?
YOU, WHATEVER YOUR NAME IS...TAKE ANNABELLE AND GET HER TO SAFETY.
WHAT? KAINE, NO!
NOW, BEFORE IT...
...BEFORE IT MOLESTS THAT BULL.
LOOK! I CAN BE A ⸗HIC!⸗ RODEO STAR! I CAN RIDE A HORSE!
LOOK AT ME!

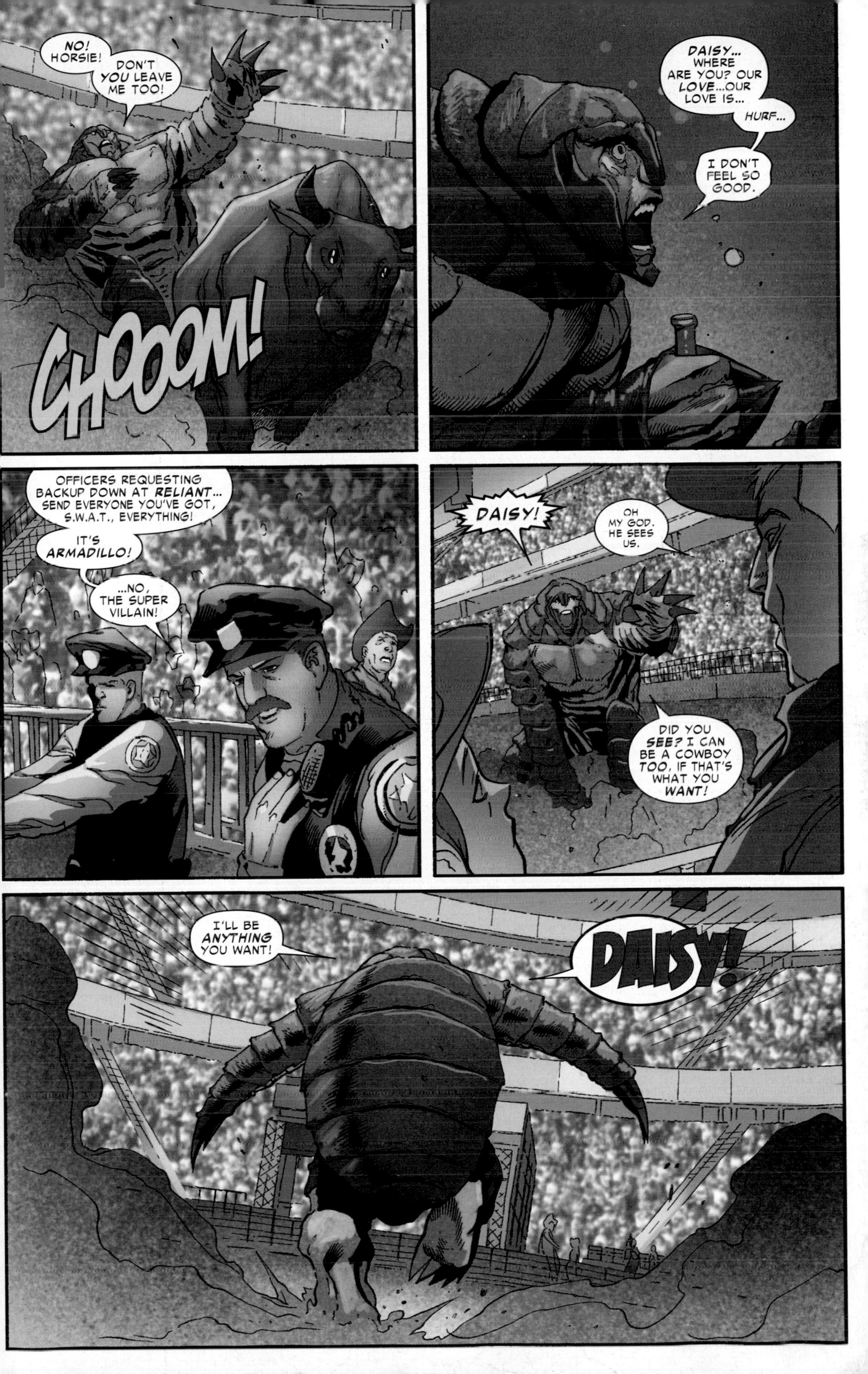
NO! HORSIE!
DON'T YOU LEAVE ME TOO!
CHOOOM!
DAISY... WHERE ARE YOU? OUR LOVE...OUR LOVE IS...
HURF...
I DON'T FEEL SO GOOD.
OFFICERS REQUESTING BACKUP DOWN AT RELIANT... SEND EVERYONE YOU'VE GOT, S.W.A.T., EVERYTHING!
IT'S ARMADILLO!
...NO, THE SUPER VILLAIN!
DAISY!
OH MY GOD. HE SEES US.
DID YOU SEE? I CAN BE A COWBOY TOO, IF THAT'S WHAT YOU WANT!
I'LL BE ANYTHING YOU WANT!
DAISY!

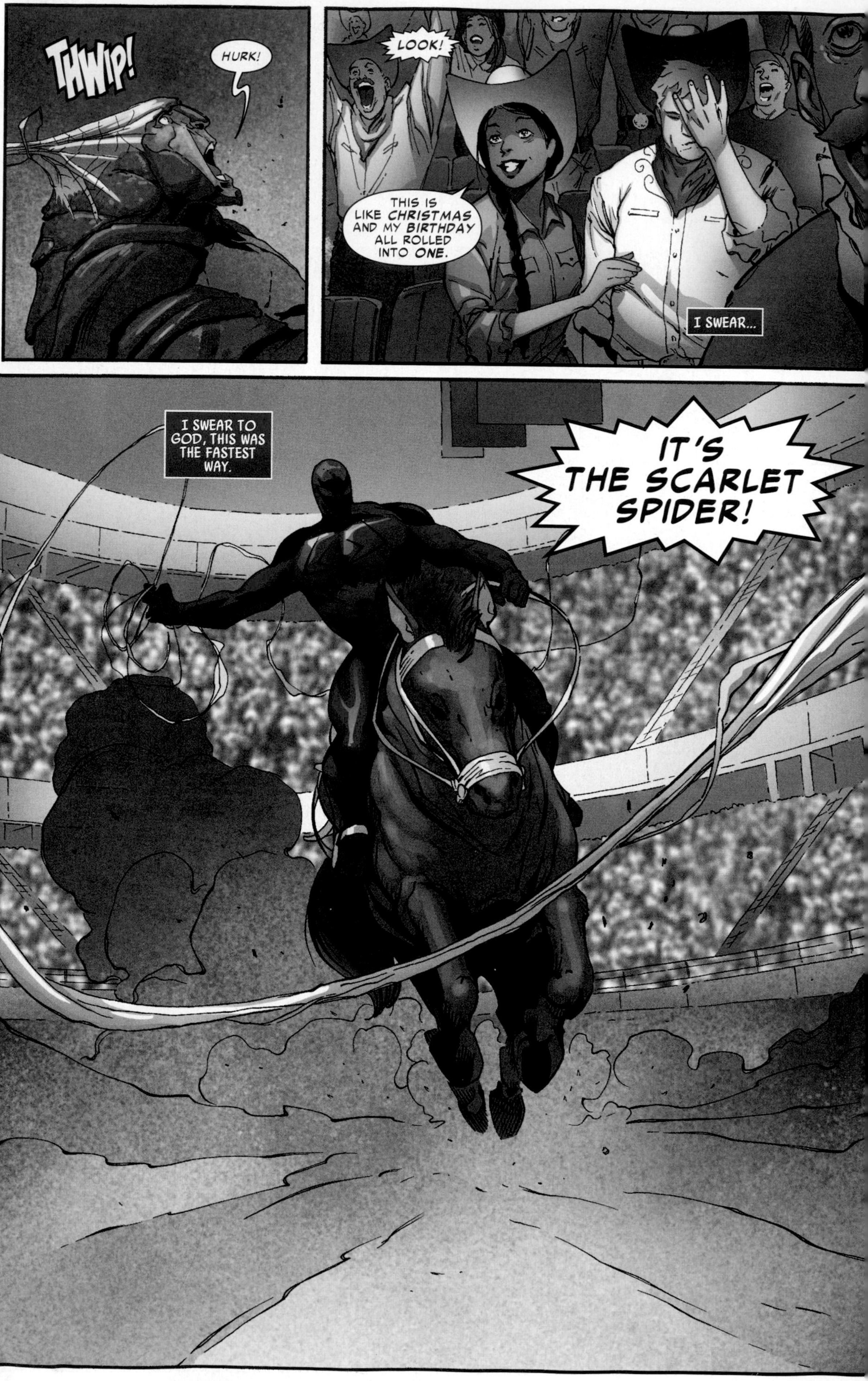
THWIP!
HURK!
LOOK!
THIS IS LIKE CHRISTMAS AND MY BIRTHDAY ALL ROLLED INTO ONE.
I SWEAR...
I SWEAR TO GOD, THIS WAS THE FASTEST WAY.
IT'S THE SCARLET SPIDER!

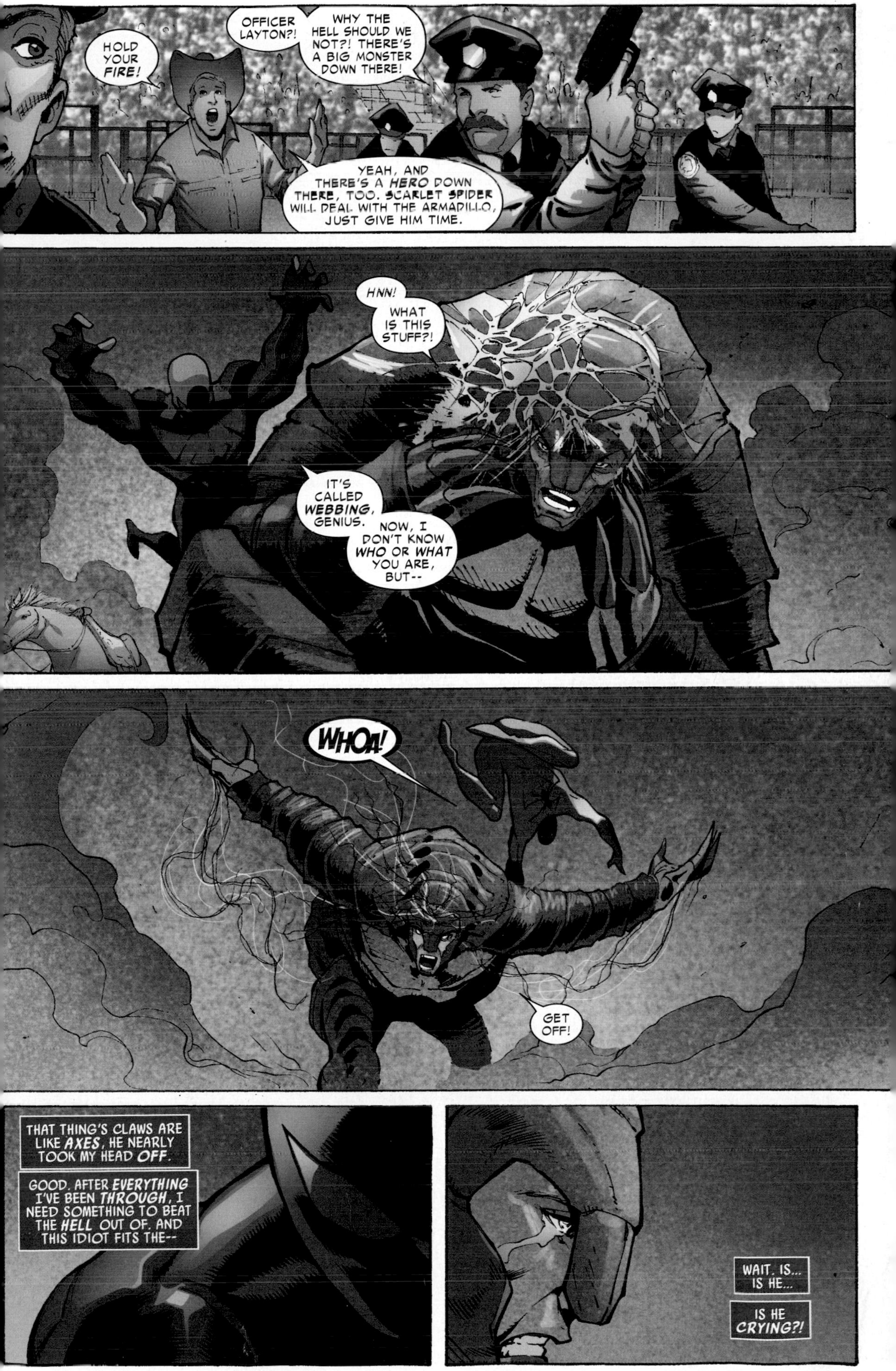
HOLD YOUR FIRE!
OFFICER LAYTON?!
WHY THE HELL SHOULD WE NOT?! THERE'S A BIG MONSTER DOWN THERE!
YEAH, AND THERE'S A HERO DOWN THERE, TOO. SCARLET SPIDER WILL DEAL WITH THE ARMADILLO, JUST GIVE HIM TIME.
HNN!
WHAT IS THIS STUFF?!
IT'S CALLED WEBBING, GENIUS.
NOW, I DON'T KNOW WHO OR WHAT YOU ARE, BUT--
WHOA!
GET OFF!
THAT THING'S CLAWS ARE LIKE AXES, HE NEARLY TOOK MY HEAD OFF.
GOOD. AFTER EVERYTHING I'VE BEEN THROUGH, I NEED SOMETHING TO BEAT THE HELL OUT OF. AND THIS IDIOT FITS THE--
WAIT. IS... IS HE...
IS HE CRYING?!

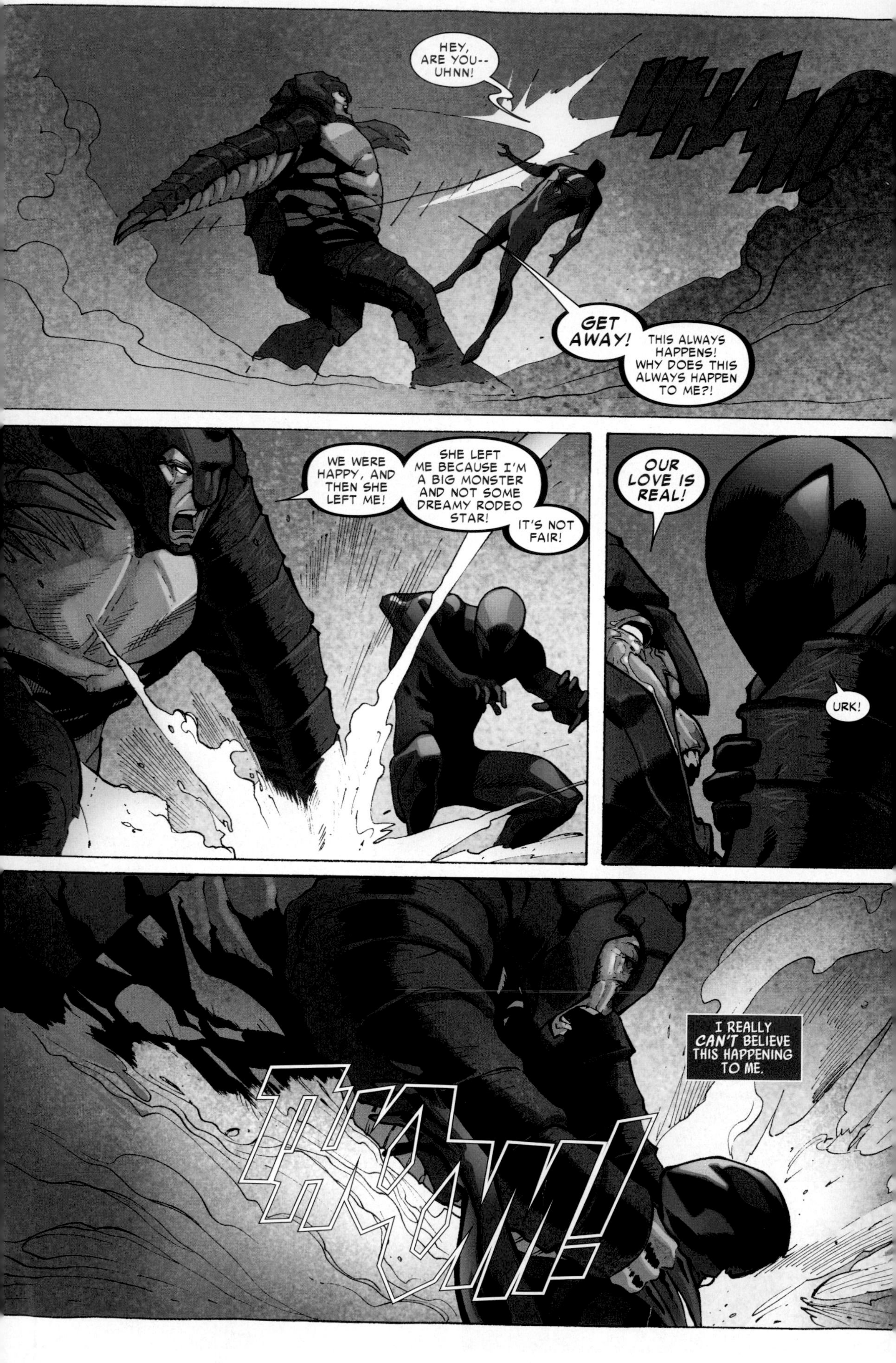
HEY, ARE YOU-- UHNN!
WHAM!
GET AWAY!
THIS ALWAYS HAPPENS! WHY DOES THIS ALWAYS HAPPEN TO ME?!
WE WERE HAPPY, AND THEN SHE LEFT ME!
SHE LEFT ME BECAUSE I'M A BIG MONSTER AND NOT SOME DREAMY RODEO STAR!
IT'S NOT FAIR!
OUR LOVE IS REAL!
URK!
I REALLY CAN'T BELIEVE THIS HAPPENING TO ME.
THWOM!

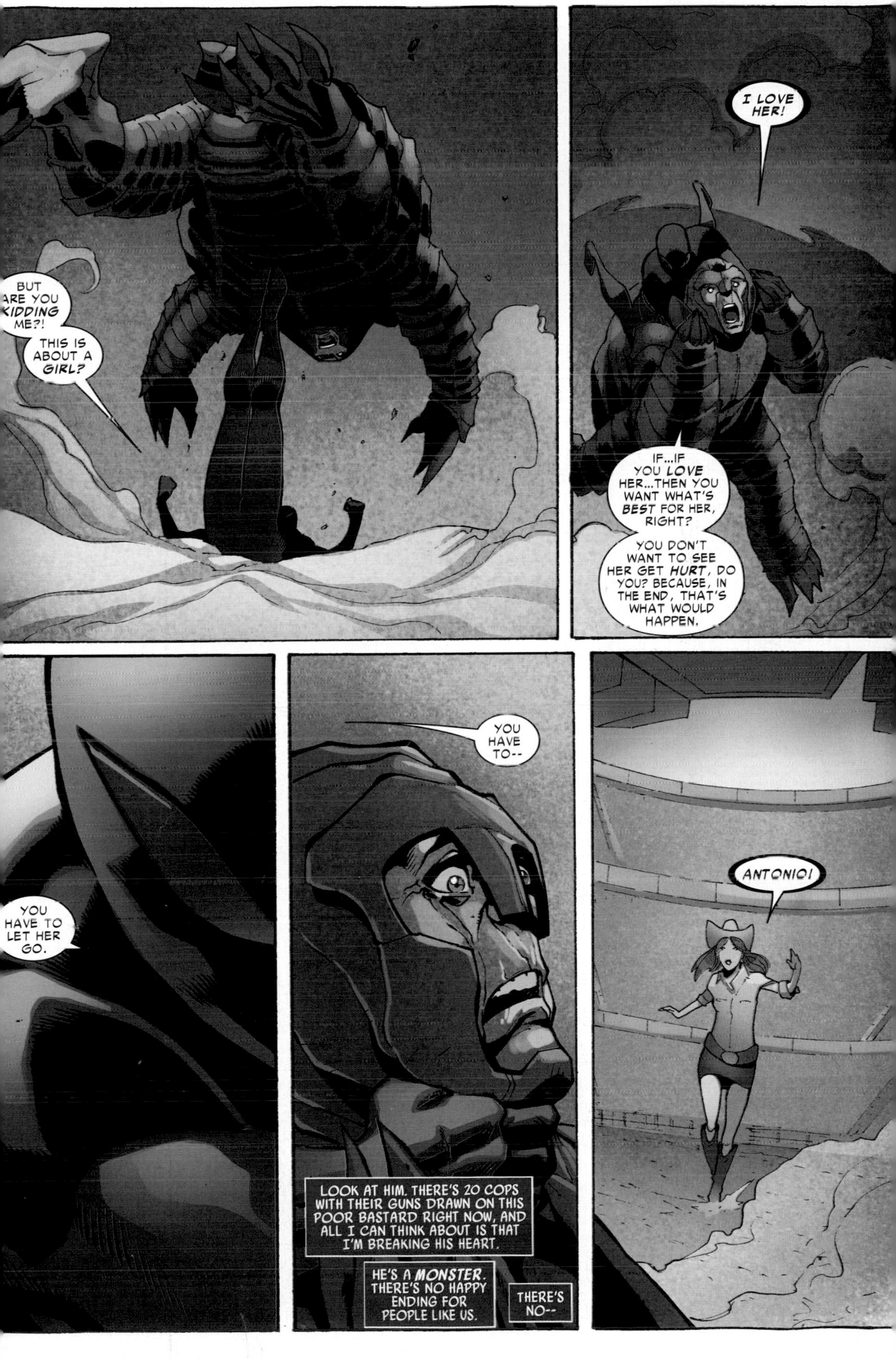
BUT ARE YOU KIDDING ME?!
THIS IS ABOUT A GIRL?
I LOVE HER!
IF...IF YOU LOVE HER...THEN YOU WANT WHAT'S BEST FOR HER, RIGHT?
YOU DON'T WANT TO SEE HER GET HURT, DO YOU? BECAUSE, IN THE END, THAT'S WHAT WOULD HAPPEN.
YOU HAVE TO LET HER GO.
YOU HAVE TO--
LOOK AT HIM. THERE'S 20 COPS WITH THEIR GUNS DRAWN ON THIS POOR BASTARD RIGHT NOW, AND ALL I CAN THINK ABOUT IS THAT I'M BREAKING HIS HEART.
HE'S A MONSTER. THERE'S NO HAPPY ENDING FOR PEOPLE LIKE US.
THERE'S NO--
ANTONIO!

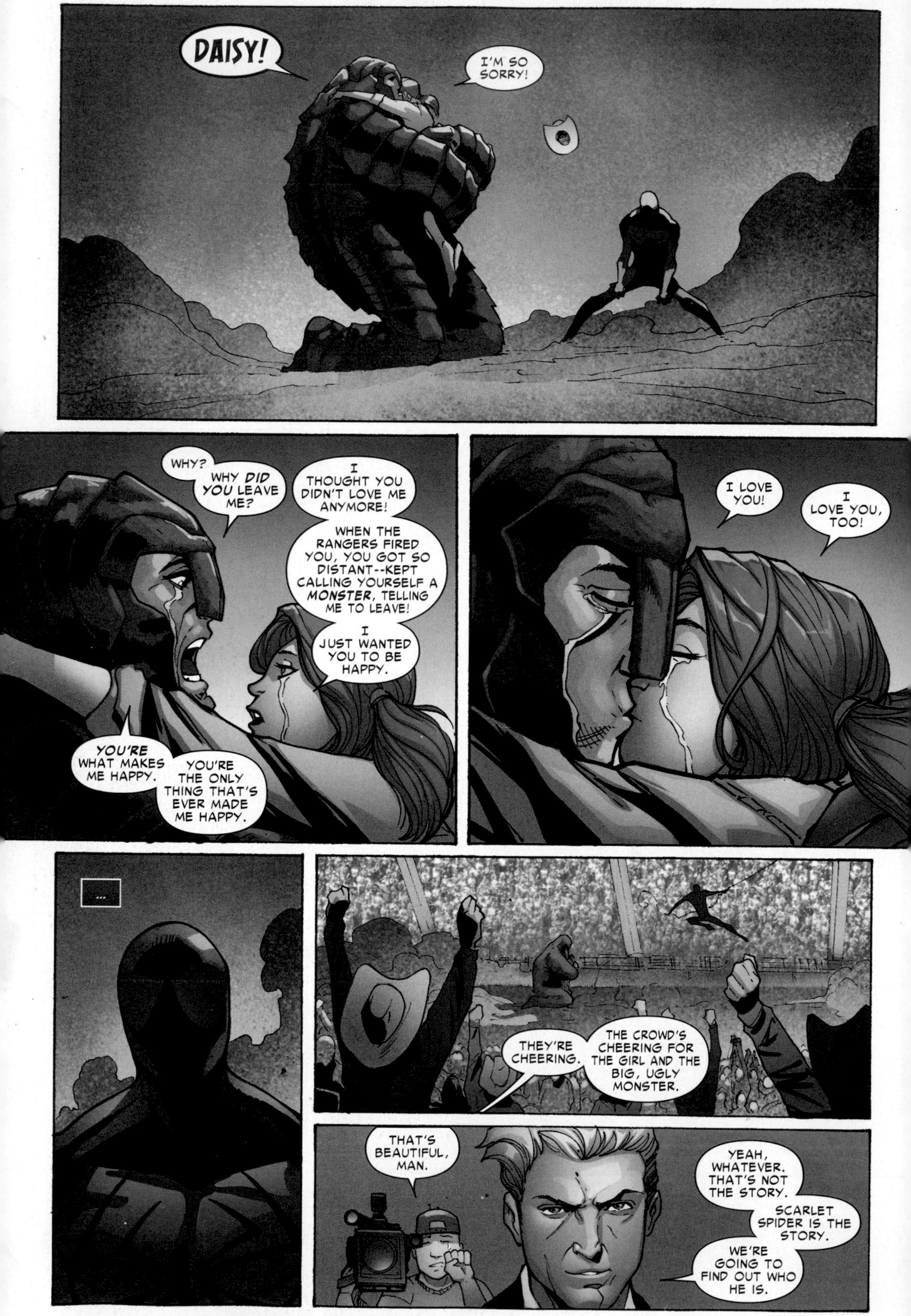
DAISY!
I'M SO SORRY!
WHY? WHY DID YOU LEAVE ME?
I THOUGHT YOU DIDN'T LOVE ME ANYMORE!
WHEN THE RANGERS FIRED YOU, YOU GOT SO DISTANT--KEPT CALLING YOURSELF A MONSTER, TELLING ME TO LEAVE!
I JUST WANTED YOU TO BE HAPPY.
YOU'RE WHAT MAKES ME HAPPY.
YOU'RE THE ONLY THING THAT'S EVER MADE ME HAPPY.
I LOVE YOU!
I LOVE YOU, TOO!
...
THEY'RE CHEERING.
THE CROWD'S CHEERING FOR THE GIRL AND THE BIG, UGLY MONSTER.
THAT'S BEAUTIFUL, MAN.
YEAH, WHATEVER. THAT'S NOT THE STORY.
SCARLET SPIDER IS THE STORY.
WE'RE GOING TO FIND OUT WHO HE IS.

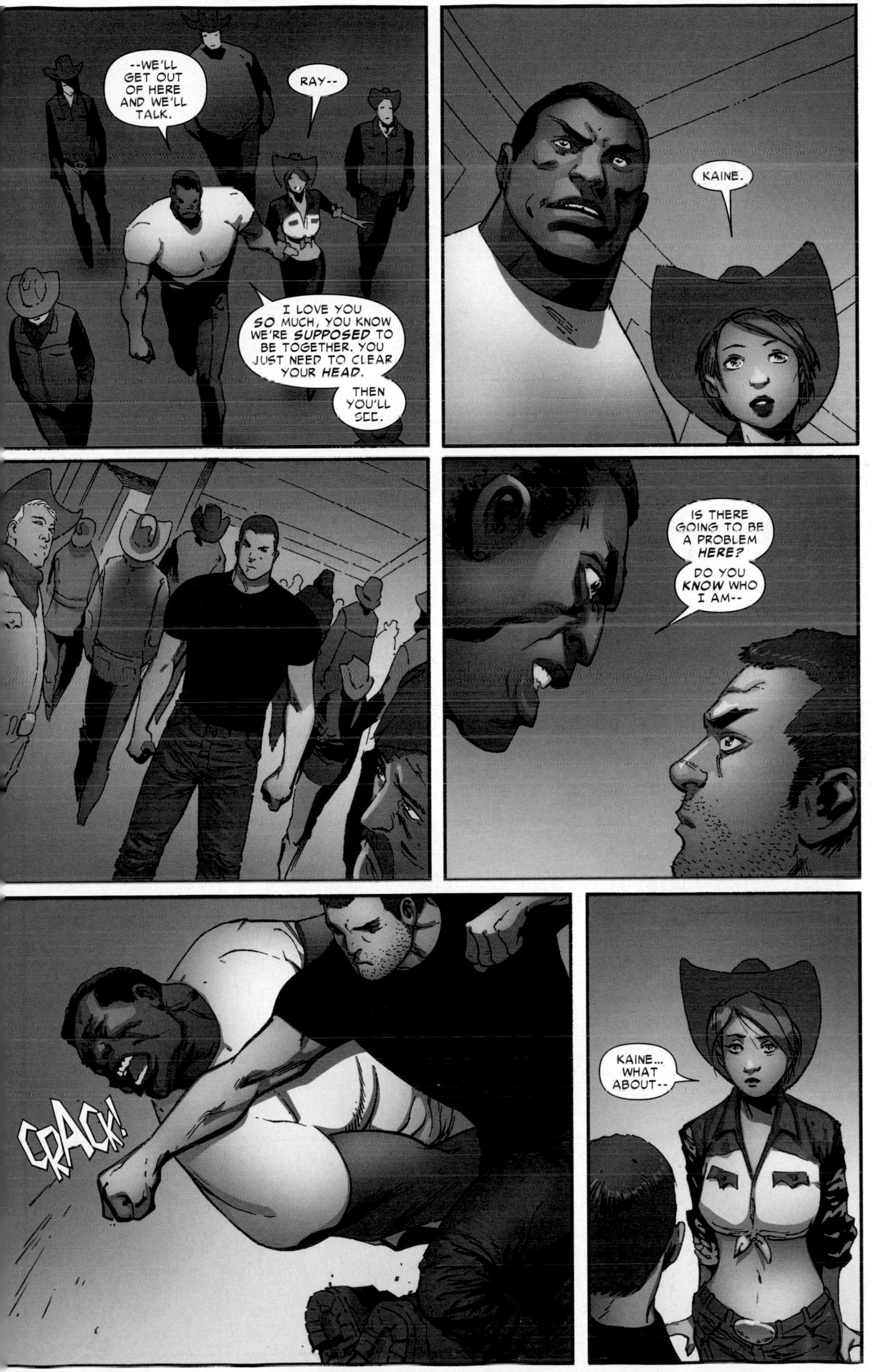
--WE'LL GET OUT OF HERE AND WE'LL TALK.
RAY--
I LOVE YOU SO MUCH, YOU KNOW WE'RE SUPPOSED TO BE TOGETHER. YOU JUST NEED TO CLEAR YOUR HEAD.
THEN YOU'LL SEE.
KAINE.
IS THERE GOING TO BE A PROBLEM HERE?
DO YOU KNOW WHO I AM--
CRACK!
KAINE... WHAT ABOUT--

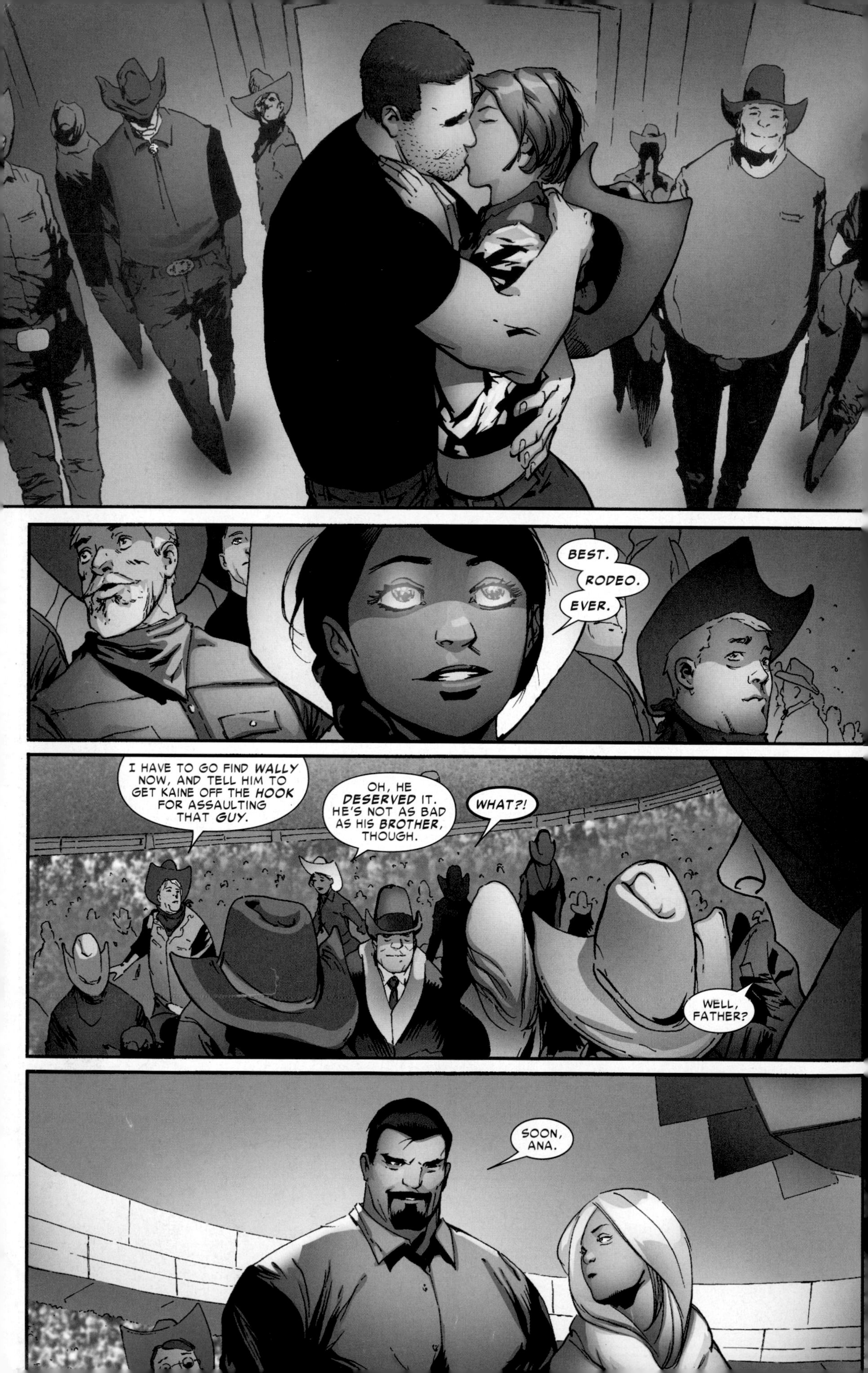
BEST.
RODEO.
EVER.
I HAVE TO GO FIND WALLY NOW, AND TELL HIM TO GET KAINE OFF THE HOOK FOR ASSAULTING THAT GUY.
OH, HE DESERVED IT. HE'S NOT AS BAD AS HIS BROTHER, THOUGH.
WHAT?!
WELL, FATHER?
SOON, ANA.

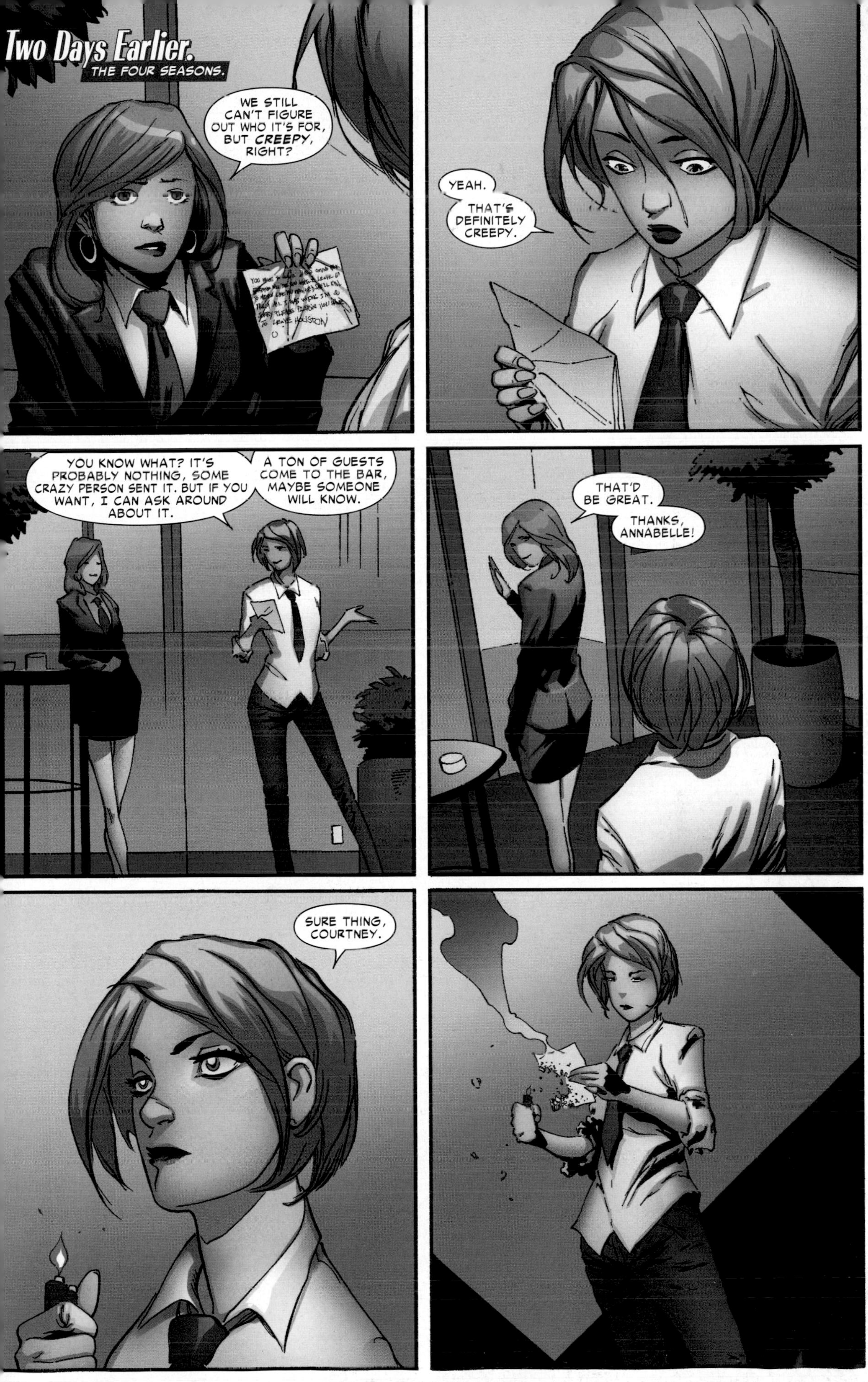
Two Days Earlier.
THE FOUR SEASONS.
WE STILL CAN'T FIGURE OUT WHO IT'S FOR, BUT CREEPY, RIGHT?
YEAH.
THAT'S DEFINITELY CREEPY.
YOU KNOW WHAT? IT'S PROBABLY NOTHING, SOME CRAZY PERSON SENT IT. BUT IF YOU WANT, I CAN ASK AROUND ABOUT IT.
A TON OF GUESTS COME TO THE BAR, MAYBE SOMEONE WILL KNOW.
THAT'D BE GREAT.
THANKS, ANNABELLE!
SURE THING, COURTNEY.

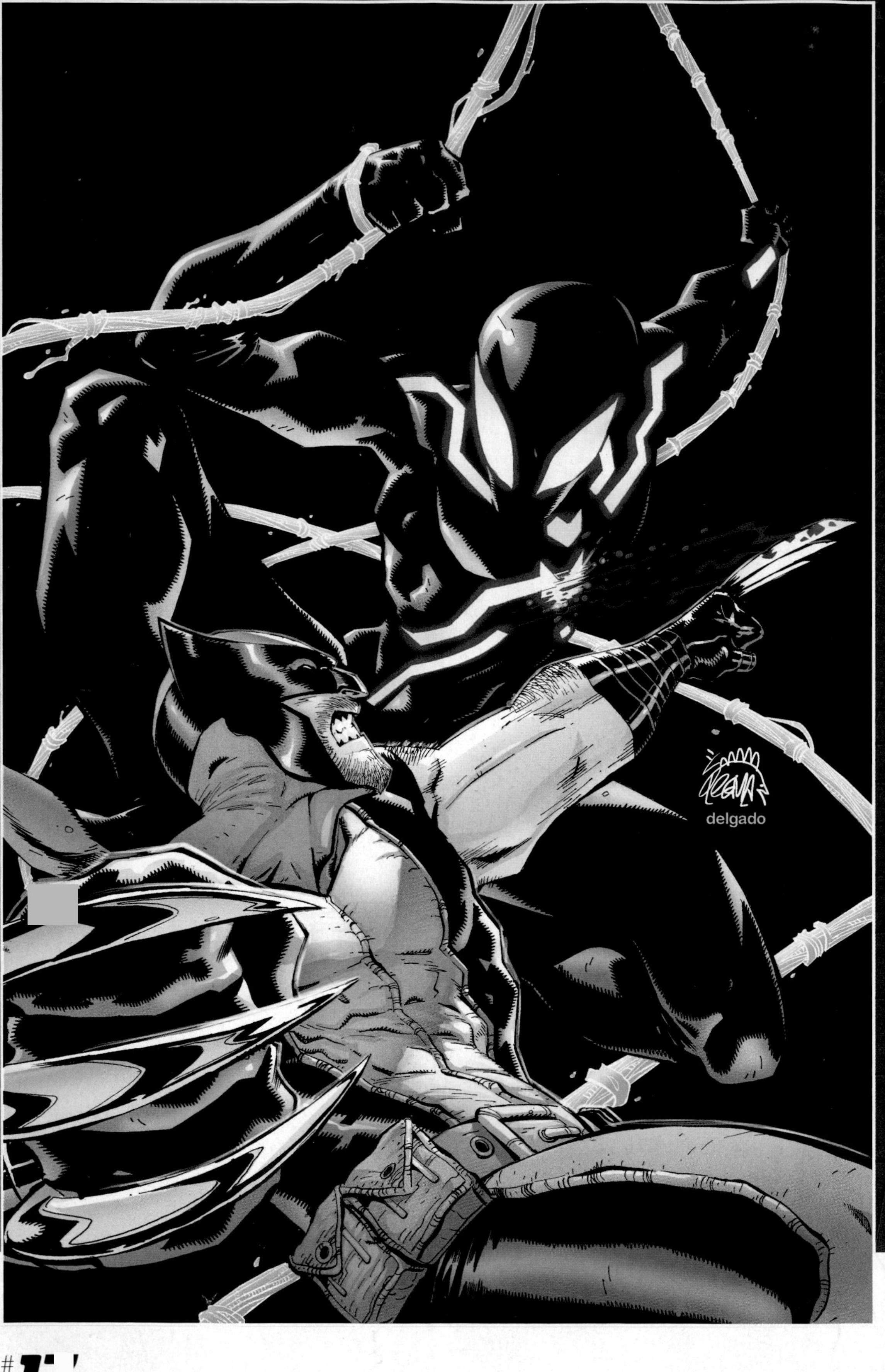
delgado

#17

"WRATH, PART 1"

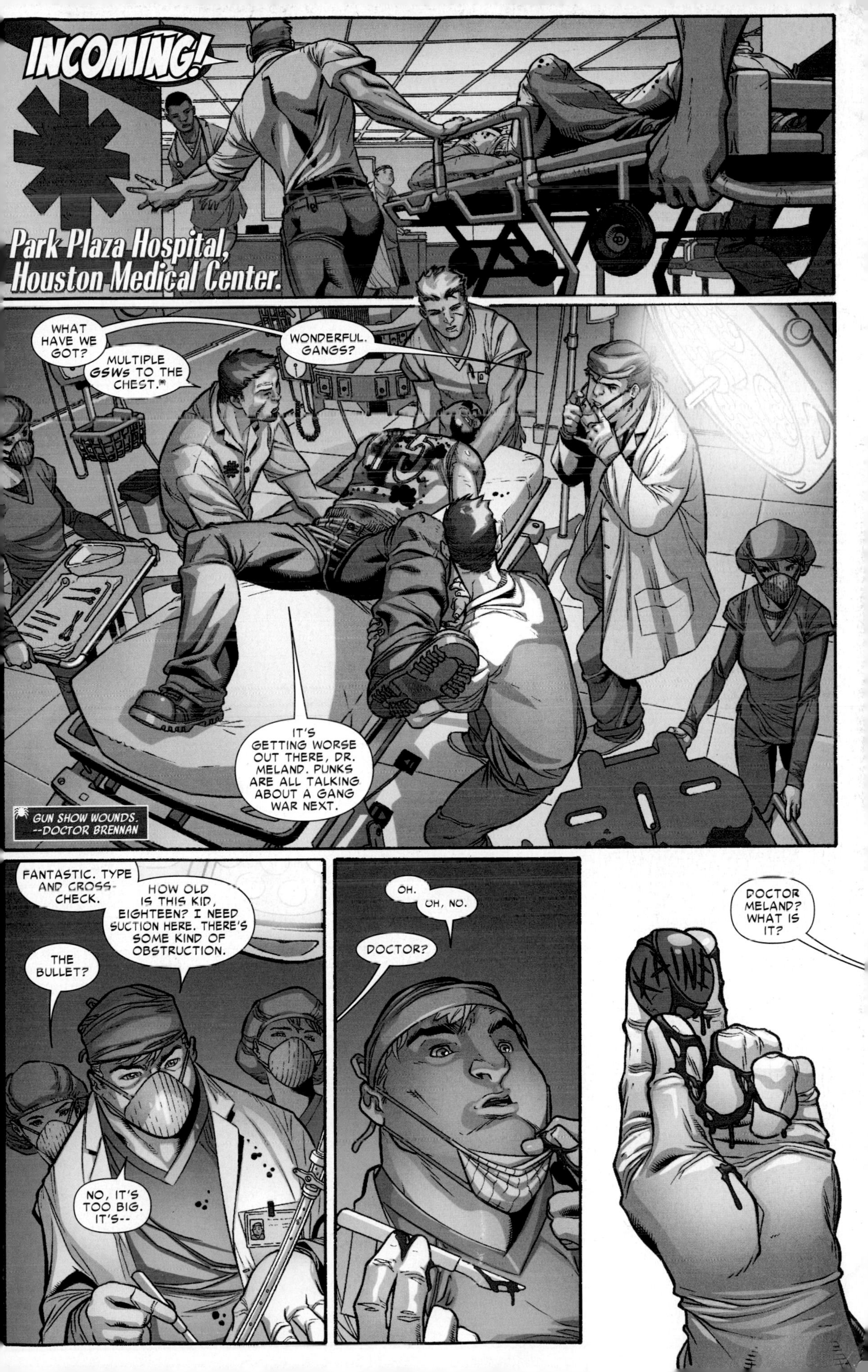
INCOMING!
Park Plaza Hospital, Houston Medical Center.
WHAT HAVE WE GOT?
MULTIPLE GSWs TO THE CHEST.*
WONDERFUL. GANGS?
IT'S GETTING WORSE OUT THERE, DR. MELAND. PUNKS ARE ALL TALKING ABOUT A GANG WAR NEXT.
*GUN SHOT WOUNDS. --DOCTOR BRENNAN
FANTASTIC. TYPE AND CROSS-CHECK.
HOW OLD IS THIS KID, EIGHTEEN? I NEED SUCTION HERE. THERE'S SOME KIND OF OBSTRUCTION.
THE BULLET?
NO, IT'S TOO BIG. IT'S--
OH.
OH, NO.
DOCTOR?
DOCTOR MELAND? WHAT IS IT?
KAINE

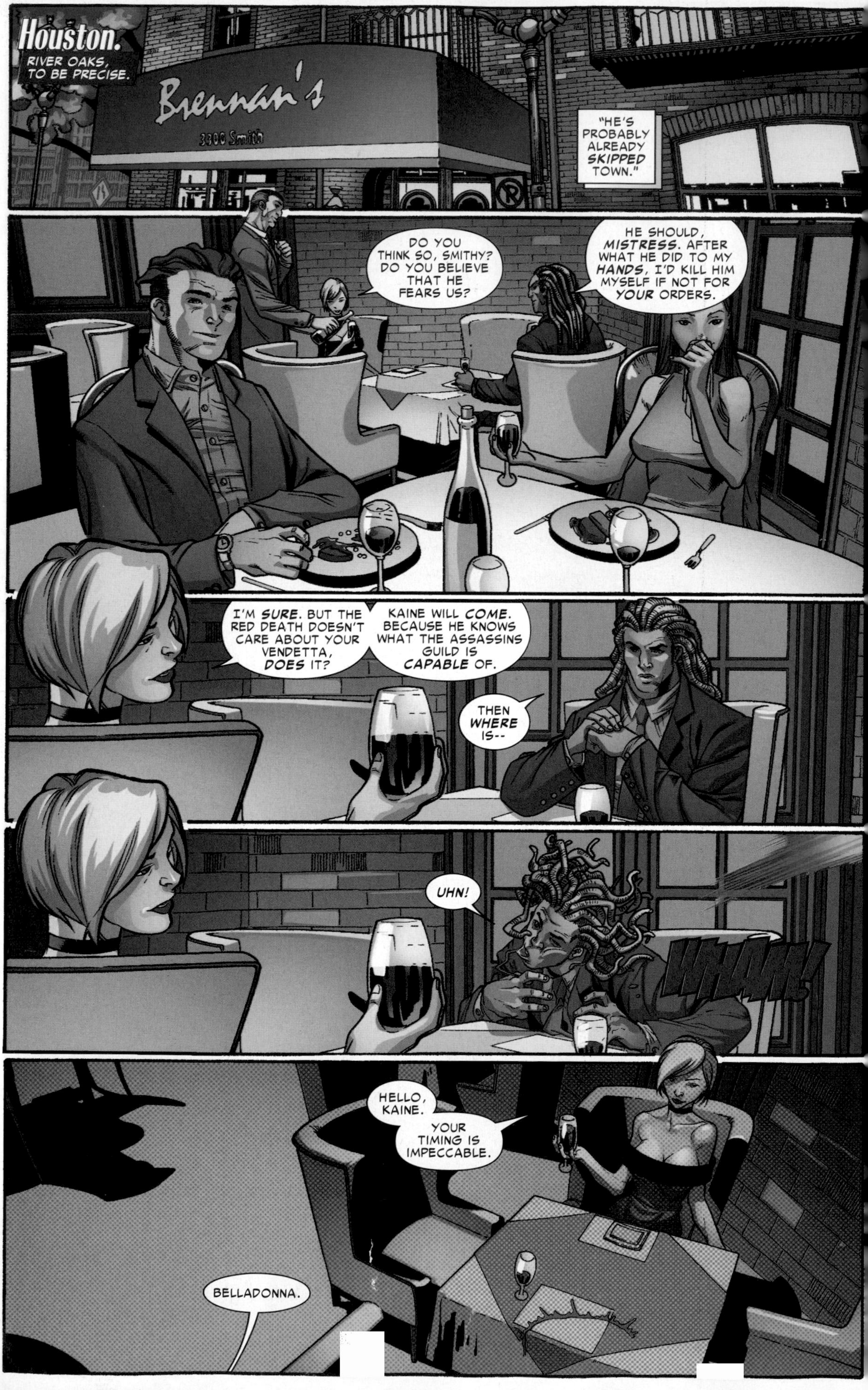
Houston.
RIVER OAKS, TO BE PRECISE.
Brennan's
3300 Smith
"HE'S PROBABLY ALREADY SKIPPED TOWN."
DO YOU THINK SO, SMITHY? DO YOU BELIEVE THAT HE FEARS US?
HE SHOULD, MISTRESS. AFTER WHAT HE DID TO MY HANDS, I'D KILL HIM MYSELF IF NOT FOR YOUR ORDERS.
I'M SURE. BUT THE RED DEATH DOESN'T CARE ABOUT YOUR VENDETTA, DOES IT?
KAINE WILL COME. BECAUSE HE KNOWS WHAT THE ASSASSINS GUILD IS CAPABLE OF.
THEN WHERE IS--
UHN!
WHAM!
HELLO, KAINE.
YOUR TIMING IS IMPECCABLE.
BELLADONNA.

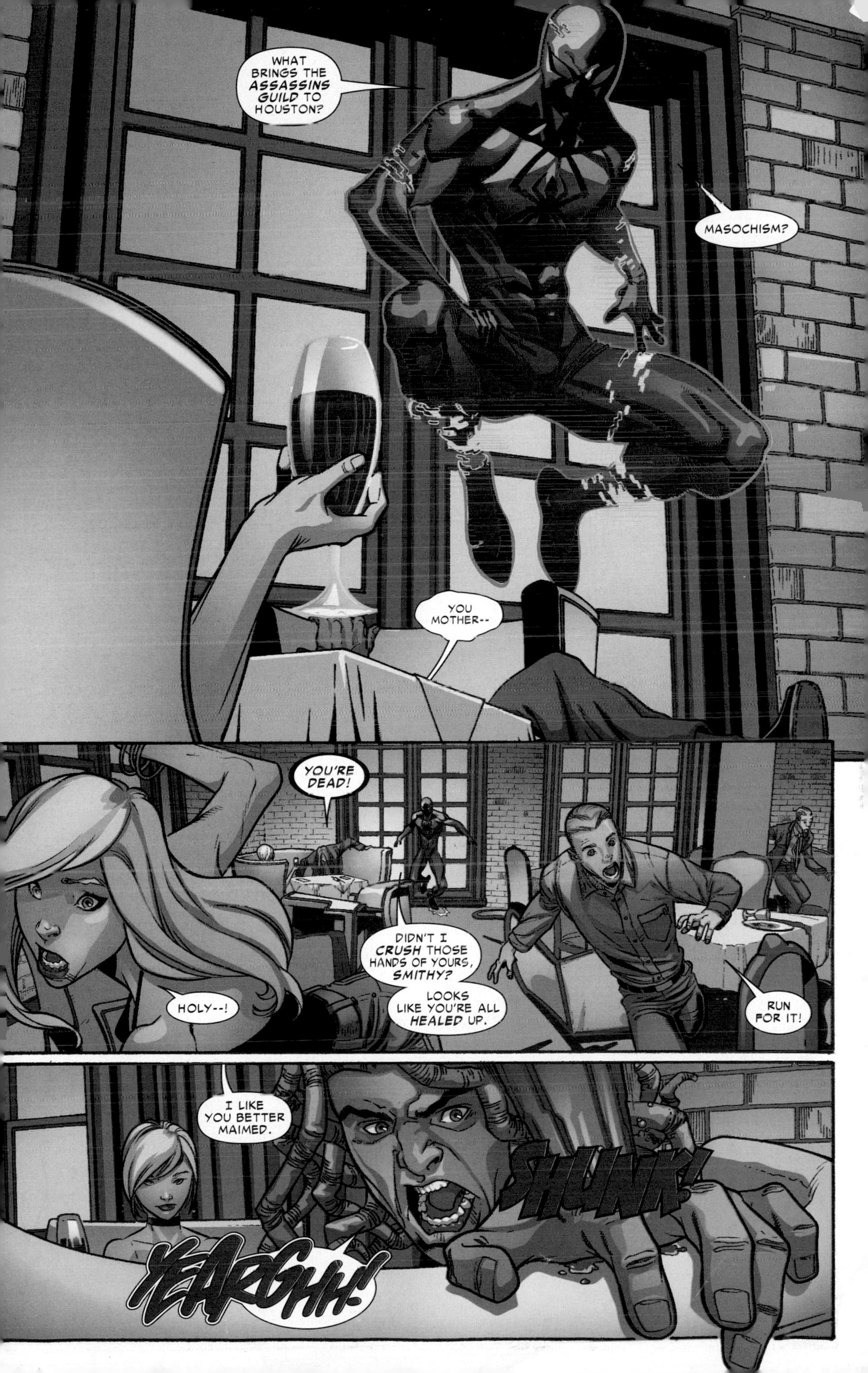
WHAT BRINGS THE ASSASSINS GUILD TO HOUSTON?
MASOCHISM?
YOU MOTHER--
YOU'RE DEAD!
DIDN'T I CRUSH THOSE HANDS OF YOURS, SMITHY?
LOOKS LIKE YOU'RE ALL HEALED UP.
HOLY--!
RUN FOR IT!
I LIKE YOU BETTER MAIMED.
SHUNK!
YEARGHH!

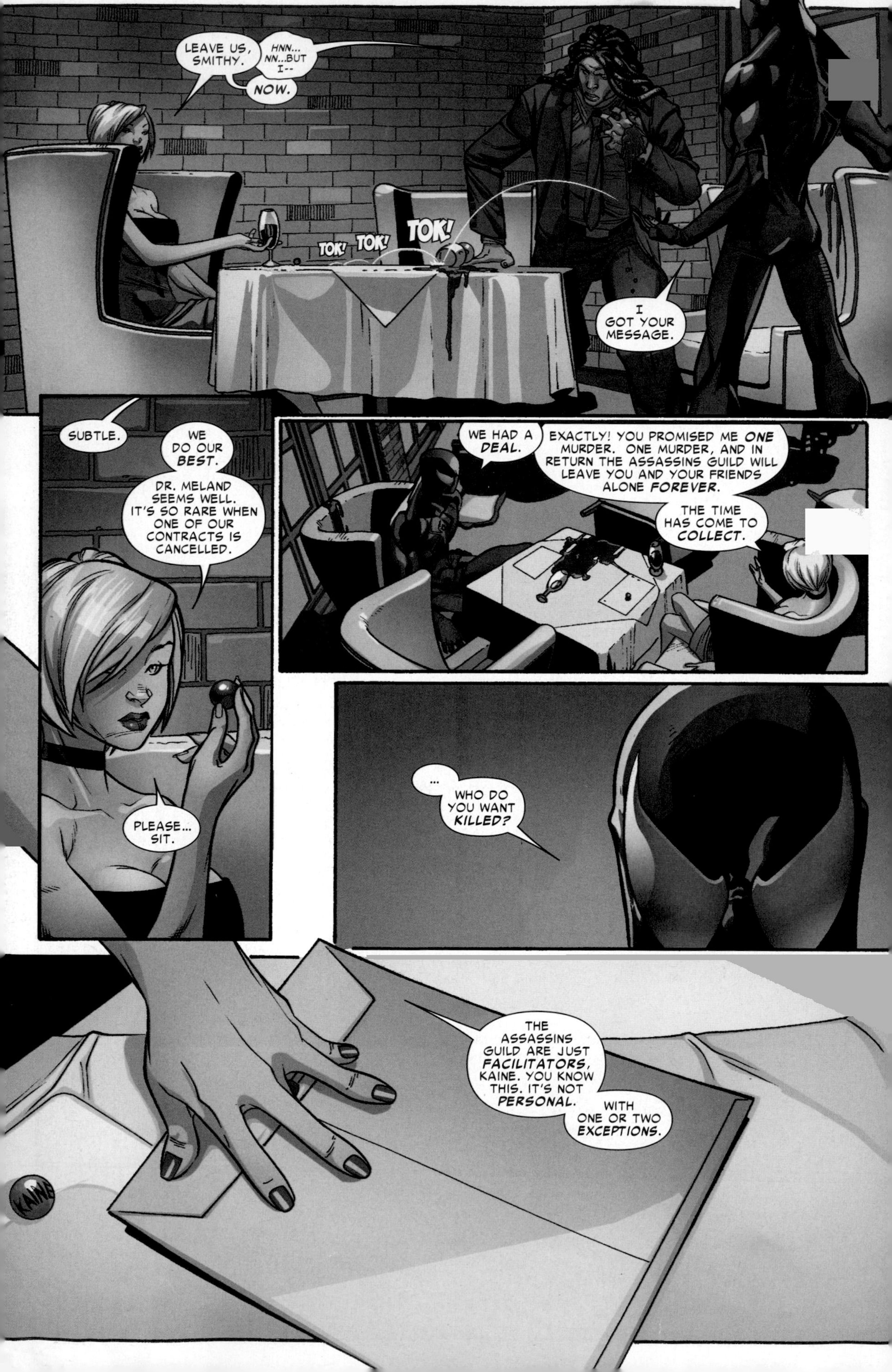
LEAVE US, SMITHY.
HNN... NN...BUT I--
NOW.
TOK! TOK! TOK!
I GOT YOUR MESSAGE.
SUBTLE.
WE DO OUR BEST.
DR. MELAND SEEMS WELL. IT'S SO RARE WHEN ONE OF OUR CONTRACTS IS CANCELLED.
PLEASE... SIT.
WE HAD A DEAL.
EXACTLY! YOU PROMISED ME ONE MURDER. ONE MURDER, AND IN RETURN THE ASSASSINS GUILD WILL LEAVE YOU AND YOUR FRIENDS ALONE FOREVER.
THE TIME HAS COME TO COLLECT.
...
WHO DO YOU WANT KILLED?
THE ASSASSINS GUILD ARE JUST FACILITATORS, KAINE. YOU KNOW THIS. IT'S NOT PERSONAL.
WITH ONE OR TWO EXCEPTIONS.
KAINE

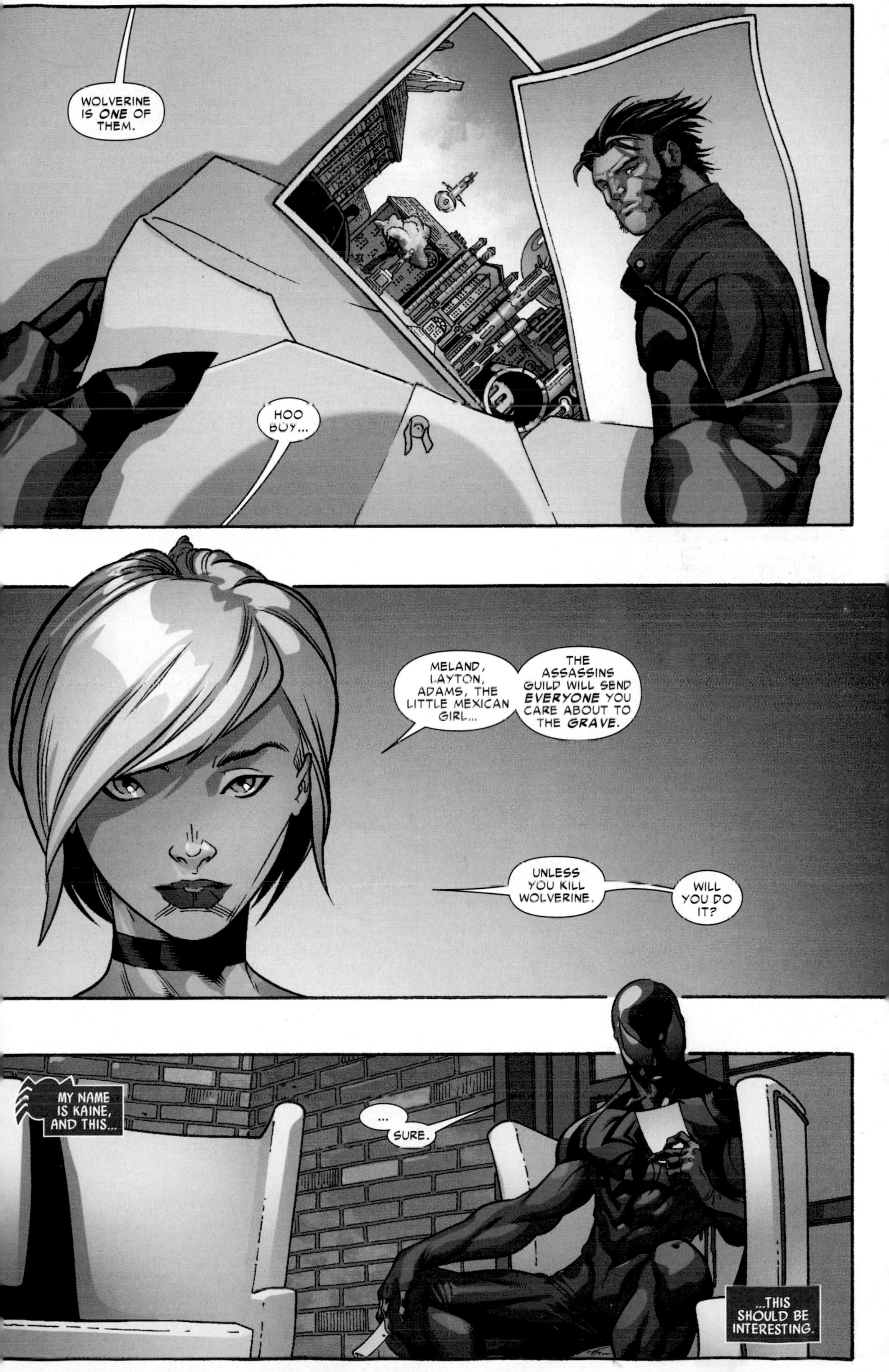
WOLVERINE IS ONE OF THEM.
HOO BOY...
MELAND, LAYTON, ADAMS, THE LITTLE MEXICAN GIRL...
THE ASSASSINS GUILD WILL SEND EVERYONE YOU CARE ABOUT TO THE GRAVE.
UNLESS YOU KILL WOLVERINE.
WILL YOU DO IT?
MY NAME IS KAINE, AND THIS...
...
SURE.
...THIS SHOULD BE INTERESTING.

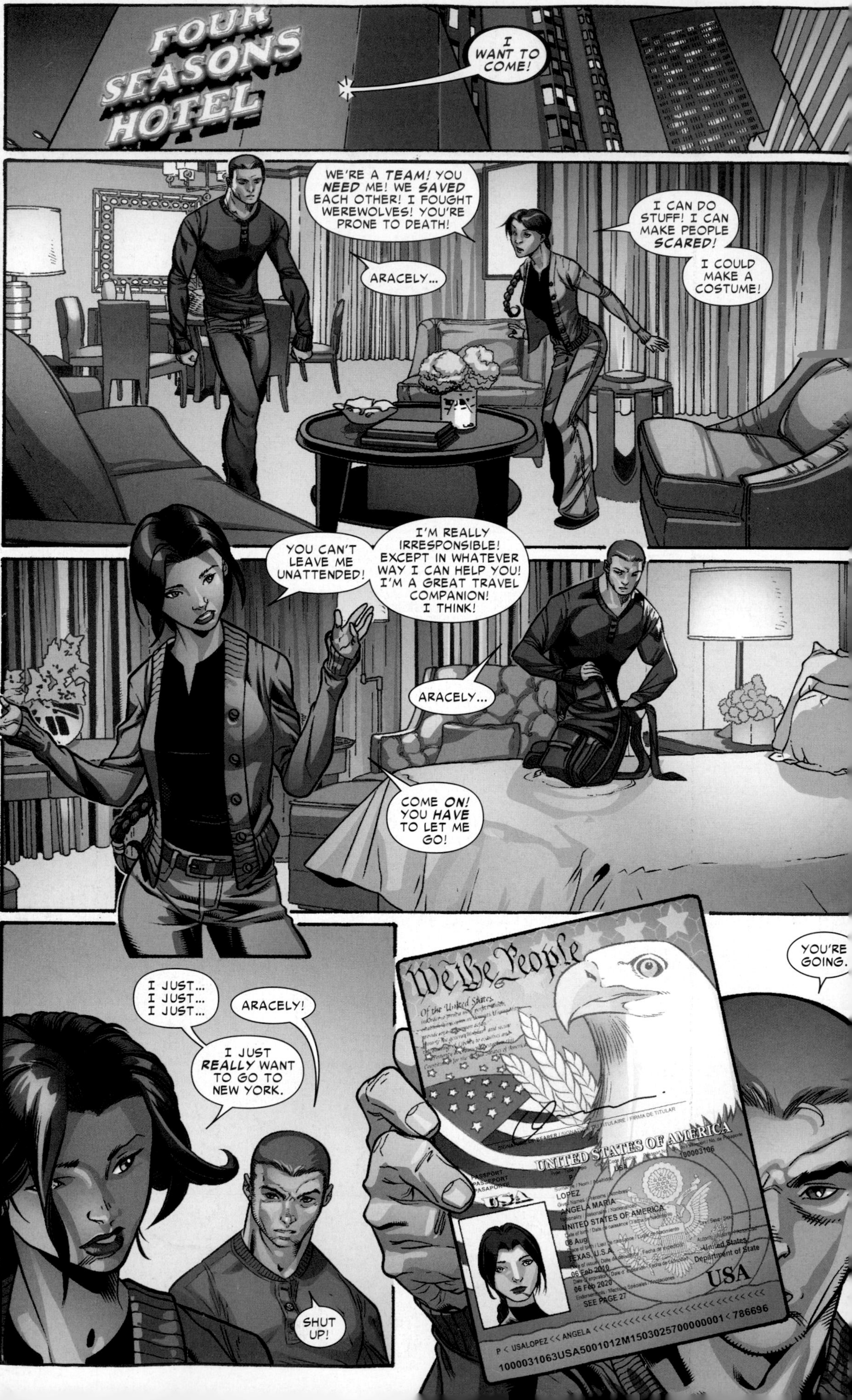
FOUR SEASONS HOTEL
I WANT TO COME!
WE'RE A TEAM! YOU NEED ME! WE SAVED EACH OTHER! I FOUGHT WEREWOLVES! YOU'RE PRONE TO DEATH!
ARACELY...
I CAN DO STUFF! I CAN MAKE PEOPLE SCARED!
I COULD MAKE A COSTUME!
YOU CAN'T LEAVE ME UNATTENDED!
I'M REALLY IRRESPONSIBLE! EXCEPT IN WHATEVER WAY I CAN HELP YOU! I'M A GREAT TRAVEL COMPANION! I THINK!
ARACELY...
COME ON! YOU HAVE TO LET ME GO!
I JUST... I JUST... I JUST...
ARACELY!
I JUST REALLY WANT TO GO TO NEW YORK.
SHUT UP!
YOU'RE GOING.
We the People
UNITED STATES OF AMERICA
LOPEZ
ANGELA MARIA
UNITED STATES OF AMERICA
TEXAS, U.S.A.
06 Feb 2010
06 Feb 2020
United States Department of State
USA
SEE PAGE 27
P < USALOPEZ << ANGELA <<<<<<<<<<<<<<<<<<<<<<<<<<<
1000031063USA5001012M1503025700000001 < 786696

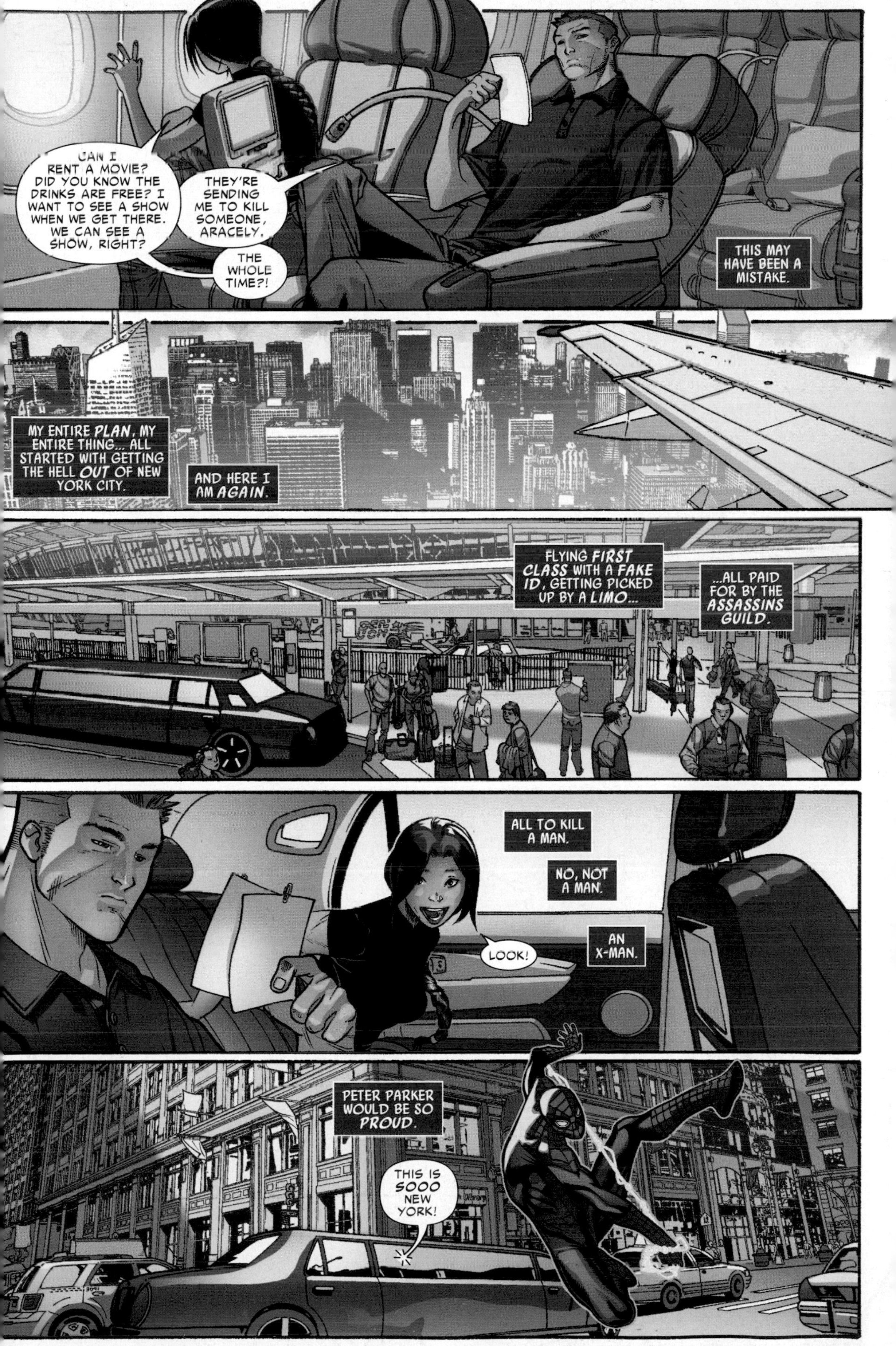
CAN I RENT A MOVIE? DID YOU KNOW THE DRINKS ARE FREE? I WANT TO SEE A SHOW WHEN WE GET THERE. WE CAN SEE A SHOW, RIGHT?
THEY'RE SENDING ME TO KILL SOMEONE, ARACELY.
THE WHOLE TIME?!
THIS MAY HAVE BEEN A MISTAKE.
MY ENTIRE PLAN, MY ENTIRE THING... ALL STARTED WITH GETTING THE HELL OUT OF NEW YORK CITY.
AND HERE I AM AGAIN.
FLYING FIRST CLASS WITH A FAKE ID, GETTING PICKED UP BY A LIMO...
...ALL PAID FOR BY THE ASSASSINS GUILD.
ALL TO KILL A MAN.
NO, NOT A MAN.
AN X-MAN.
LOOK!
PETER PARKER WOULD BE SO PROUD.
THIS IS SOOO NEW YORK!

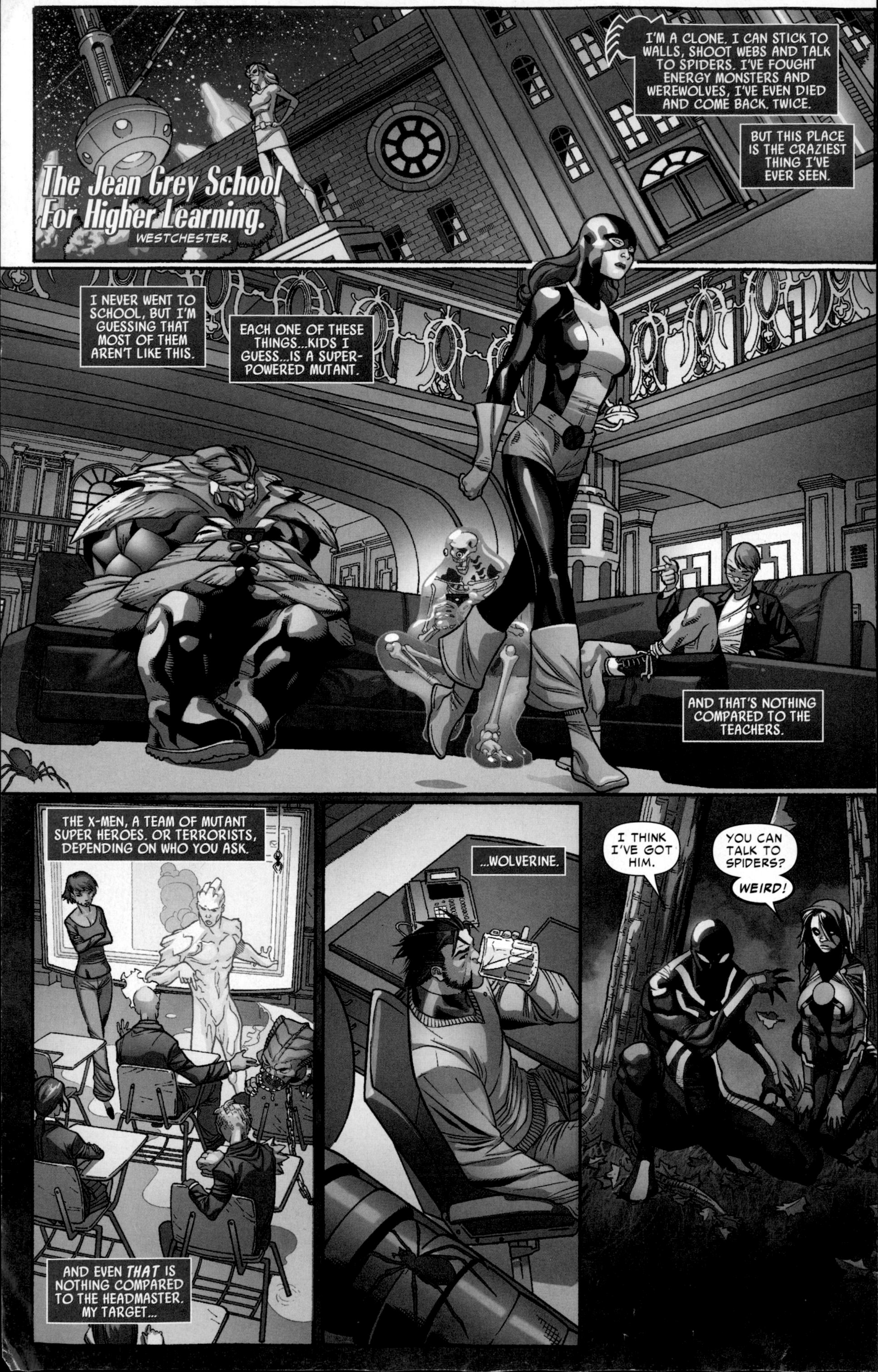
I'M A CLONE. I CAN STICK TO WALLS, SHOOT WEBS AND TALK TO SPIDERS. I'VE FOUGHT ENERGY MONSTERS AND WEREWOLVES, I'VE EVEN DIED AND COME BACK. TWICE.
BUT THIS PLACE IS THE CRAZIEST THING I'VE EVER SEEN.
The Jean Grey School For Higher Learning.
WESTCHESTER.
I NEVER WENT TO SCHOOL, BUT I'M GUESSING THAT MOST OF THEM AREN'T LIKE THIS.
EACH ONE OF THESE THINGS...KIDS I GUESS...IS A SUPER-POWERED MUTANT.
AND THAT'S NOTHING COMPARED TO THE TEACHERS.
THE X-MEN, A TEAM OF MUTANT SUPER HEROES. OR TERRORISTS, DEPENDING ON WHO YOU ASK.
AND EVEN THAT IS NOTHING COMPARED TO THE HEADMASTER. MY TARGET...
...WOLVERINE.
I THINK I'VE GOT HIM.
YOU CAN TALK TO SPIDERS?
WEIRD!

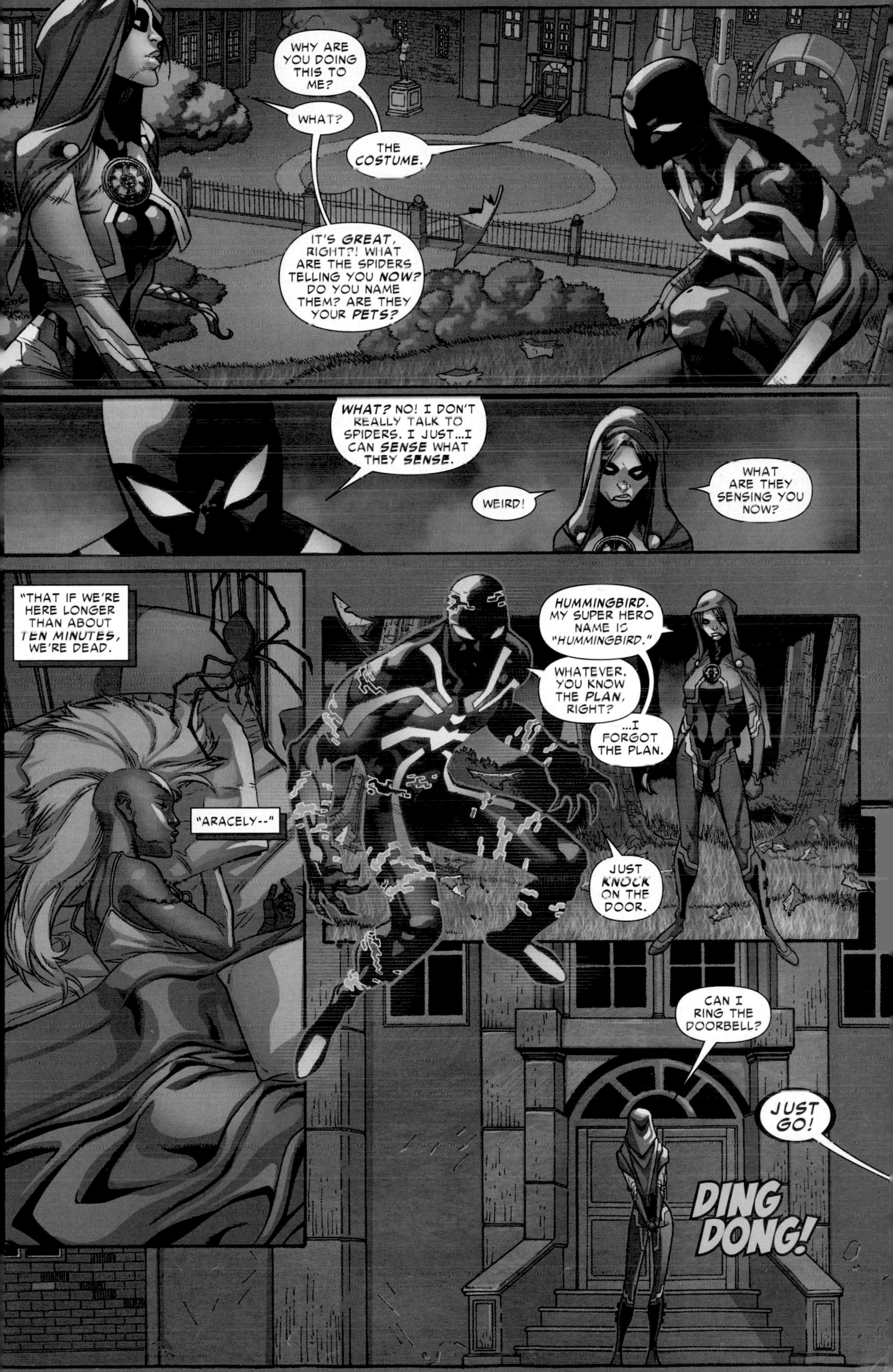

WHY ARE YOU DOING THIS TO ME?
WHAT?
THE *COSTUME*.
IT'S *GREAT*, RIGHT?! WHAT ARE THE SPIDERS TELLING YOU *NOW*? DO YOU NAME THEM? ARE THEY YOUR *PETS*?
WHAT? NO! I DON'T REALLY TALK TO SPIDERS. I JUST...I CAN ***SENSE*** WHAT THEY ***SENSE***.
WEIRD!
WHAT ARE THEY SENSING YOU NOW?
"THAT IF WE'RE HERE LONGER THAN ABOUT *TEN MINUTES*, WE'RE DEAD.
"ARACELY--"
HUMMINGBIRD. MY SUPER HERO NAME IS "*HUMMINGBIRD*."
WHATEVER, YOU KNOW THE *PLAN*, RIGHT?
...I FORGOT THE PLAN.
JUST ***KNOCK*** ON THE DOOR.
CAN I RING THE DOORBELL?
JUST GO!
DING DONG!

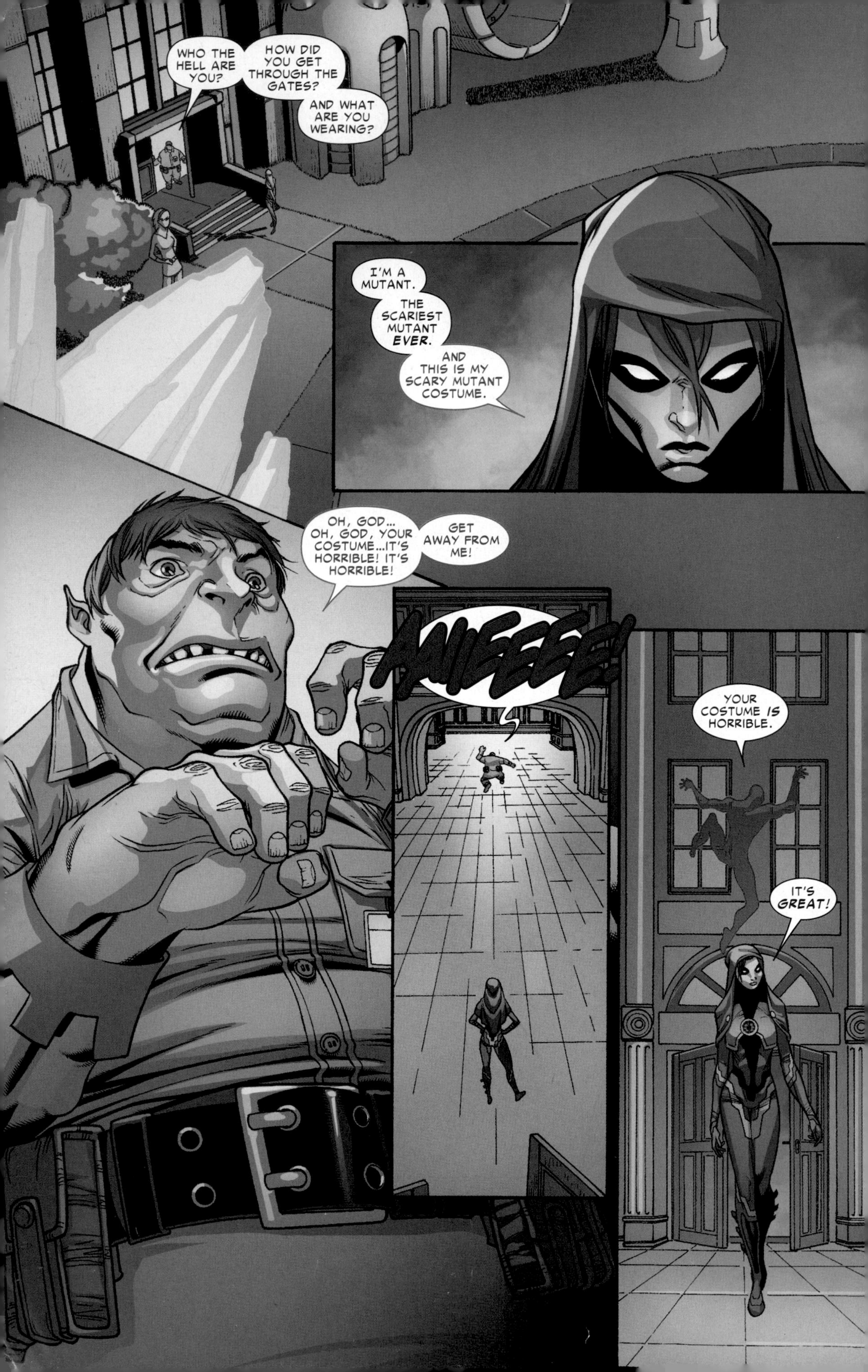

WHO THE HELL ARE YOU?
HOW DID YOU GET THROUGH THE GATES?
AND WHAT ARE YOU WEARING?
I'M A MUTANT.
THE SCARIEST MUTANT *EVER*.
AND THIS IS MY SCARY MUTANT COSTUME.
OH, GOD... OH, GOD, YOUR COSTUME...IT'S HORRIBLE! IT'S HORRIBLE!
GET AWAY FROM ME!
AAIIEEEE!
YOUR COSTUME *IS* HORRIBLE.
IT'S *GREAT*!

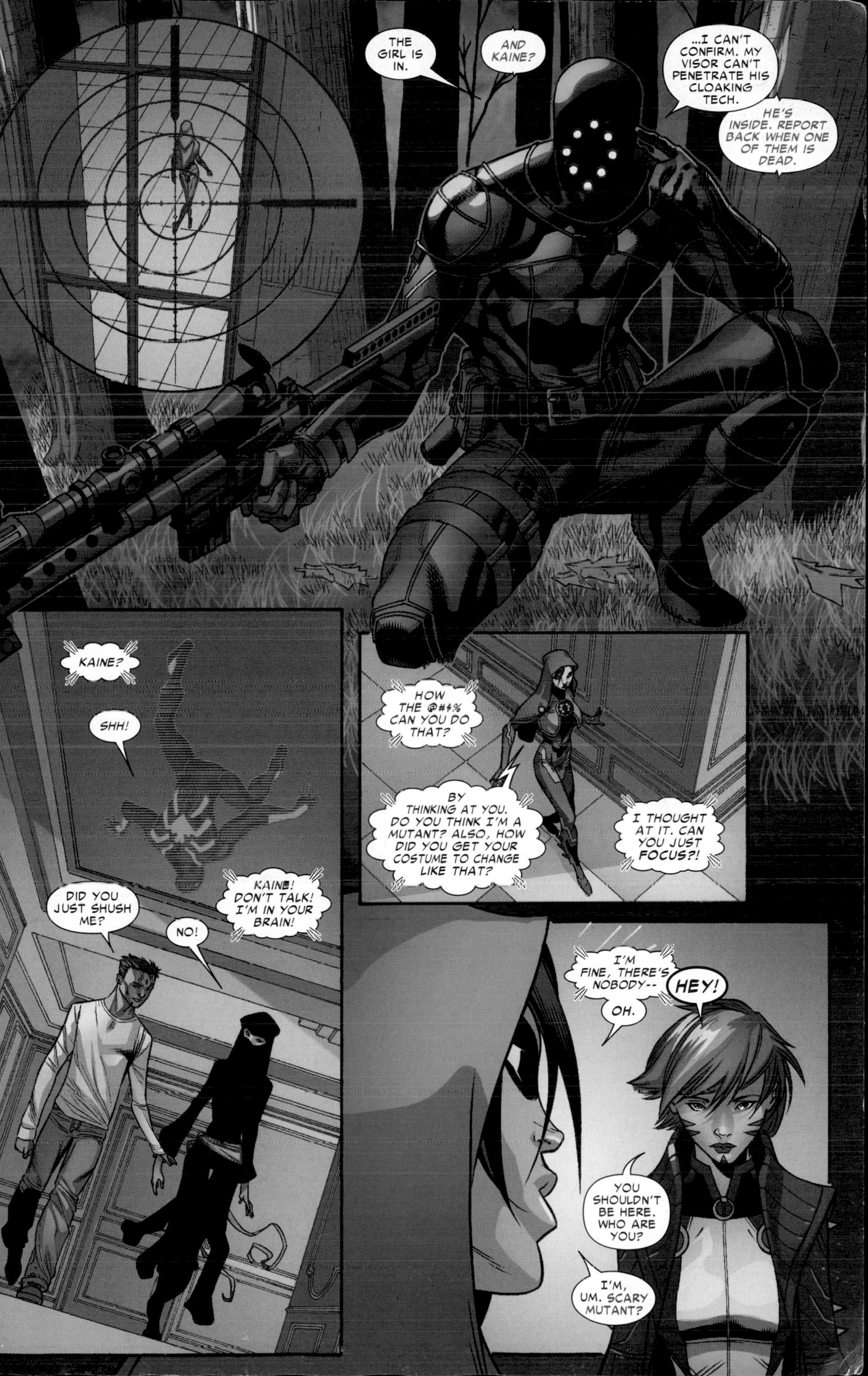
THE GIRL IS IN.
AND KAINE?
...I CAN'T CONFIRM. MY VISOR CAN'T PENETRATE HIS CLOAKING TECH.
HE'S INSIDE. REPORT BACK WHEN ONE OF THEM IS DEAD.
KAINE?
SHH!
DID YOU JUST SHUSH ME?
NO!
KAINE! DON'T TALK! I'M IN YOUR BRAIN!
HOW THE @#$% CAN YOU DO THAT?
BY THINKING AT YOU. DO YOU THINK I'M A MUTANT? ALSO, HOW DID YOU GET YOUR COSTUME TO CHANGE LIKE THAT?
I THOUGHT AT IT. CAN YOU JUST FOCUS?!
I'M FINE, THERE'S NOBODY--
HEY!
OH.
YOU SHOULDN'T BE HERE. WHO ARE YOU?
I'M, UM. SCARY MUTANT?

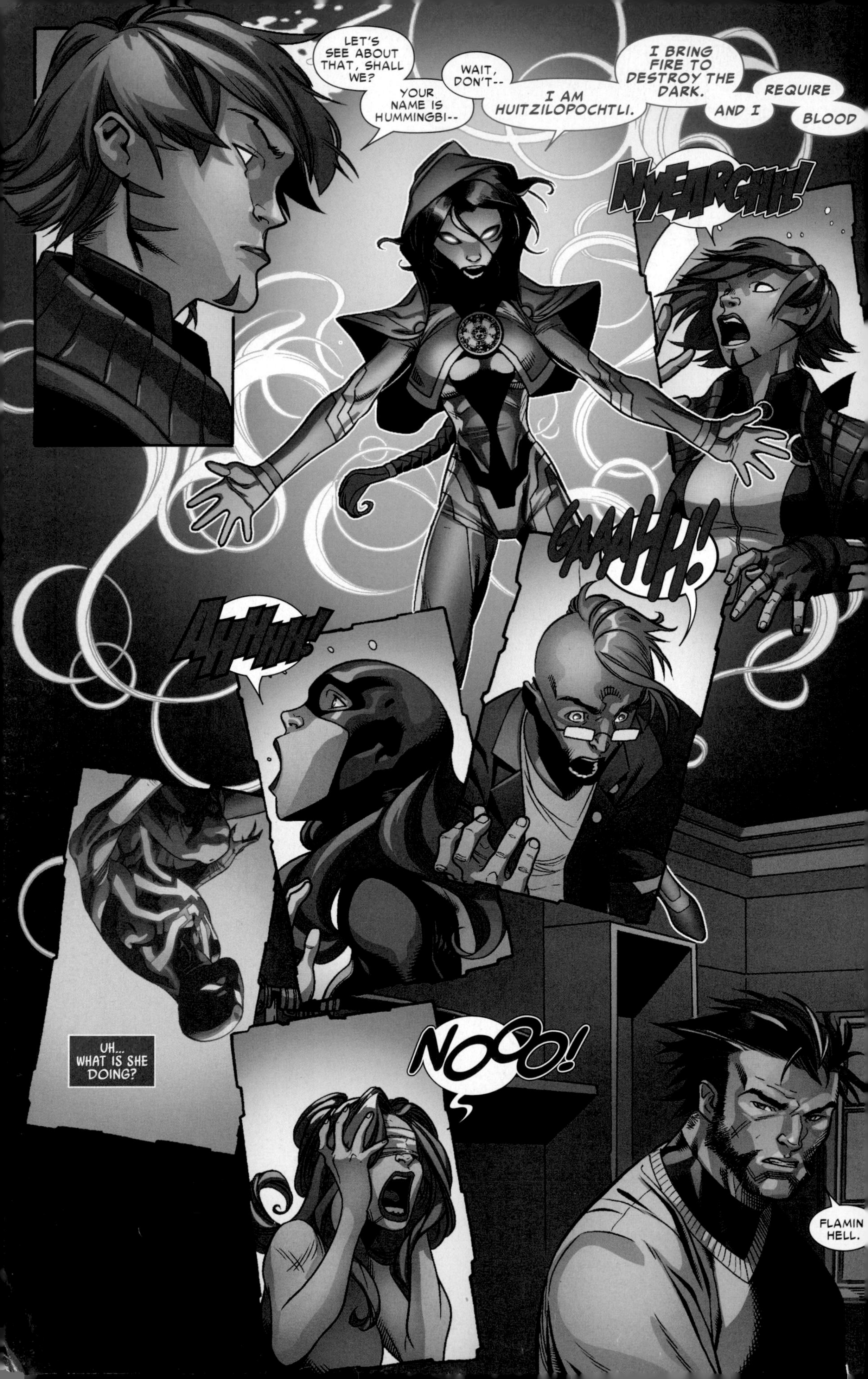
LET'S SEE ABOUT THAT, SHALL WE?
YOUR NAME IS HUMMINGBI--
WAIT, DON'T--
I AM HUITZILOPOCHTLI.
I BRING FIRE TO DESTROY THE DARK.
AND I
REQUIRE
BLOOD
NYEARGHH!
GAAAHH!
AHHHH!
UH... WHAT IS SHE DOING?
NOOOO!
FLAMIN HELL.

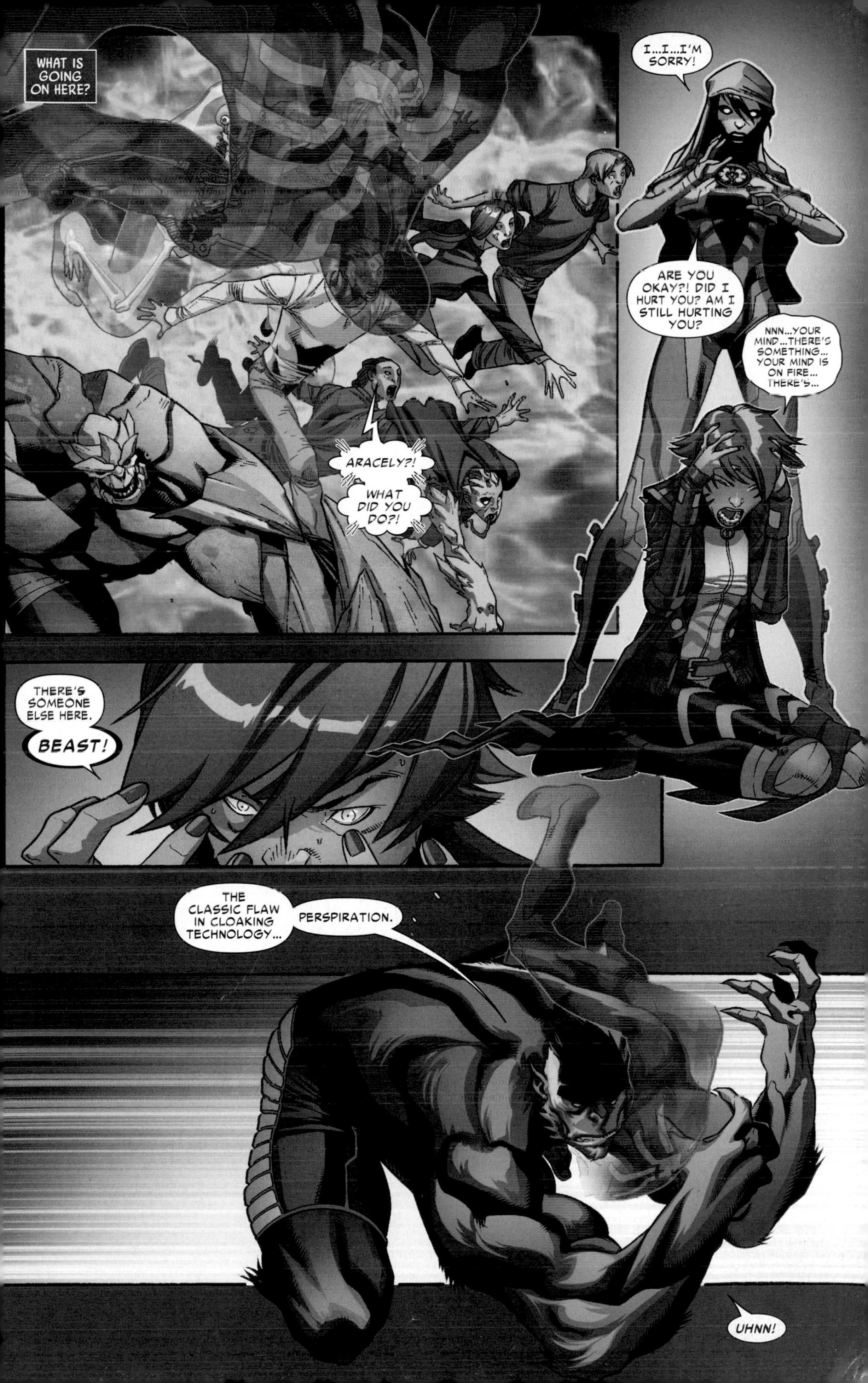
WHAT IS GOING ON HERE?
I...I...I'M SORRY!
ARE YOU OKAY?! DID I HURT YOU? AM I STILL HURTING YOU?
NNN...YOUR MIND...THERE'S SOMETHING... YOUR MIND IS ON FIRE... THERE'S...
ARACELY?!
WHAT DID YOU DO?!
THERE'S SOMEONE ELSE HERE.
BEAST!
THE CLASSIC FLAW IN CLOAKING TECHNOLOGY...
PERSPIRATION.
UHNN!

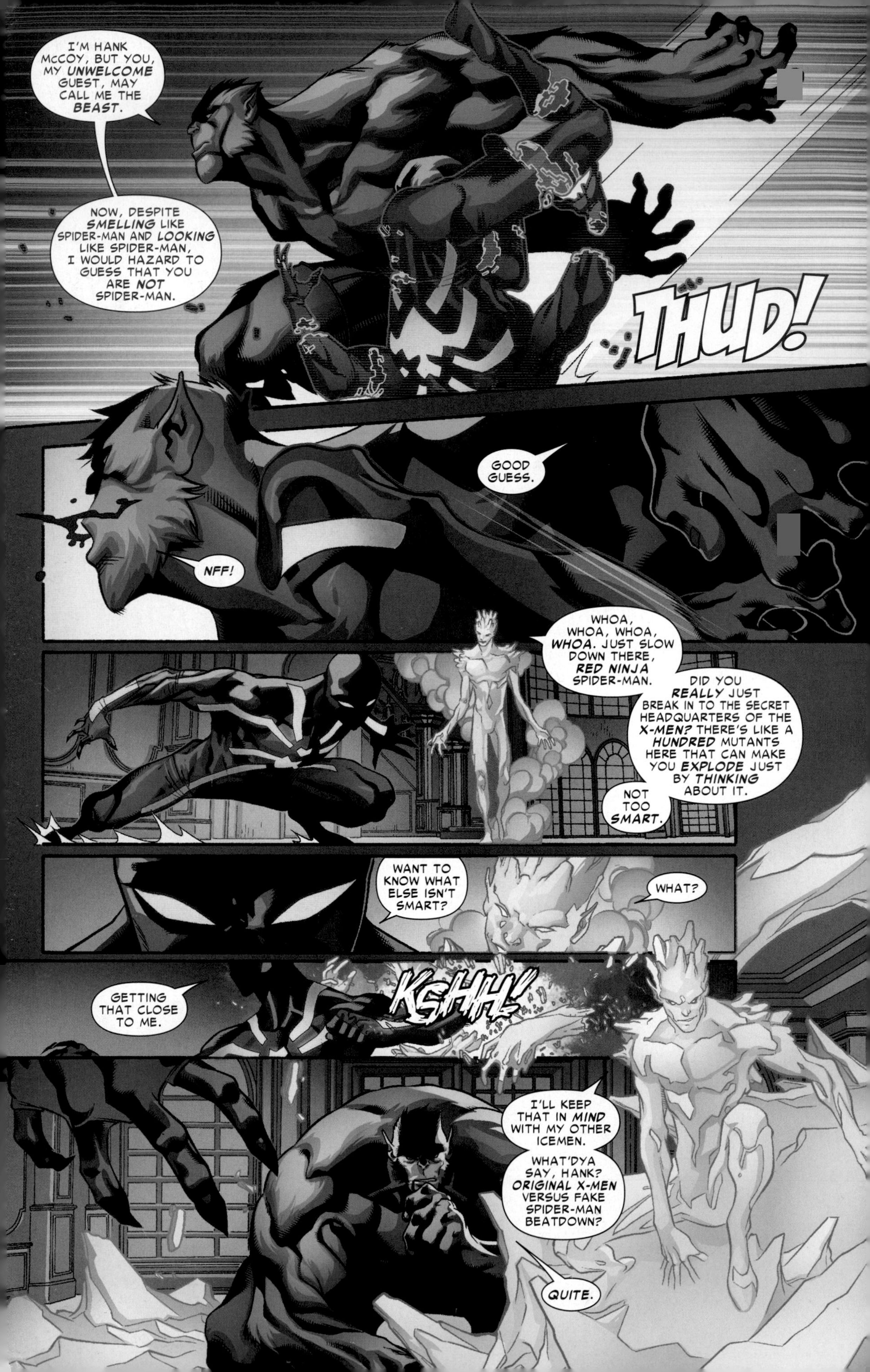

I'M HANK McCOY, BUT YOU, MY UNWELCOME GUEST, MAY CALL ME THE BEAST.
NOW, DESPITE SMELLING LIKE SPIDER-MAN AND LOOKING LIKE SPIDER-MAN, I WOULD HAZARD TO GUESS THAT YOU ARE NOT SPIDER-MAN.
THUD!
GOOD GUESS.
NFF!
WHOA, WHOA, WHOA, WHOA. JUST SLOW DOWN THERE, RED NINJA SPIDER-MAN.
DID YOU REALLY JUST BREAK IN TO THE SECRET HEADQUARTERS OF THE X-MEN? THERE'S LIKE A HUNDRED MUTANTS HERE THAT CAN MAKE YOU EXPLODE JUST BY THINKING ABOUT IT.
NOT TOO SMART.
WANT TO KNOW WHAT ELSE ISN'T SMART?
WHAT?
KSHHL!
GETTING THAT CLOSE TO ME.
I'LL KEEP THAT IN MIND WITH MY OTHER ICEMEN.
WHAT'DYA SAY, HANK? ORIGINAL X-MEN VERSUS FAKE SPIDER-MAN BEATDOWN?
QUITE.

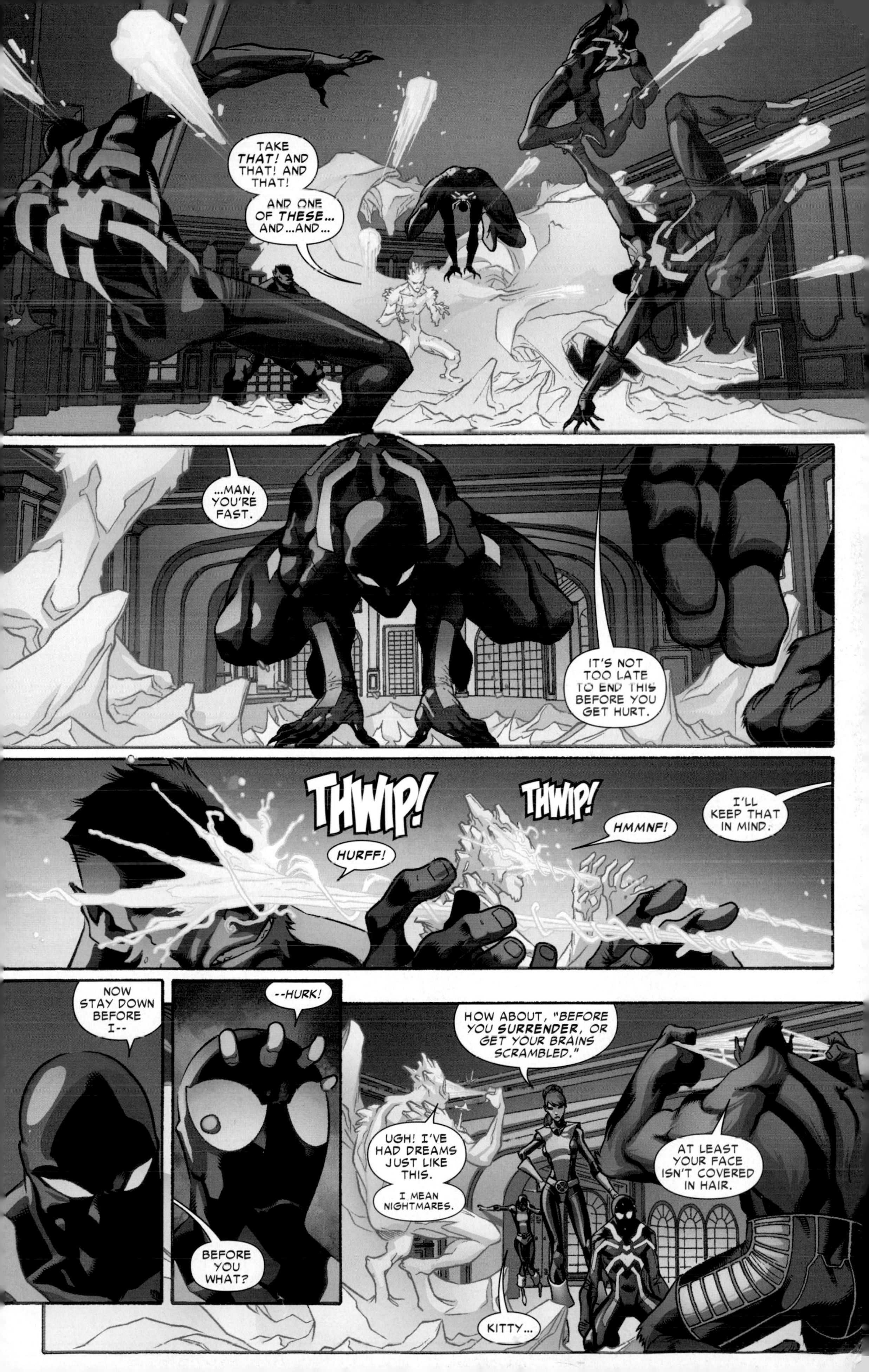
TAKE THAT! AND THAT! AND THAT!
AND ONE OF THESE... AND...AND...
...MAN, YOU'RE FAST.
IT'S NOT TOO LATE TO END THIS BEFORE YOU GET HURT.
THWIP!
HURFF!
THWIP!
HMMNF!
I'LL KEEP THAT IN MIND.
NOW STAY DOWN BEFORE I--
--HURK!
BEFORE YOU WHAT?
HOW ABOUT, "BEFORE YOU SURRENDER, OR GET YOUR BRAINS SCRAMBLED."
UGH! I'VE HAD DREAMS JUST LIKE THIS.
I MEAN NIGHTMARES.
AT LEAST YOUR FACE ISN'T COVERED IN HAIR.
KITTY...

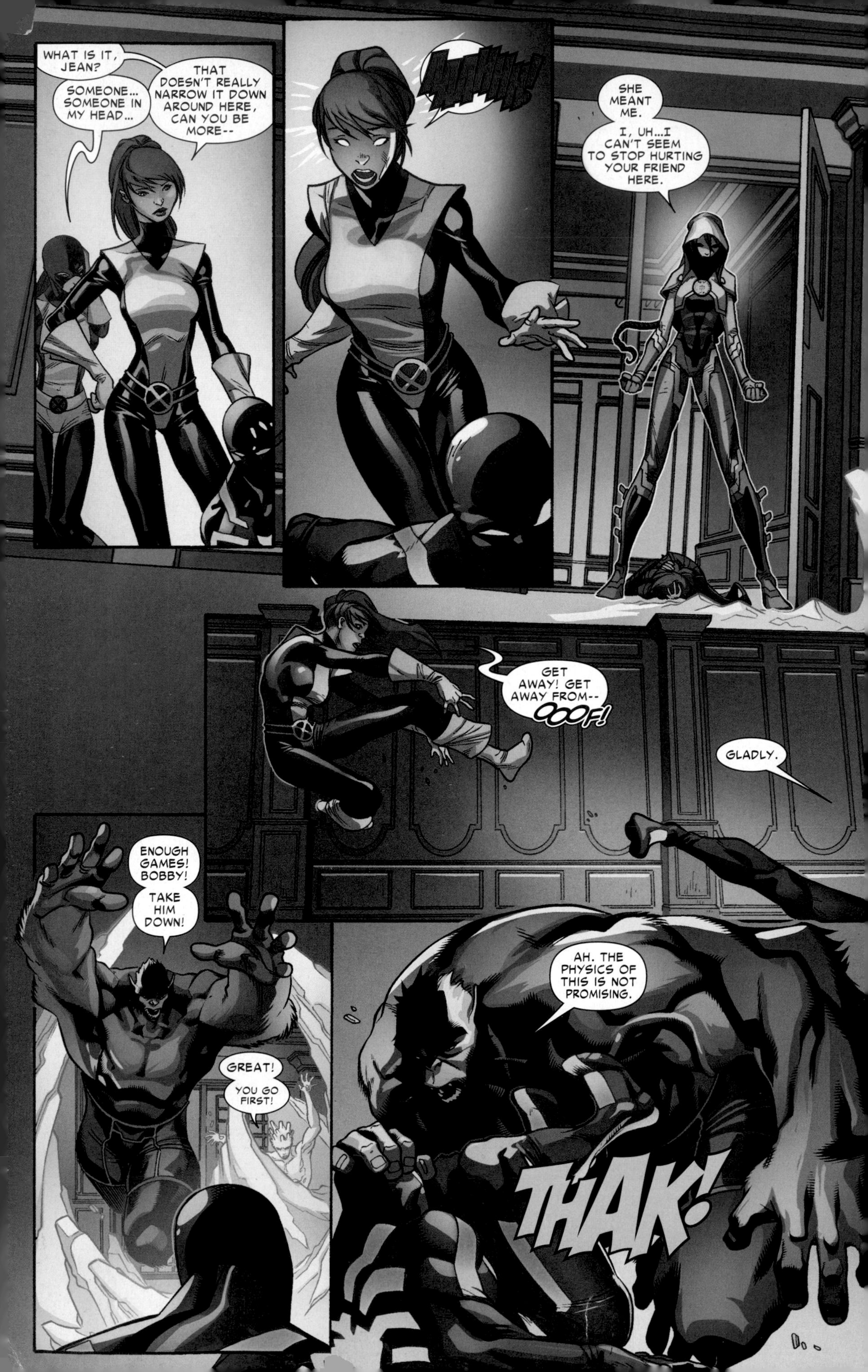
WHAT IS IT, JEAN?
SOMEONE... SOMEONE IN MY HEAD...
THAT DOESN'T REALLY NARROW IT DOWN AROUND HERE, CAN YOU BE MORE--
SHE MEANT ME.
I, UH...I CAN'T SEEM TO STOP HURTING YOUR FRIEND HERE.
GET AWAY! GET AWAY FROM-- OOOF!
GLADLY.
ENOUGH GAMES! BOBBY!
TAKE HIM DOWN!
GREAT!
YOU GO FIRST!
AH. THE PHYSICS OF THIS IS NOT PROMISING.
THAK!

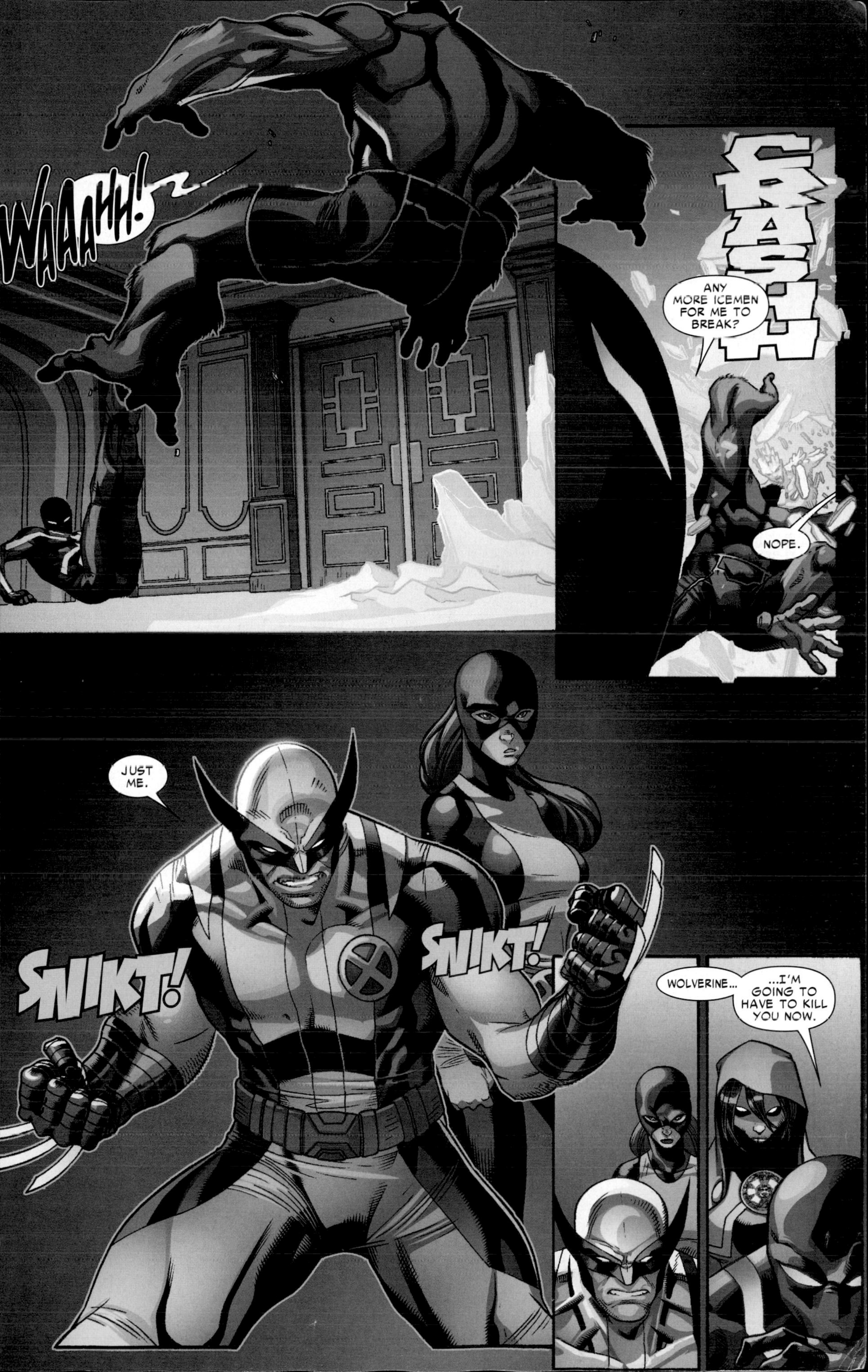
WAAAHH!
CRASH
ANY MORE ICEMEN FOR ME TO BREAK?
NOPE.
JUST ME.
SNIKT!
SNIKT!
WOLVERINE...
...I'M GOING TO HAVE TO KILL YOU NOW.

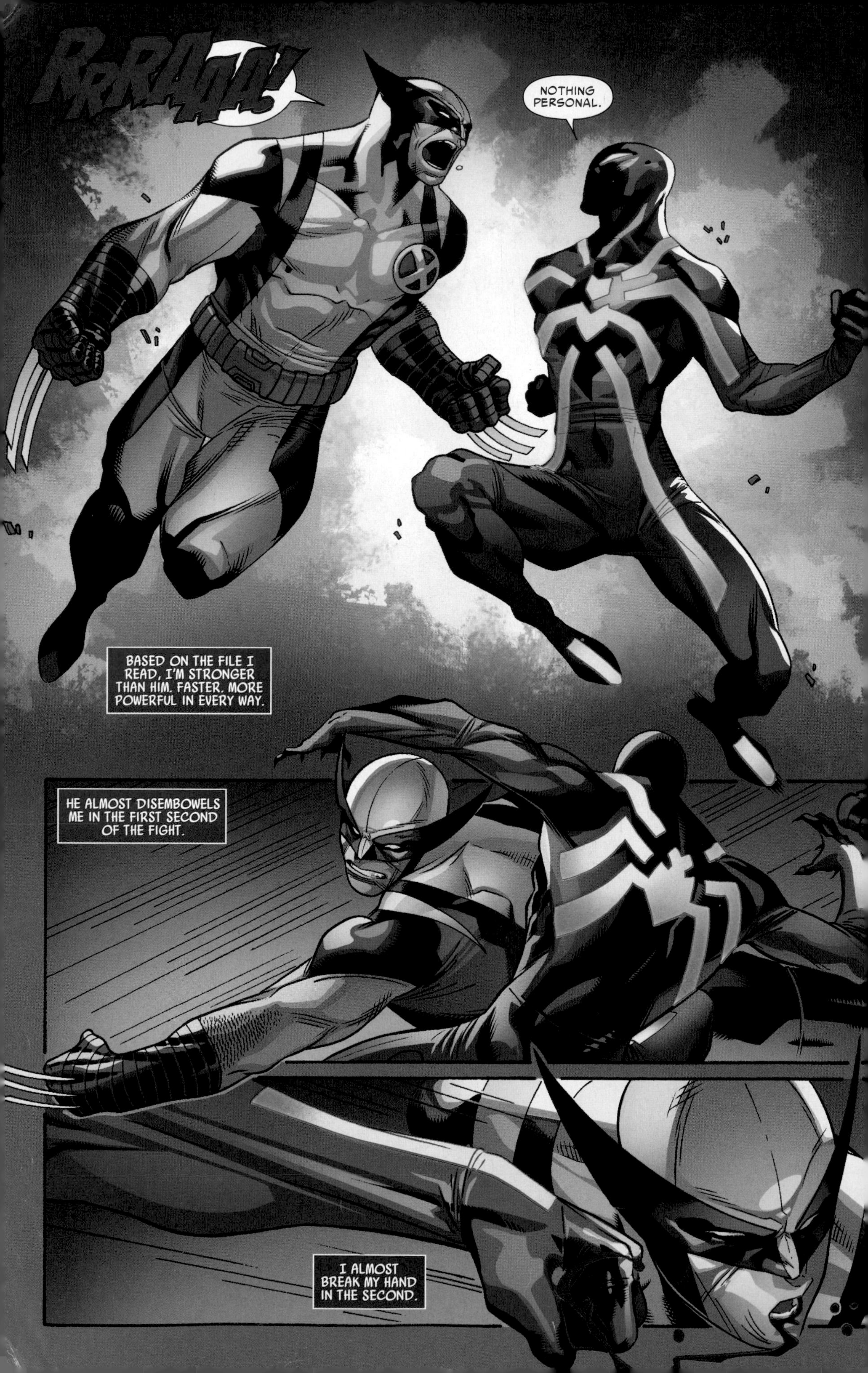
RRRAAAA!
NOTHING PERSONAL.
BASED ON THE FILE I READ, I'M STRONGER THAN HIM. FASTER. MORE POWERFUL IN EVERY WAY.
HE ALMOST DISEMBOWELS ME IN THE FIRST SECOND OF THE FIGHT.
I ALMOST BREAK MY HAND IN THE SECOND.

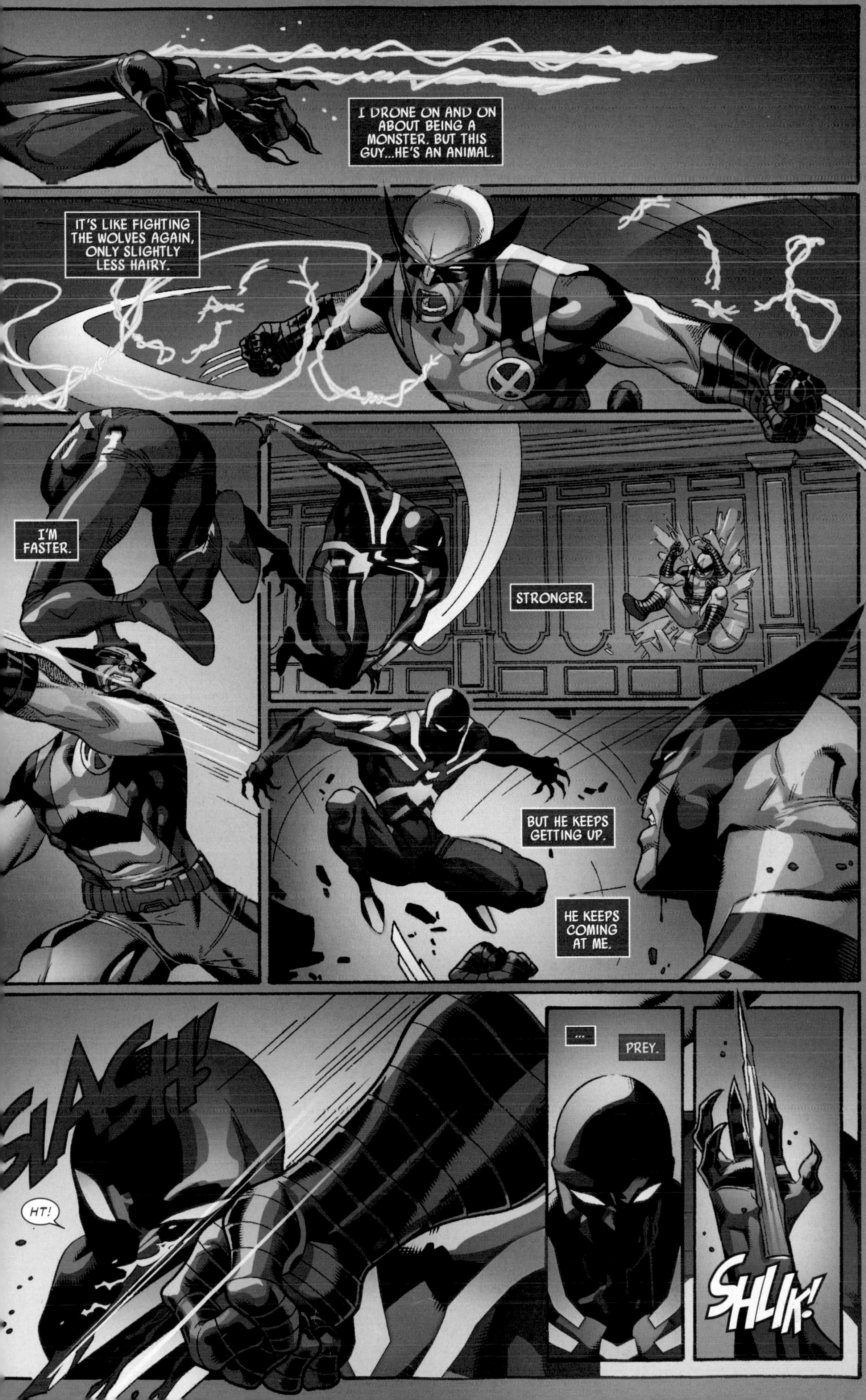
I DRONE ON AND ON ABOUT BEING A MONSTER. BUT THIS GUY...HE'S AN ANIMAL.
IT'S LIKE FIGHTING THE WOLVES AGAIN, ONLY SLIGHTLY LESS HAIRY.
I'M FASTER.
STRONGER.
BUT HE KEEPS GETTING UP.
HE KEEPS COMING AT ME.
GASH!
HT!
...
PREY.
SHLIK!

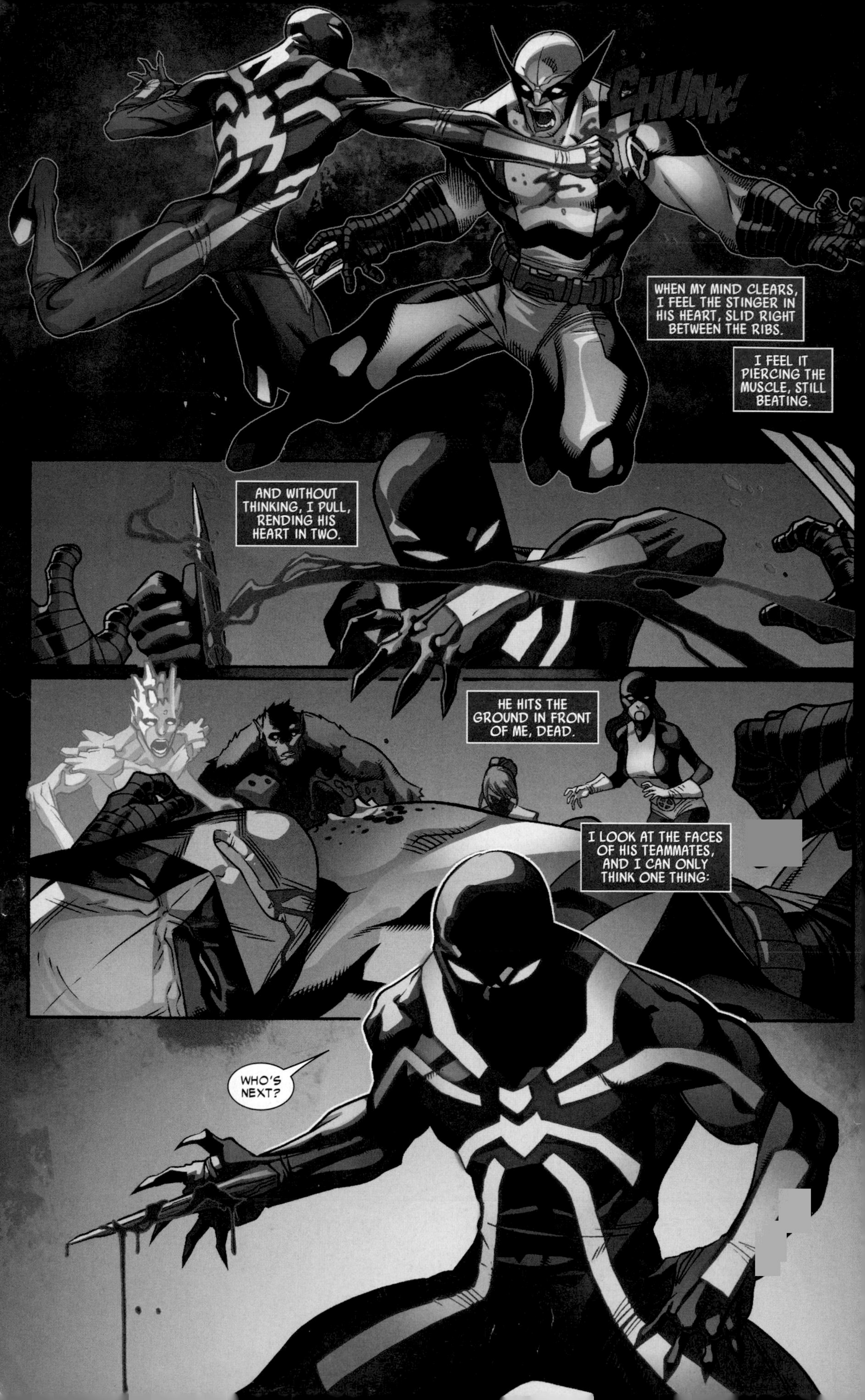
CHUNK!
WHEN MY MIND CLEARS, I FEEL THE STINGER IN HIS HEART, SLID RIGHT BETWEEN THE RIBS.
I FEEL IT PIERCING THE MUSCLE, STILL BEATING.
AND WITHOUT THINKING, I PULL, RENDING HIS HEART IN TWO.
HE HITS THE GROUND IN FRONT OF ME, DEAD.
I LOOK AT THE FACES OF HIS TEAMMATES, AND I CAN ONLY THINK ONE THING:
WHO'S NEXT?

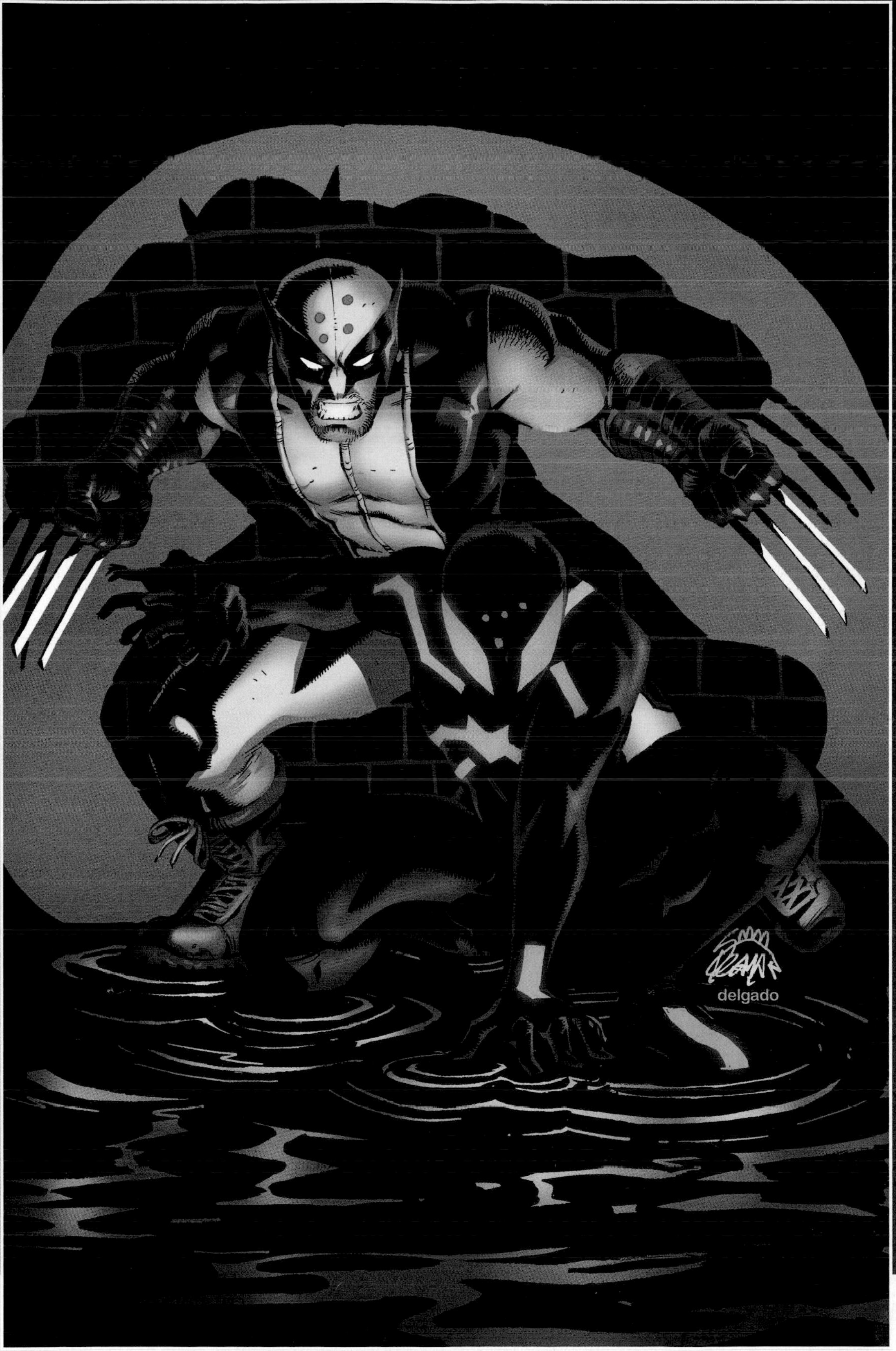
delgado

"WRATH, PART 2"

#18

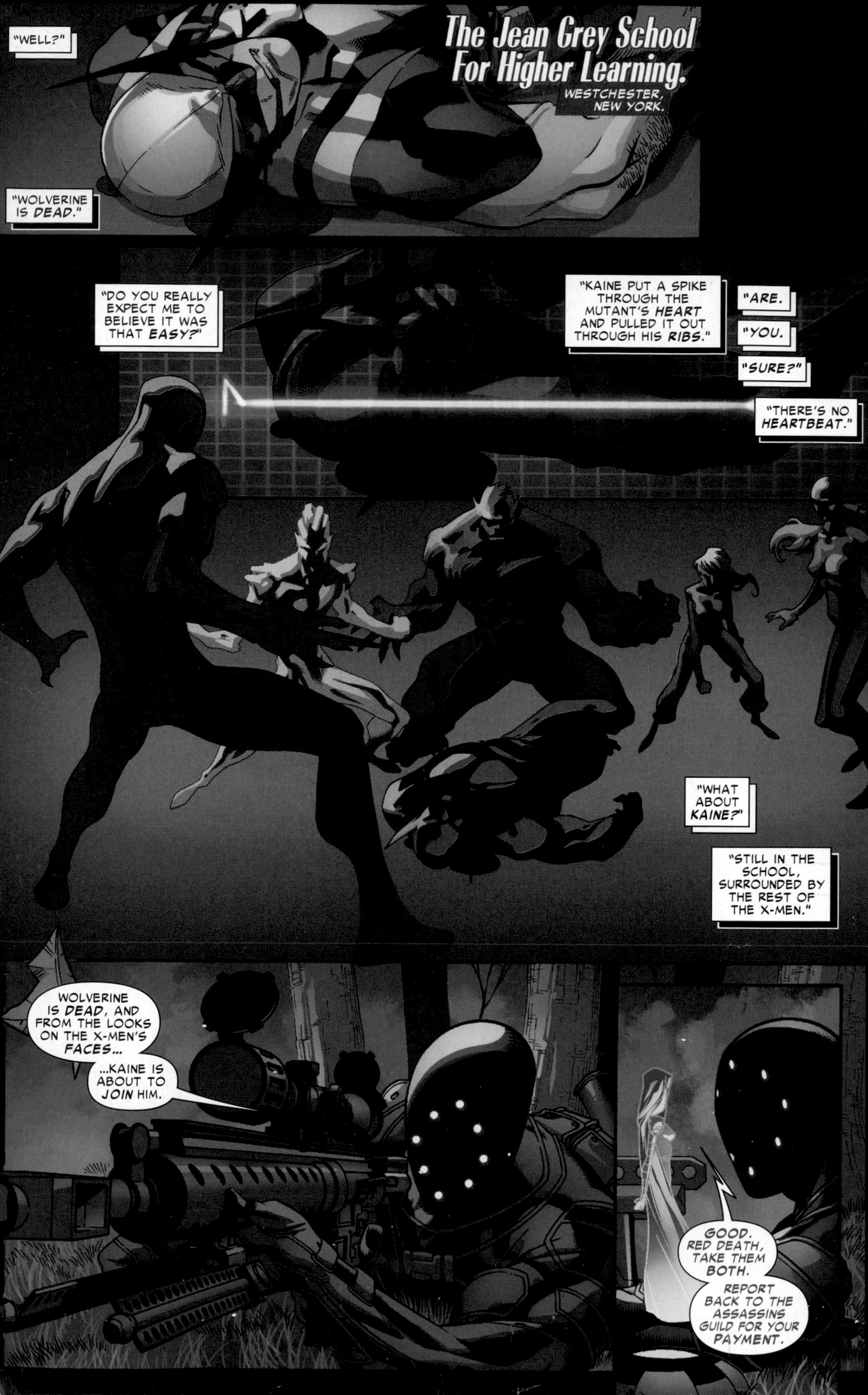
"WELL?"
The Jean Grey School For Higher Learning.
WESTCHESTER, NEW YORK.
"WOLVERINE IS DEAD."
"DO YOU REALLY EXPECT ME TO BELIEVE IT WAS THAT EASY?"
"KAINE PUT A SPIKE THROUGH THE MUTANT'S HEART AND PULLED IT OUT THROUGH HIS RIBS."
"ARE.
"YOU.
"SURE?"
"THERE'S NO HEARTBEAT."
"WHAT ABOUT KAINE?"
"STILL IN THE SCHOOL, SURROUNDED BY THE REST OF THE X-MEN."
WOLVERINE IS DEAD, AND FROM THE LOOKS ON THE X-MEN'S FACES...
...KAINE IS ABOUT TO JOIN HIM.
GOOD. RED DEATH, TAKE THEM BOTH.
REPORT BACK TO THE ASSASSINS GUILD FOR YOUR PAYMENT.

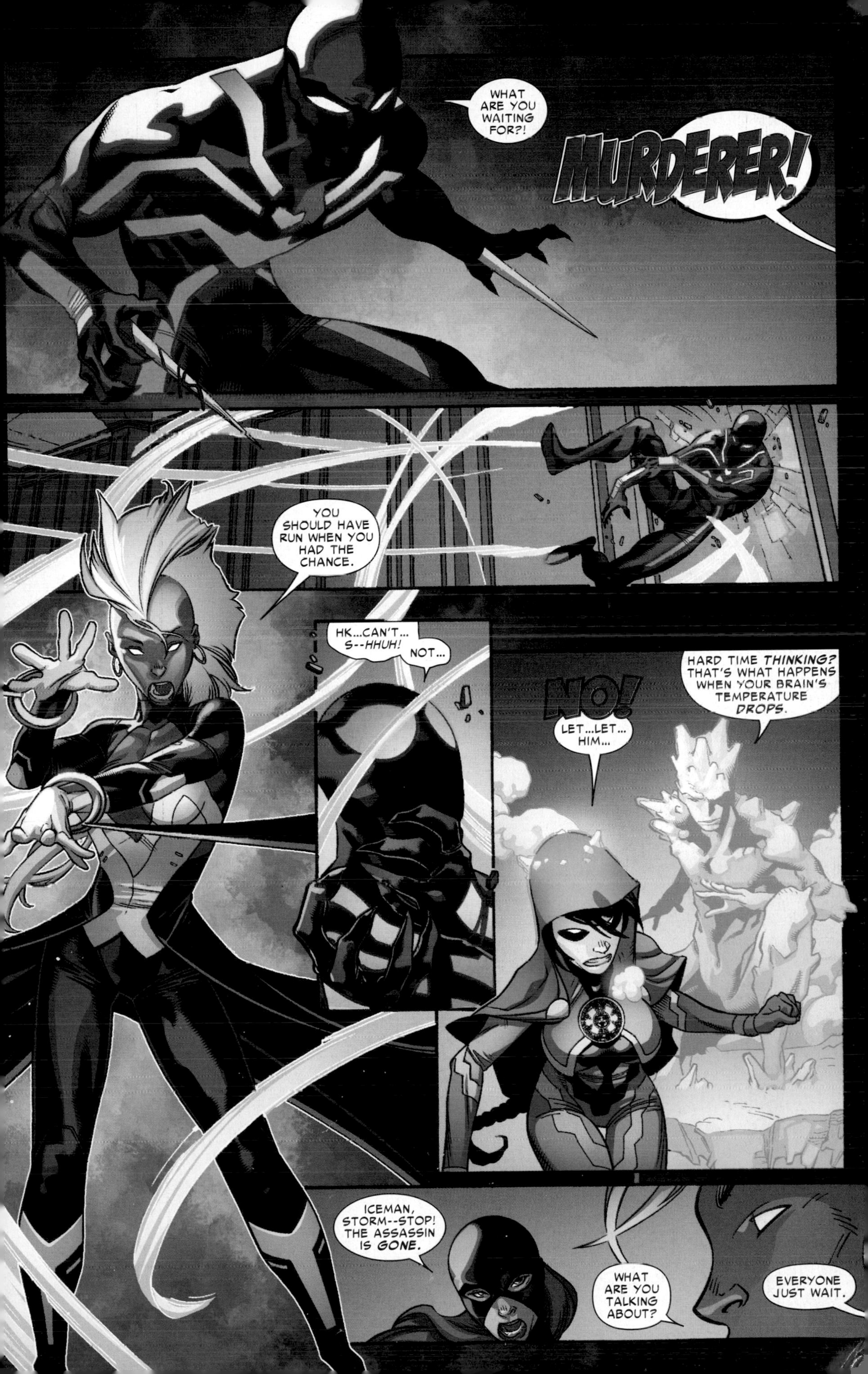
WHAT ARE YOU WAITING FOR?!
MURDERER!
YOU SHOULD HAVE RUN WHEN YOU HAD THE CHANCE.
HK...CAN'T... S--HHUH!
NOT...
NO!
LET...LET... HIM...
HARD TIME THINKING? THAT'S WHAT HAPPENS WHEN YOUR BRAIN'S TEMPERATURE DROPS.
ICEMAN, STORM--STOP! THE ASSASSIN IS GONE.
WHAT ARE YOU TALKING ABOUT?
EVERYONE JUST WAIT.

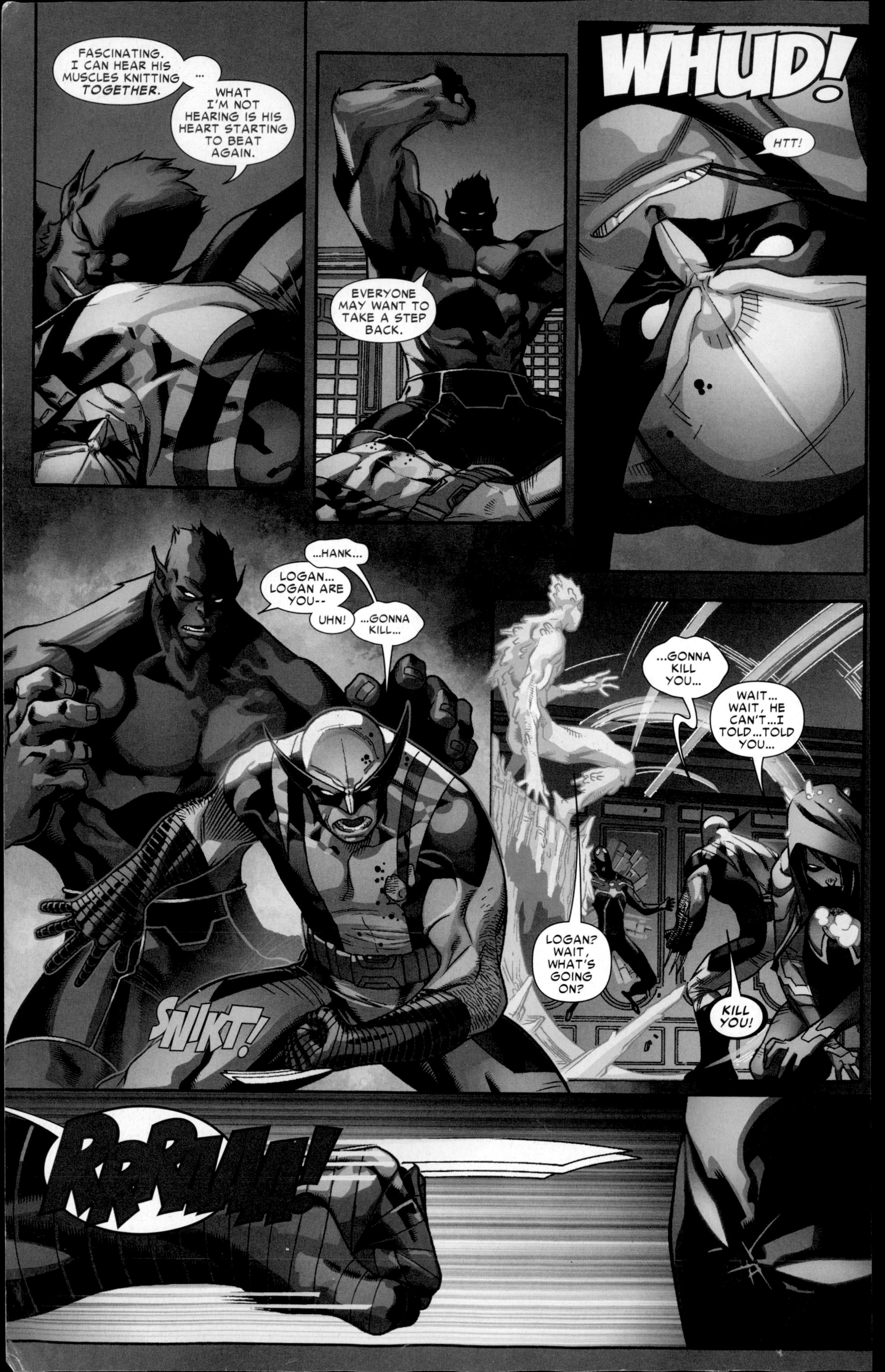
FASCINATING. I CAN HEAR HIS MUSCLES KNITTING TOGETHER.
...
WHAT I'M NOT HEARING IS HIS HEART STARTING TO BEAT AGAIN.
EVERYONE MAY WANT TO TAKE A STEP BACK.
WHUD!
HTT!
...HANK...
LOGAN... LOGAN ARE YOU--
UHN!
...GONNA KILL...
SNIKT!
...GONNA KILL YOU...
WAIT... WAIT, HE CAN'T...I TOLD...TOLD YOU...
LOGAN? WAIT, WHAT'S GOING ON?
KILL YOU!
RRRUUH!

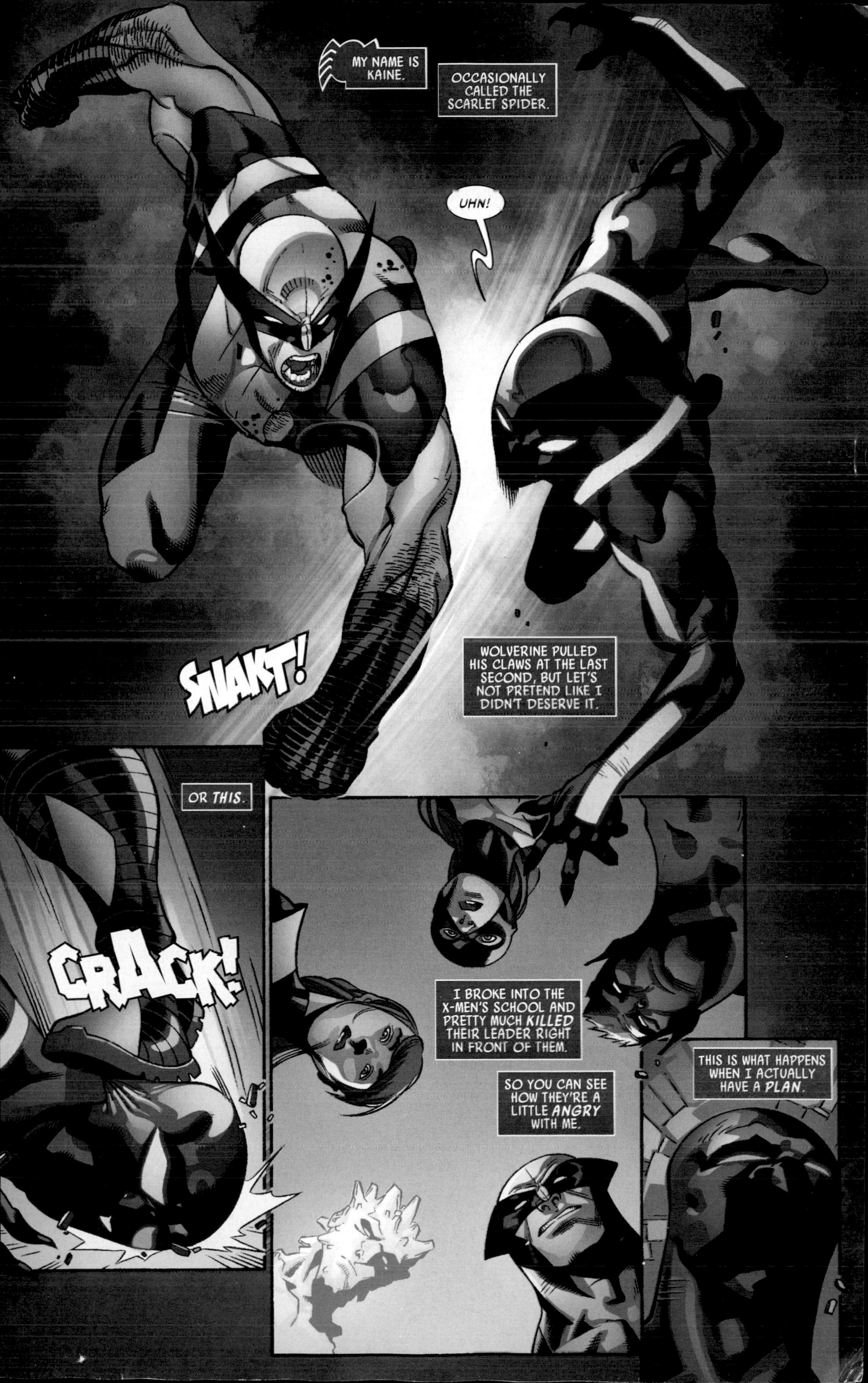
MY NAME IS KAINE.
OCCASIONALLY CALLED THE SCARLET SPIDER.
UHN!
SNAKT!
WOLVERINE PULLED HIS CLAWS AT THE LAST SECOND, BUT LET'S NOT PRETEND LIKE I DIDN'T DESERVE IT.
OR THIS.
CRACK!
I BROKE INTO THE X-MEN'S SCHOOL AND PRETTY MUCH KILLED THEIR LEADER RIGHT IN FRONT OF THEM.
SO YOU CAN SEE HOW THEY'RE A LITTLE ANGRY WITH ME.
THIS IS WHAT HAPPENS WHEN I ACTUALLY HAVE A PLAN.

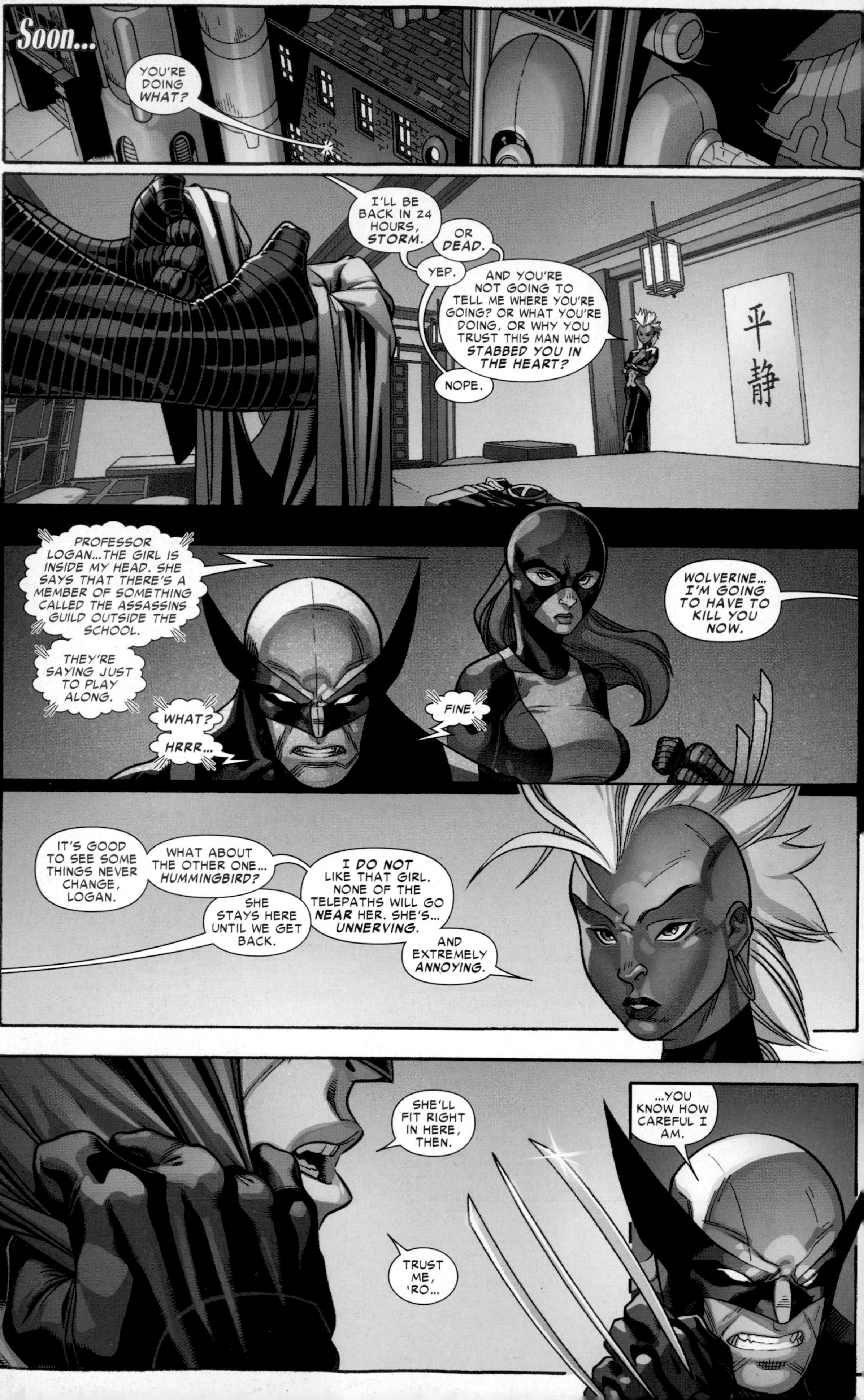
Soon...
YOU'RE DOING WHAT?
I'LL BE BACK IN 24 HOURS, STORM.
OR DEAD.
YEP.
AND YOU'RE NOT GOING TO TELL ME WHERE YOU'RE GOING? OR WHAT YOU'RE DOING, OR WHY YOU TRUST THIS MAN WHO STABBED YOU IN THE HEART?
NOPE.
平静
PROFESSOR LOGAN...THE GIRL IS INSIDE MY HEAD. SHE SAYS THAT THERE'S A MEMBER OF SOMETHING CALLED THE ASSASSINS GUILD OUTSIDE THE SCHOOL.
THEY'RE SAYING JUST TO PLAY ALONG.
WHAT?
HRRR...
WOLVERINE... I'M GOING TO HAVE TO KILL YOU NOW.
FINE.
IT'S GOOD TO SEE SOME THINGS NEVER CHANGE, LOGAN.
WHAT ABOUT THE OTHER ONE... HUMMINGBIRD?
SHE STAYS HERE UNTIL WE GET BACK.
I DO NOT LIKE THAT GIRL. NONE OF THE TELEPATHS WILL GO NEAR HER. SHE'S... UNNERVING.
AND EXTREMELY ANNOYING.
SHE'LL FIT RIGHT IN HERE, THEN.
TRUST ME, 'RO...
...YOU KNOW HOW CAREFUL I AM.

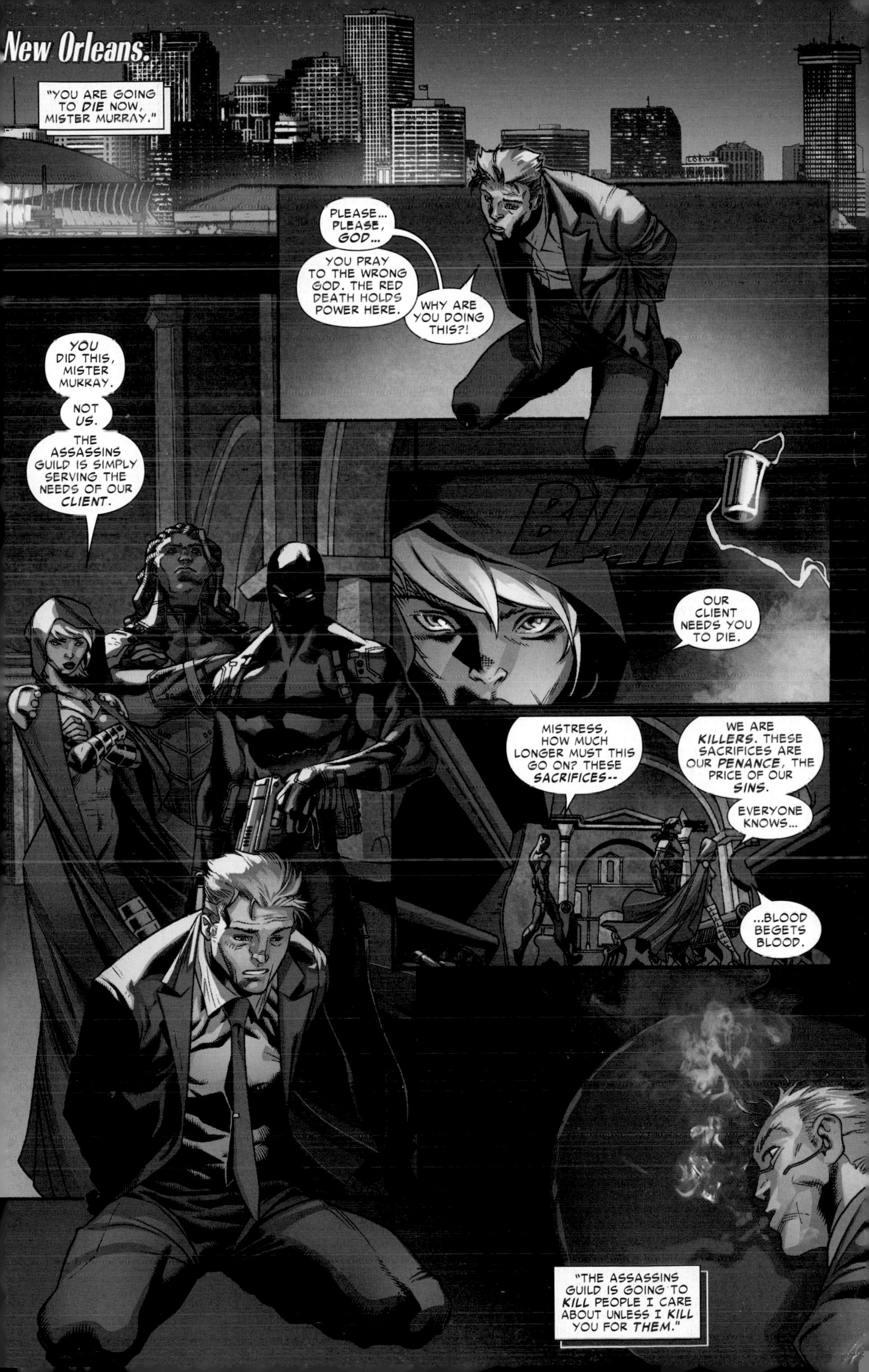
New Orleans.
"YOU ARE GOING TO *DIE* NOW, MISTER MURRAY."
PLEASE... PLEASE, *GOD*...
YOU PRAY TO THE WRONG GOD. THE RED DEATH HOLDS POWER HERE.
WHY ARE YOU DOING THIS?!
YOU DID THIS, MISTER MURRAY.
NOT *US*.
THE ASSASSINS GUILD IS SIMPLY SERVING THE NEEDS OF OUR *CLIENT*.
BLAM
OUR CLIENT NEEDS YOU TO DIE.
MISTRESS, HOW MUCH LONGER MUST THIS GO ON? THESE *SACRIFICES*--
WE ARE *KILLERS*. THESE SACRIFICES ARE OUR *PENANCE*, THE PRICE OF OUR *SINS*.
EVERYONE KNOWS...
...BLOOD BEGETS BLOOD.
"THE ASSASSINS GUILD IS GOING TO *KILL* PEOPLE I CARE ABOUT UNLESS I *KILL* YOU FOR *THEM*."

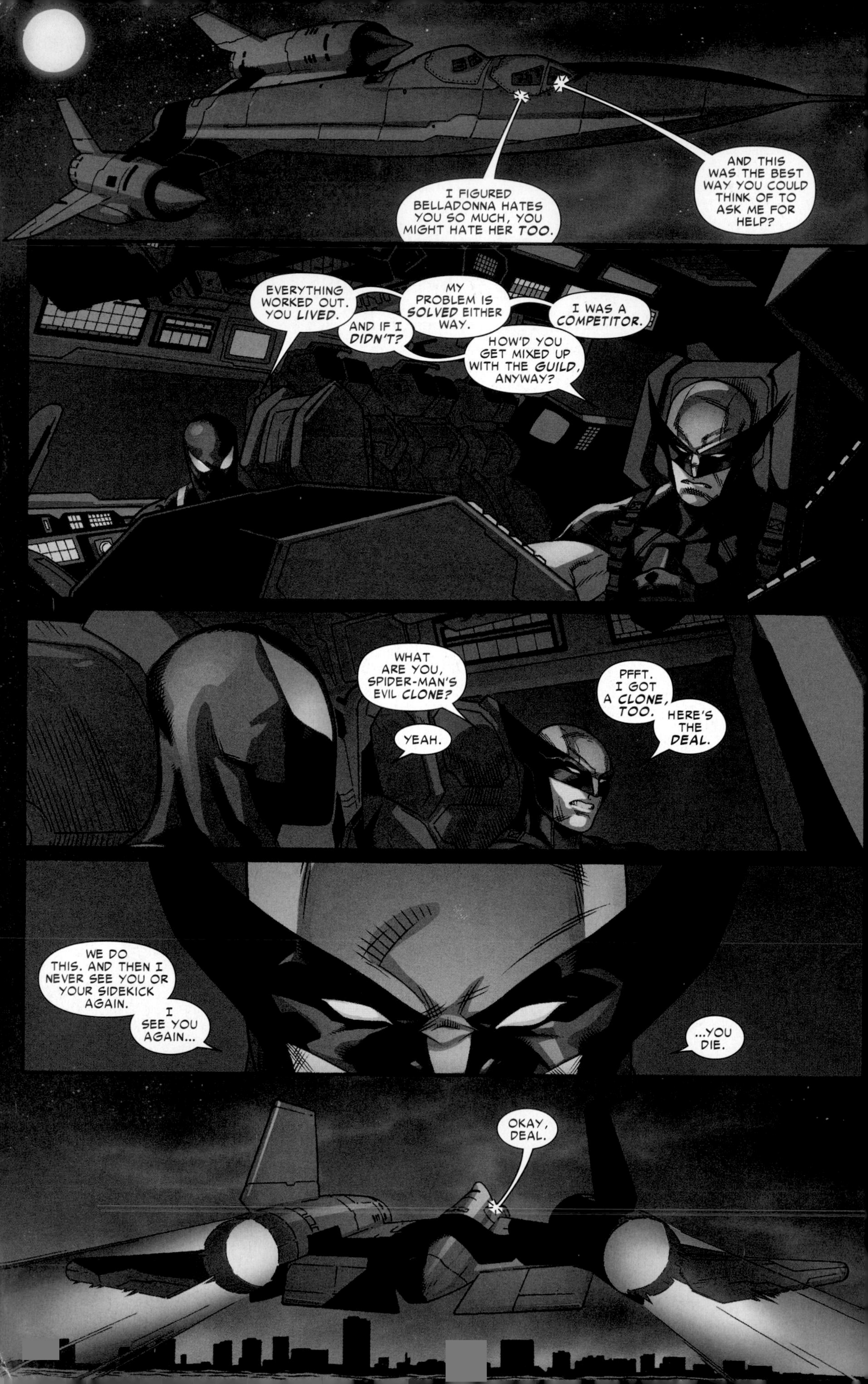
I FIGURED BELLADONNA HATES YOU SO MUCH, YOU MIGHT HATE HER TOO.
AND THIS WAS THE BEST WAY YOU COULD THINK OF TO ASK ME FOR HELP?
EVERYTHING WORKED OUT. YOU LIVED.
AND IF I DIDN'T?
MY PROBLEM IS SOLVED EITHER WAY.
I WAS A COMPETITOR.
HOW'D YOU GET MIXED UP WITH THE GUILD, ANYWAY?
WHAT ARE YOU, SPIDER-MAN'S EVIL CLONE?
YEAH.
PFFT. I GOT A CLONE, TOO.
HERE'S THE DEAL.
WE DO THIS. AND THEN I NEVER SEE YOU OR YOUR SIDEKICK AGAIN.
I SEE YOU AGAIN...
...YOU DIE.
OKAY, DEAL.

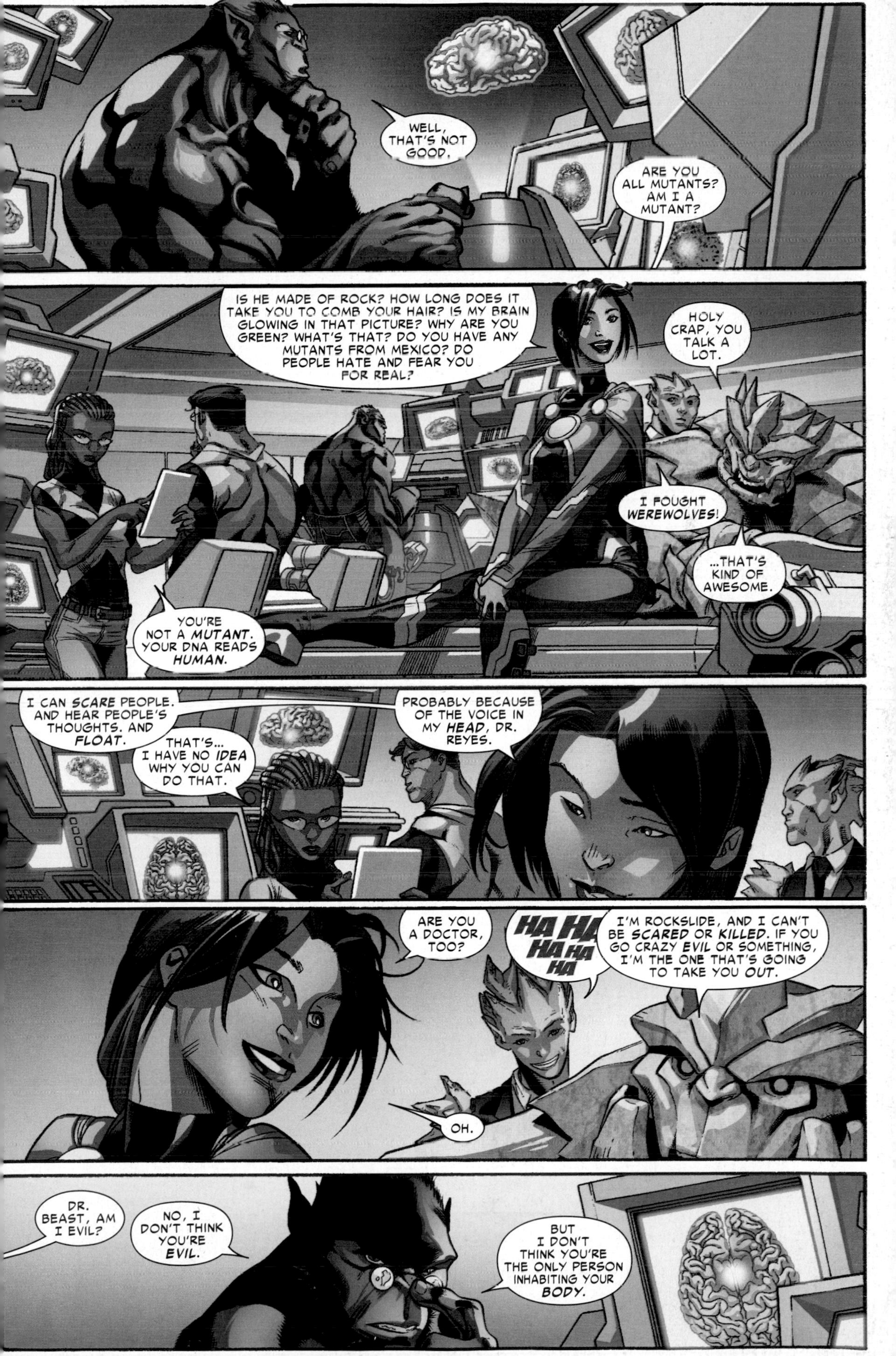

WELL, THAT'S NOT GOOD.
ARE YOU ALL MUTANTS? AM I A MUTANT?
IS HE MADE OF ROCK? HOW LONG DOES IT TAKE YOU TO COMB YOUR HAIR? IS MY BRAIN GLOWING IN THAT PICTURE? WHY ARE YOU GREEN? WHAT'S THAT? DO YOU HAVE ANY MUTANTS FROM MEXICO? DO PEOPLE HATE AND FEAR YOU FOR REAL?
HOLY CRAP, YOU TALK A LOT.
I FOUGHT WEREWOLVES!
...THAT'S KIND OF AWESOME.
YOU'RE NOT A MUTANT. YOUR DNA READS HUMAN.
I CAN SCARE PEOPLE. AND HEAR PEOPLE'S THOUGHTS. AND FLOAT.
THAT'S... I HAVE NO IDEA WHY YOU CAN DO THAT.
PROBABLY BECAUSE OF THE VOICE IN MY HEAD, DR. REYES.
ARE YOU A DOCTOR, TOO?
HA HA HA HA HA
I'M ROCKSLIDE, AND I CAN'T BE SCARED OR KILLED. IF YOU GO CRAZY EVIL OR SOMETHING, I'M THE ONE THAT'S GOING TO TAKE YOU OUT.
OH.
DR. BEAST, AM I EVIL?
NO, I DON'T THINK YOU'RE EVIL.
BUT I DON'T THINK YOU'RE THE ONLY PERSON INHABITING YOUR BODY.

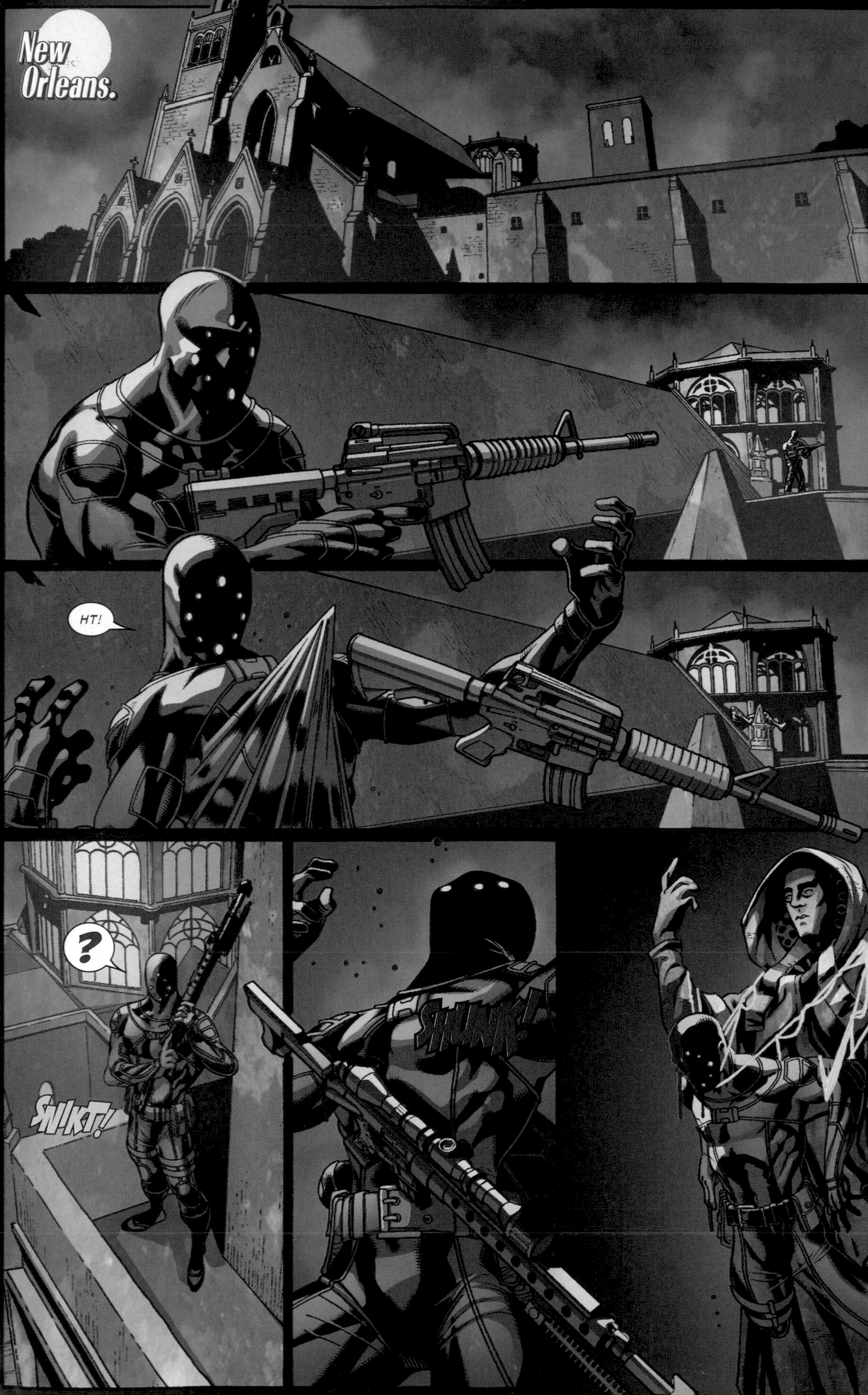
New Orleans.
HT!
?
SNIKT!
SHUNK!

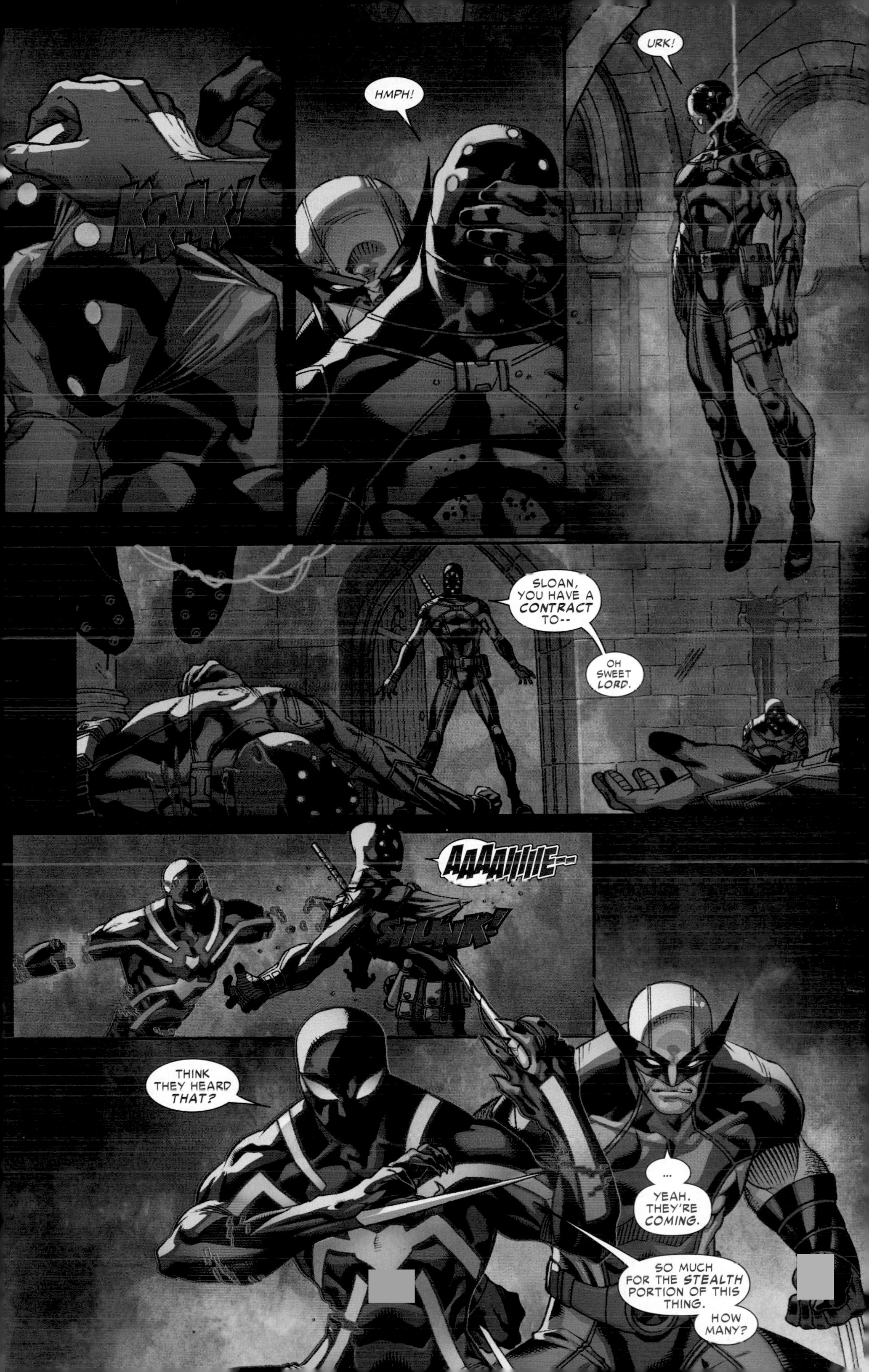

HMPH!
URK!
SLOAN, YOU HAVE A CONTRACT TO--
OH SWEET LORD.
AAAAIIIIIE--
THUNK!
THINK THEY HEARD THAT?
...
YEAH. THEY'RE COMING.
SO MUCH FOR THE STEALTH PORTION OF THIS THING.
HOW MANY?

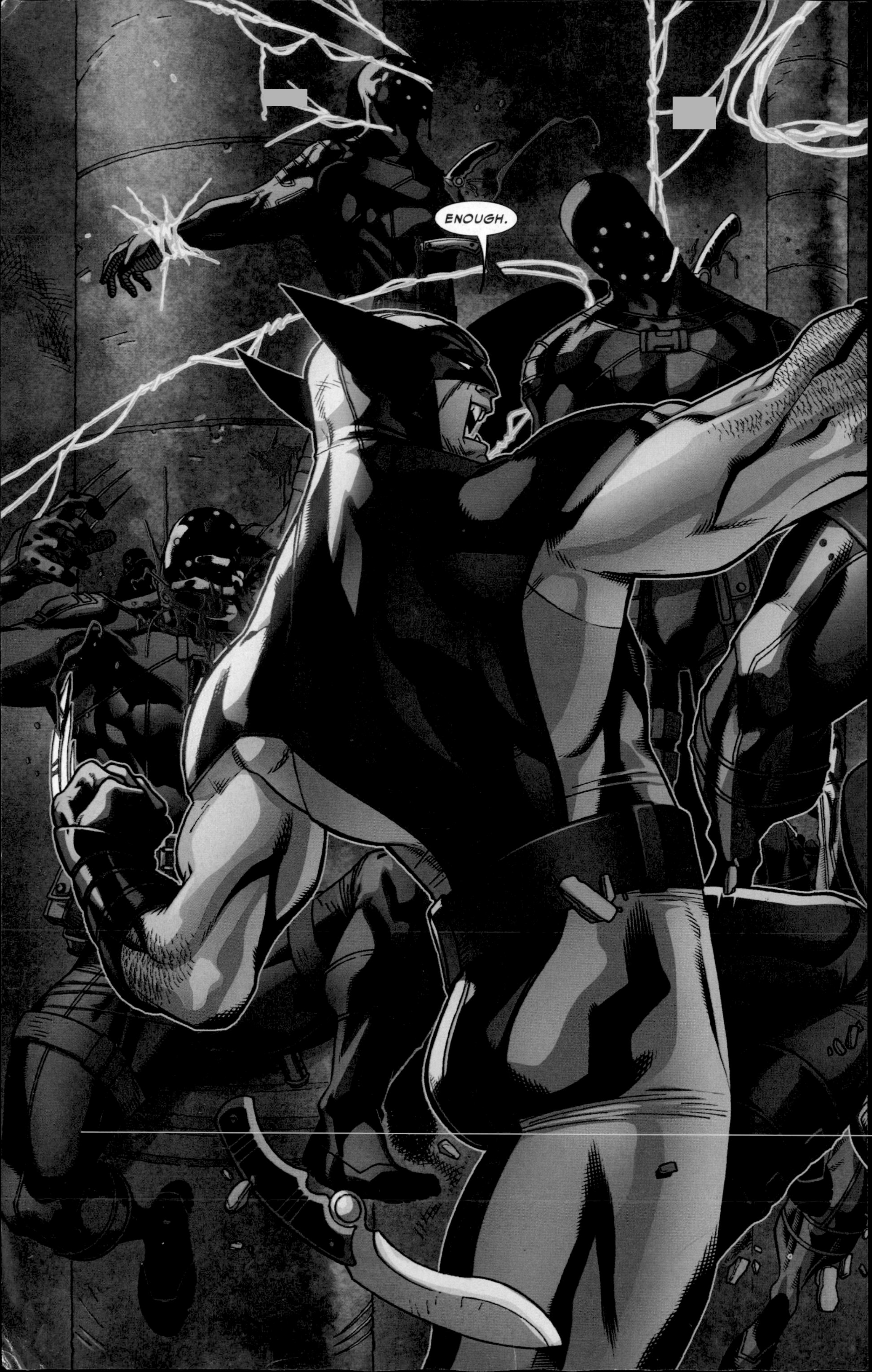
ENOUGH.

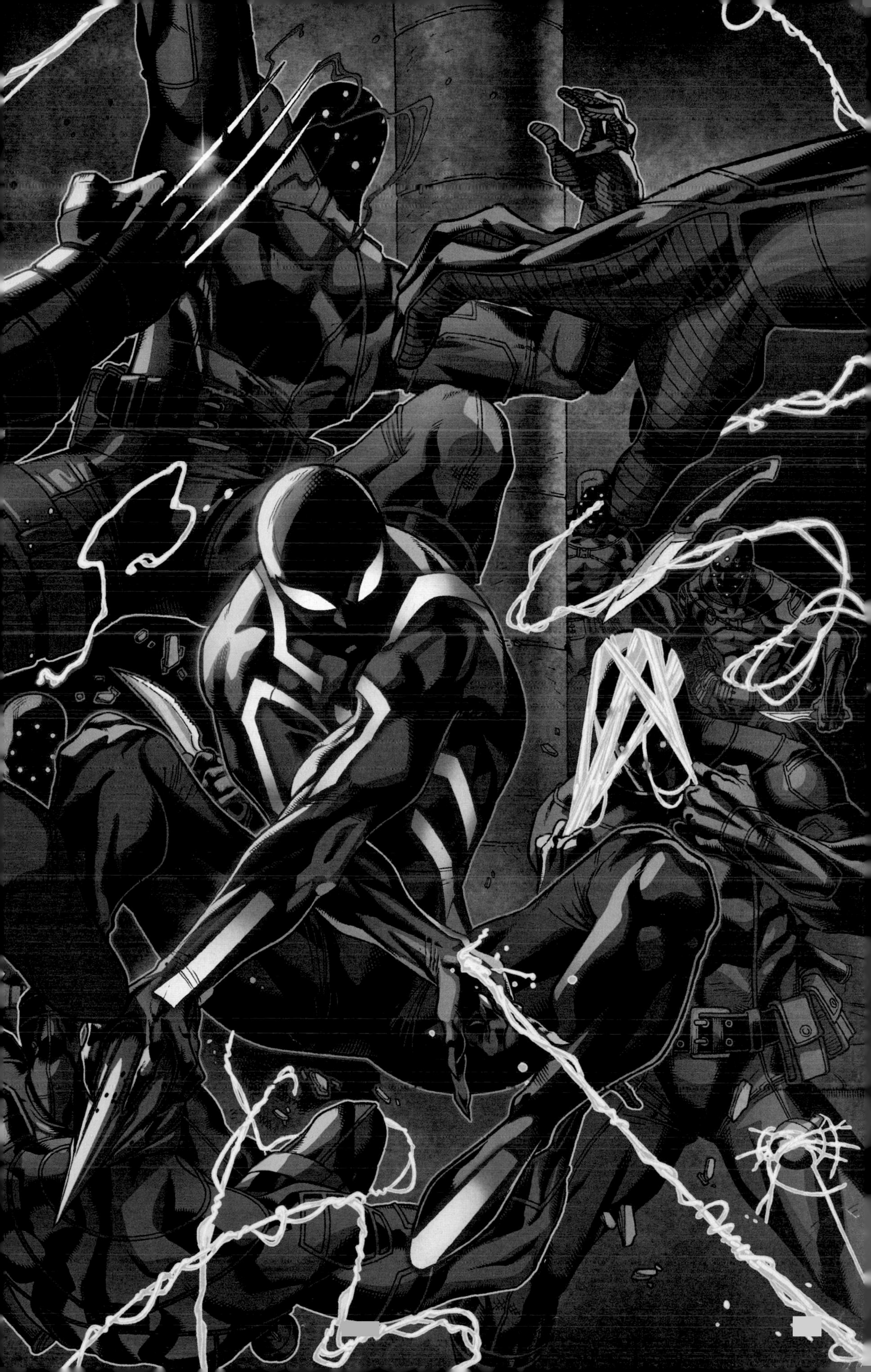

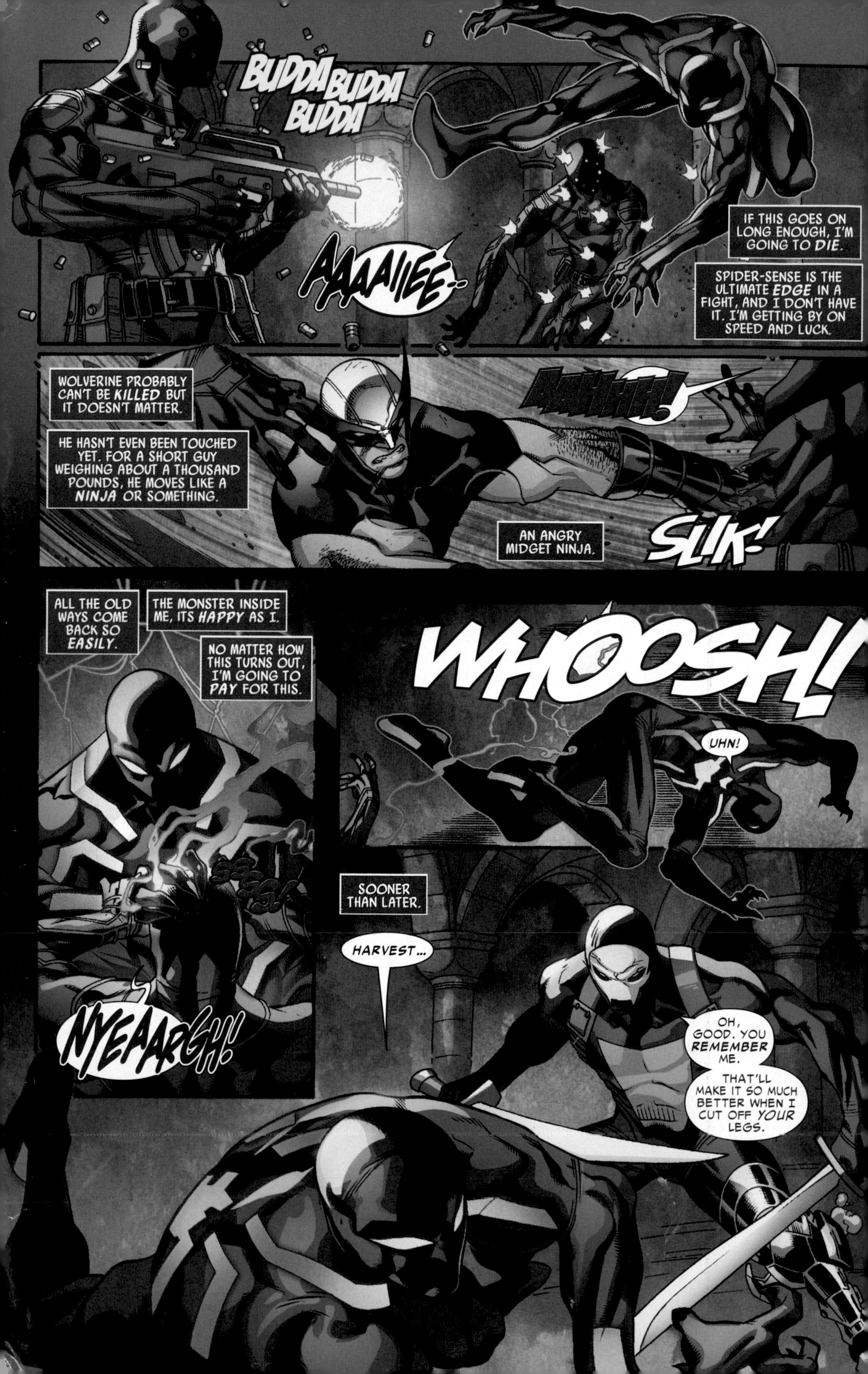
BUDDA BUDDA BUDDA
AAAAIIEE--
IF THIS GOES ON LONG ENOUGH, I'M GOING TO DIE.
SPIDER-SENSE IS THE ULTIMATE EDGE IN A FIGHT, AND I DON'T HAVE IT. I'M GETTING BY ON SPEED AND LUCK.
WOLVERINE PROBABLY CAN'T BE KILLED BUT IT DOESN'T MATTER.
HE HASN'T EVEN BEEN TOUCHED YET. FOR A SHORT GUY WEIGHING ABOUT A THOUSAND POUNDS, HE MOVES LIKE A NINJA OR SOMETHING.
AN ANGRY MIDGET NINJA.
SLIK!
ALL THE OLD WAYS COME BACK SO EASILY.
THE MONSTER INSIDE ME, ITS HAPPY AS I.
NO MATTER HOW THIS TURNS OUT, I'M GOING TO PAY FOR THIS.
NYEAARGH!
WHOOSH!
UHN!
SOONER THAN LATER.
HARVEST...
OH, GOOD. YOU REMEMBER ME.
THAT'LL MAKE IT SO MUCH BETTER WHEN I CUT OFF YOUR LEGS.

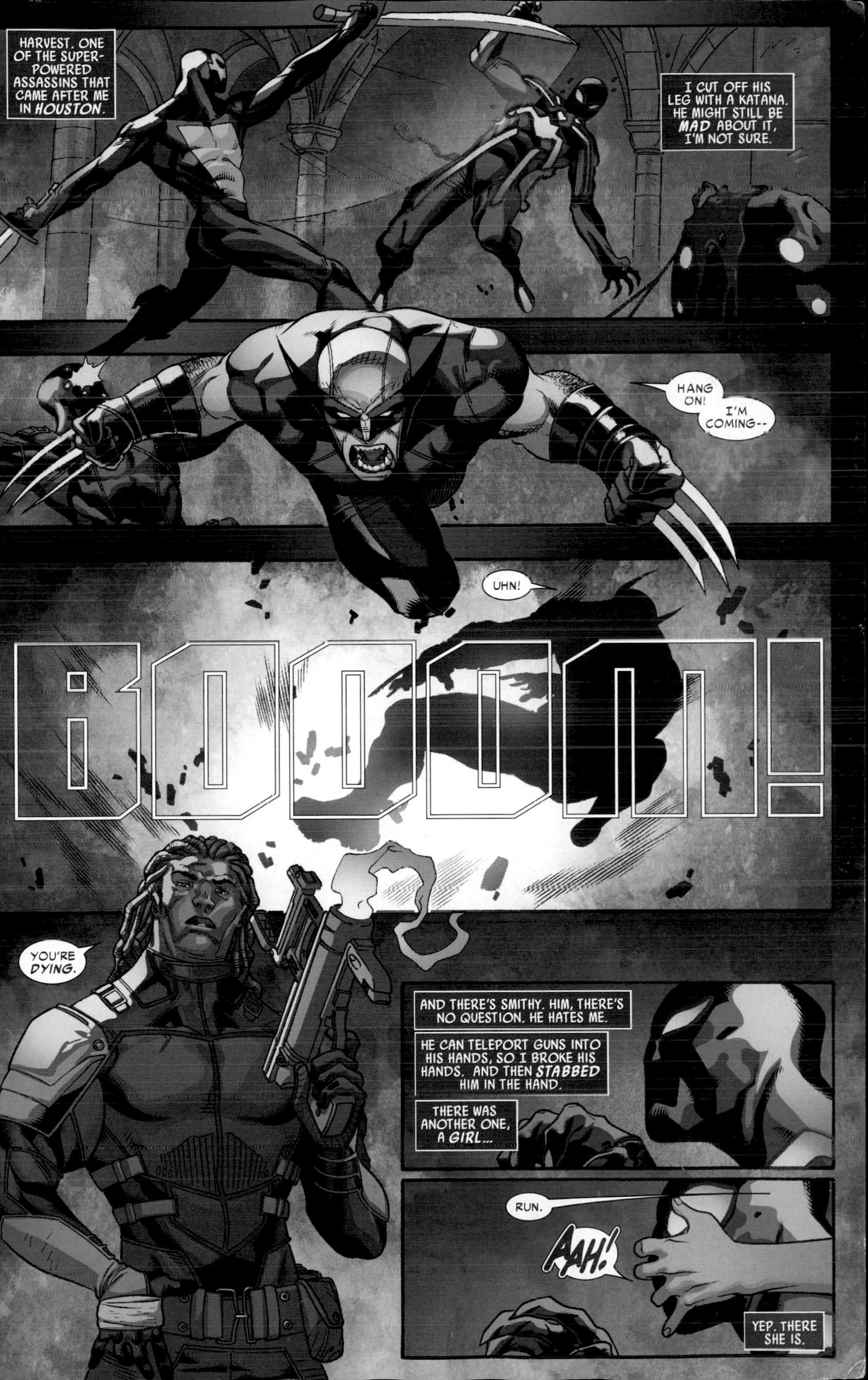
HARVEST. ONE OF THE SUPER-POWERED ASSASSINS THAT CAME AFTER ME IN HOUSTON.
I CUT OFF HIS LEG WITH A KATANA. HE MIGHT STILL BE MAD ABOUT IT, I'M NOT SURE.
HANG ON!
I'M COMING--
UHN!
BOOM!
YOU'RE DYING.
AND THERE'S SMITHY. HIM, THERE'S NO QUESTION. HE HATES ME.
HE CAN TELEPORT GUNS INTO HIS HANDS, SO I BROKE HIS HANDS. AND THEN STABBED HIM IN THE HAND.
THERE WAS ANOTHER ONE, A GIRL...
RUN.
AAH!
YEP. THERE SHE IS.

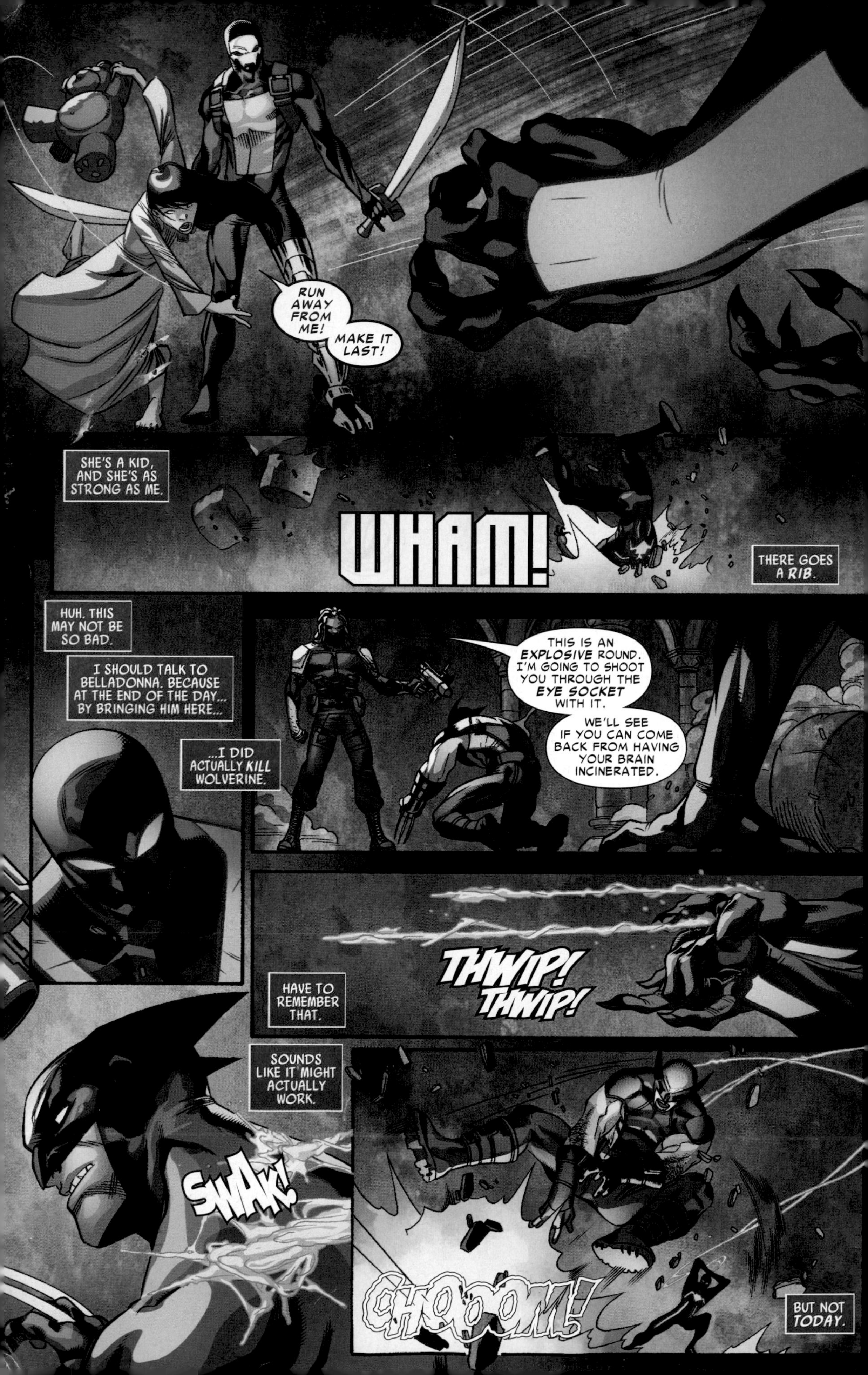

RUN AWAY FROM ME!
MAKE IT LAST!
SHE'S A KID, AND SHE'S AS STRONG AS ME.
WHAM!
THERE GOES A RIB.
HUH. THIS MAY NOT BE SO BAD.
I SHOULD TALK TO BELLADONNA. BECAUSE AT THE END OF THE DAY... BY BRINGING HIM HERE...
...I DID ACTUALLY KILL WOLVERINE.
THIS IS AN EXPLOSIVE ROUND. I'M GOING TO SHOOT YOU THROUGH THE EYE SOCKET WITH IT.
WE'LL SEE IF YOU CAN COME BACK FROM HAVING YOUR BRAIN INCINERATED.
THWIP! THWIP!
HAVE TO REMEMBER THAT.
SOUNDS LIKE IT MIGHT ACTUALLY WORK.
SWAK!
CHOOOOM!
BUT NOT TODAY.

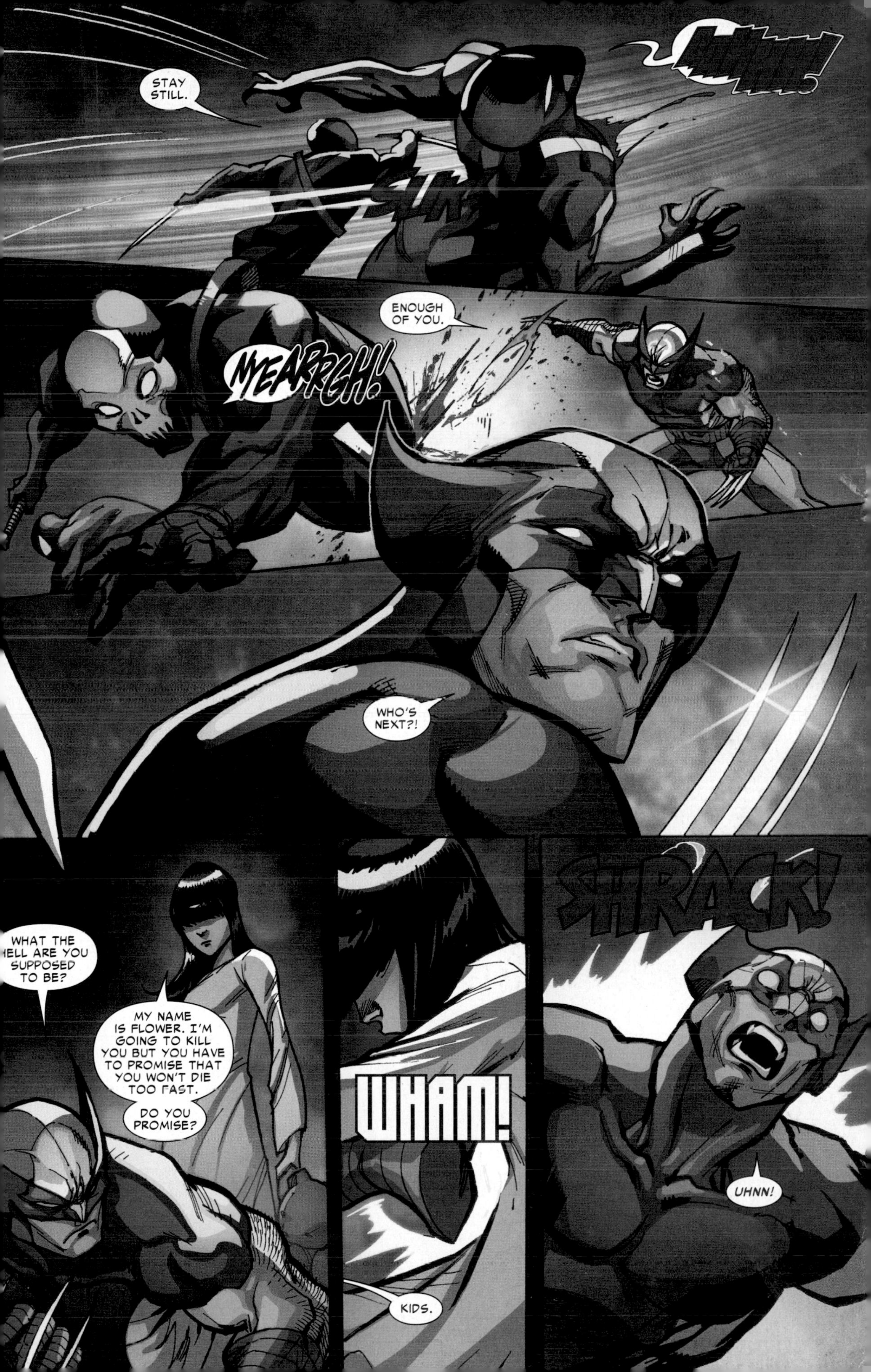

STAY STILL.
ENOUGH OF YOU.
NYEARRGH!
WHO'S NEXT?!
WHAT THE HELL ARE YOU SUPPOSED TO BE?
MY NAME IS FLOWER. I'M GOING TO KILL YOU BUT YOU HAVE TO PROMISE THAT YOU WON'T DIE TOO FAST.
DO YOU PROMISE?
WHAM!
KIDS.
SHRACK!
UHNN!

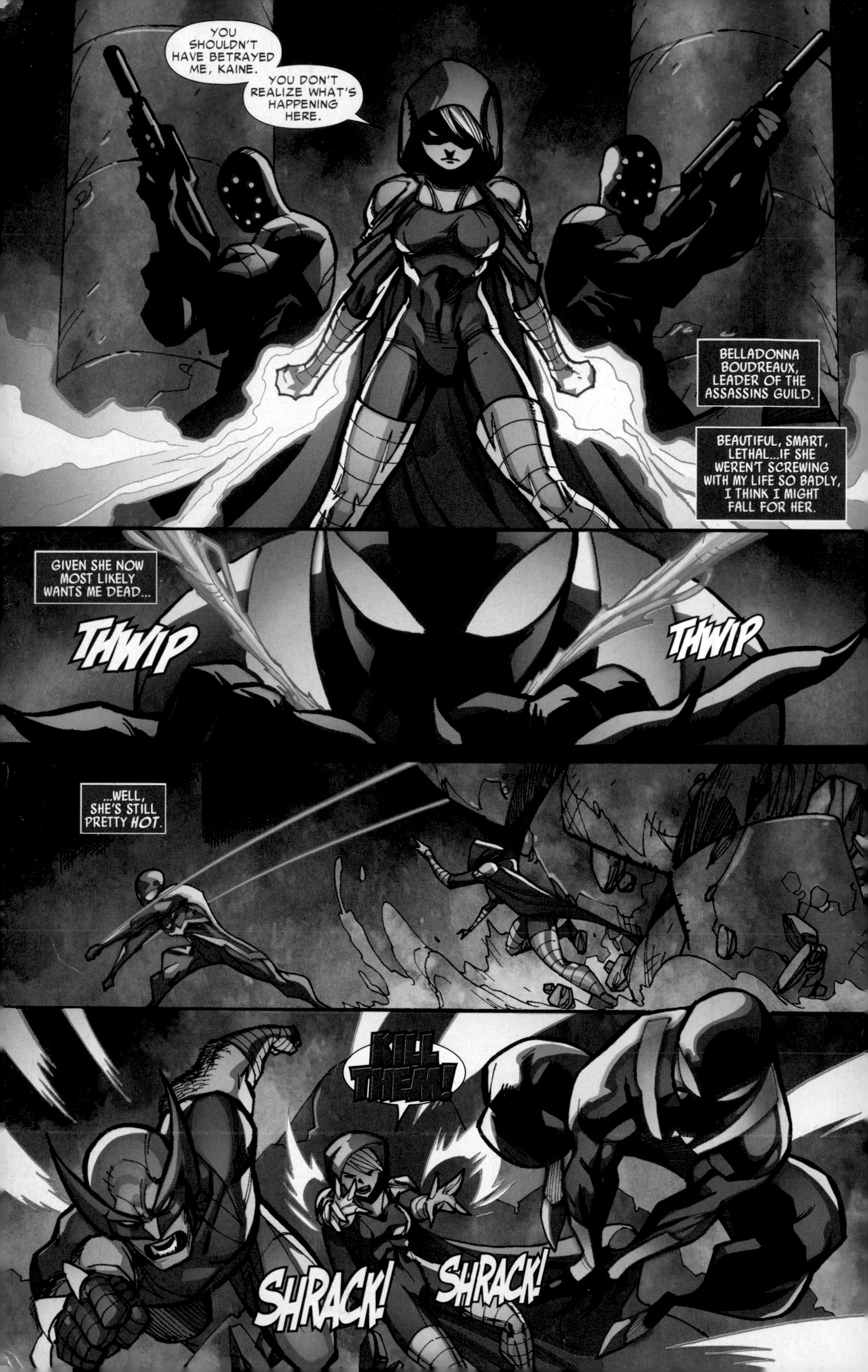
YOU SHOULDN'T HAVE BETRAYED ME, KAINE.
YOU DON'T REALIZE WHAT'S HAPPENING HERE.
BELLADONNA BOUDREAUX, LEADER OF THE ASSASSINS GUILD.
BEAUTIFUL, SMART, LETHAL...IF SHE WEREN'T SCREWING WITH MY LIFE SO BADLY, I THINK I MIGHT FALL FOR HER.
GIVEN SHE NOW MOST LIKELY WANTS ME DEAD...
THWIP
THWIP
...WELL, SHE'S STILL PRETTY HOT.
KILL THEM!
SHRACK!
SHRACK!

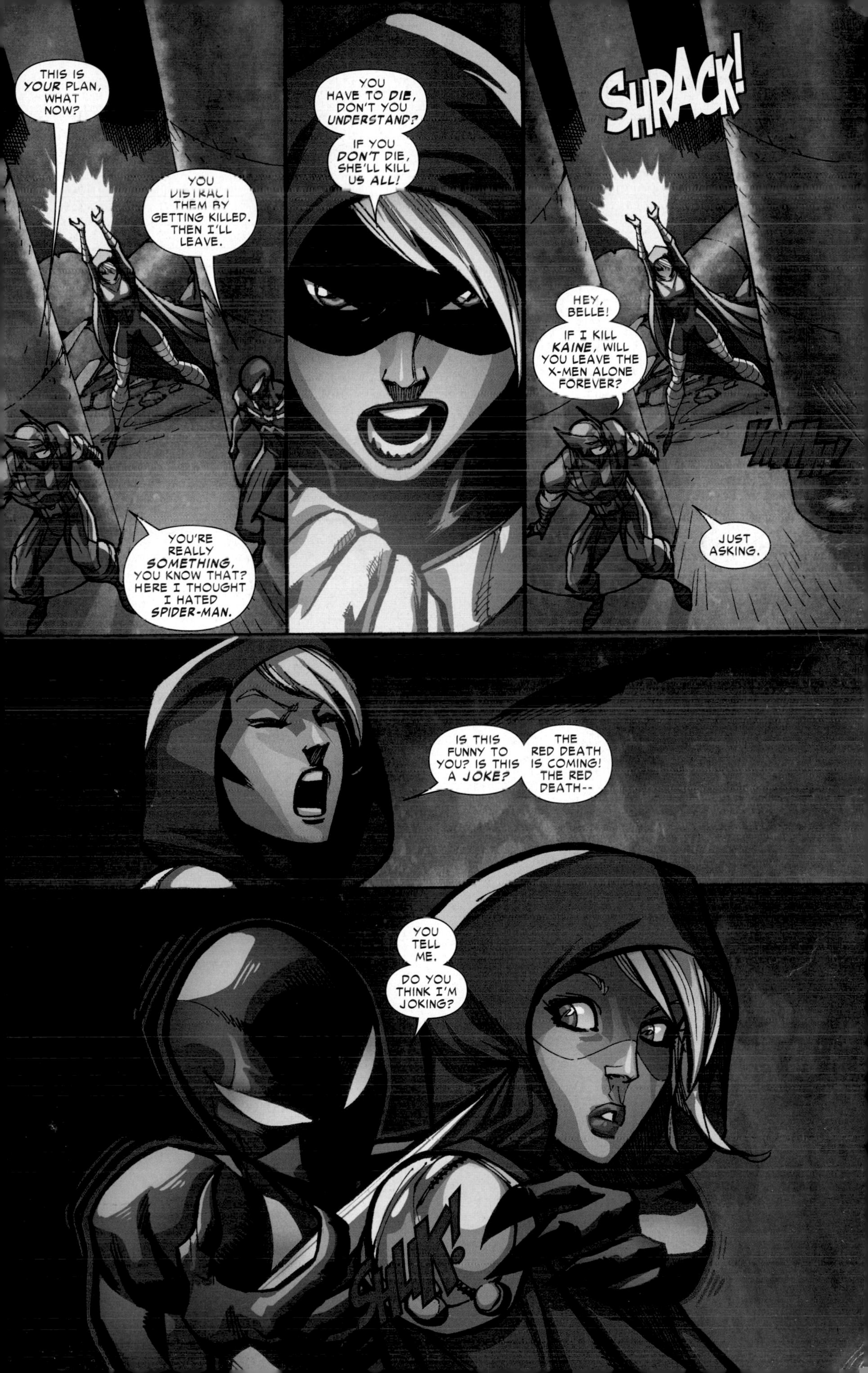
THIS IS YOUR PLAN, WHAT NOW?
YOU DISTRACT THEM BY GETTING KILLED. THEN I'LL LEAVE.
YOU'RE REALLY SOMETHING, YOU KNOW THAT? HERE I THOUGHT I HATED SPIDER-MAN.
YOU HAVE TO DIE, DON'T YOU UNDERSTAND?
IF YOU DON'T DIE, SHE'LL KILL US ALL!
SHRACK!
HEY, BELLE!
IF I KILL KAINE, WILL YOU LEAVE THE X-MEN ALONE FOREVER?
JUST ASKING.
IS THIS FUNNY TO YOU? IS THIS A JOKE?
THE RED DEATH IS COMING! THE RED DEATH--
YOU TELL ME.
DO YOU THINK I'M JOKING?
CHUK!

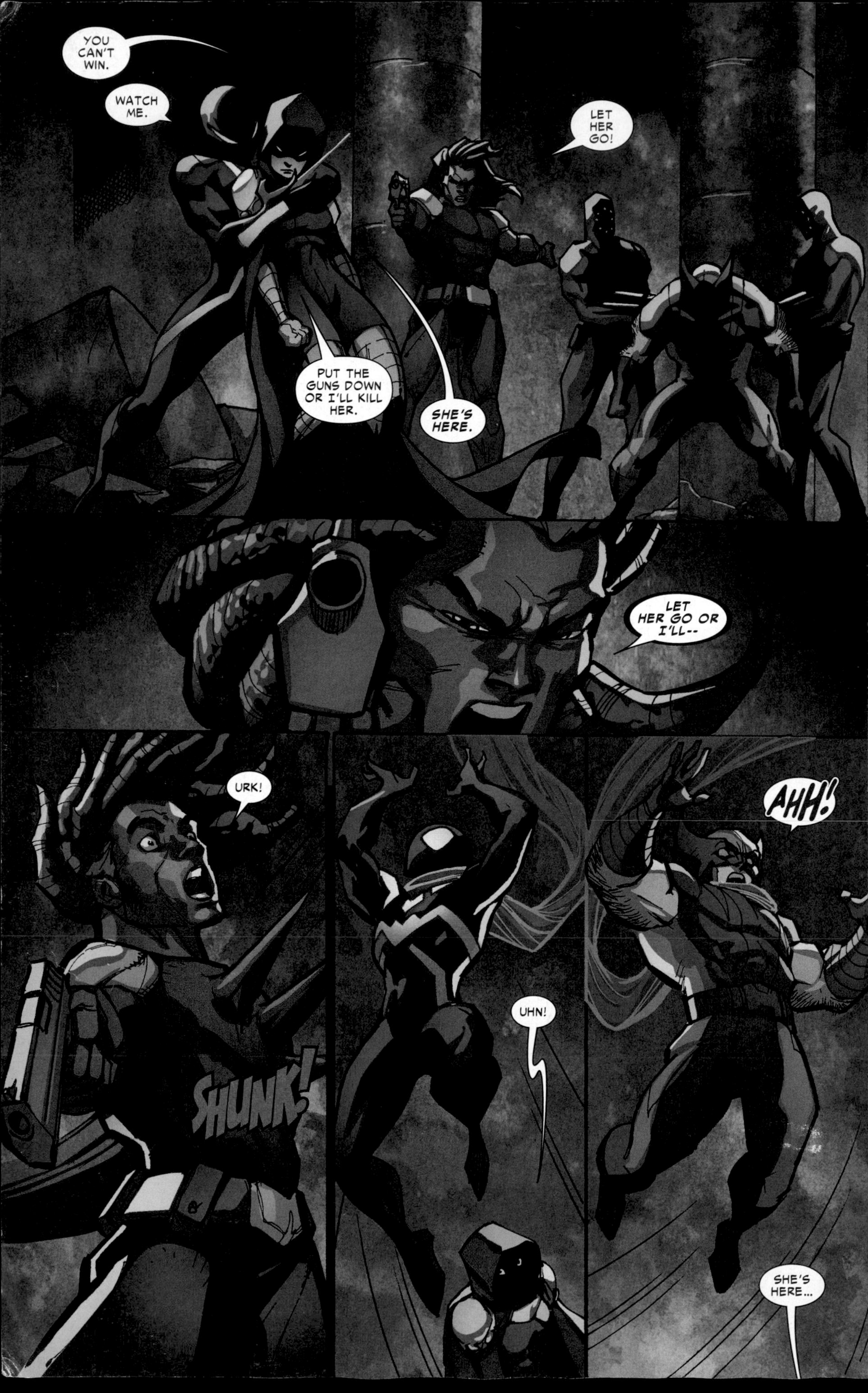
YOU CAN'T WIN.
WATCH ME.
LET HER GO!
PUT THE GUNS DOWN OR I'LL KILL HER.
SHE'S HERE.
LET HER GO OR I'LL--
URK!
SHUNK!
UHN!
AHH!
SHE'S HERE...

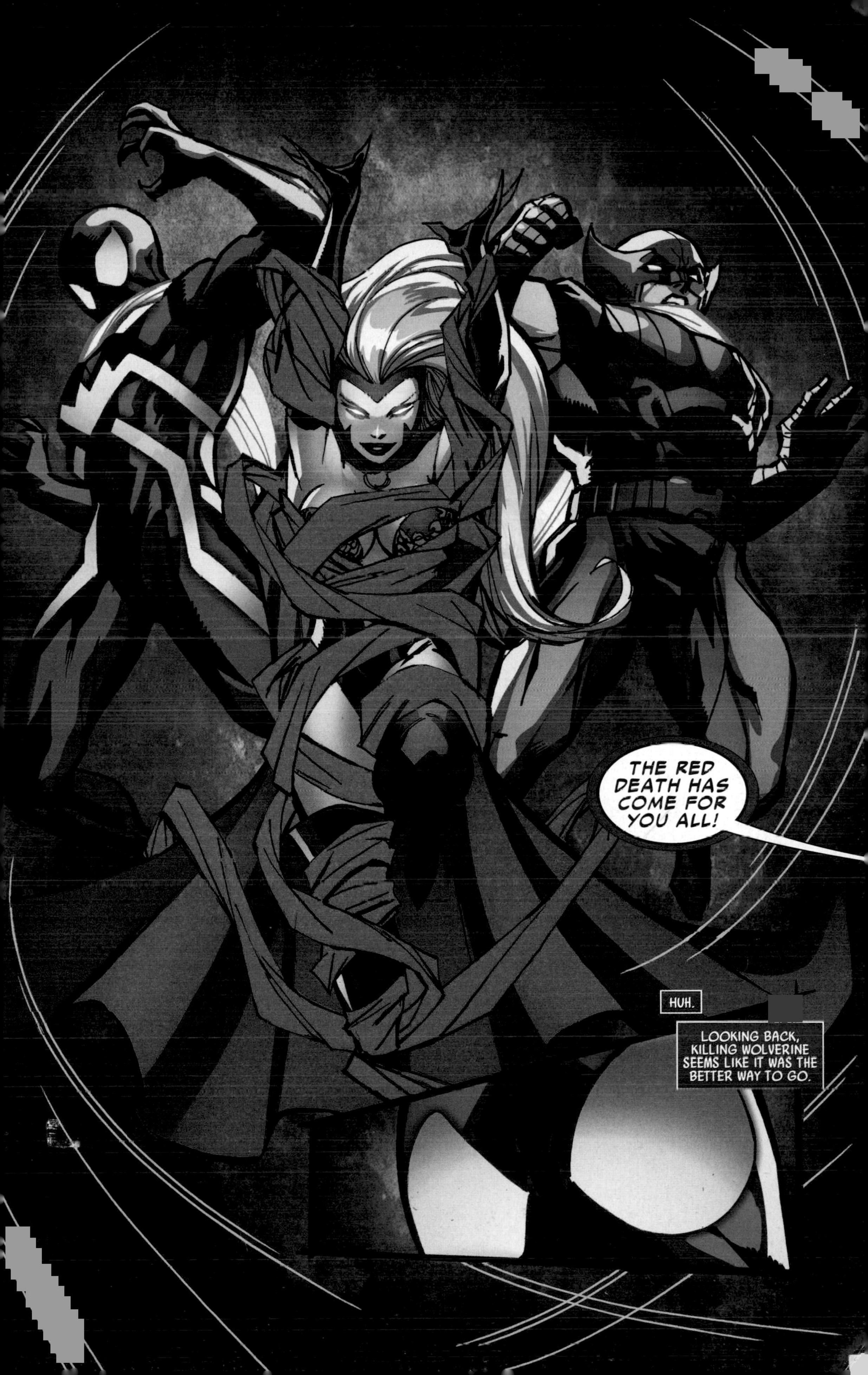
THE RED DEATH HAS COME FOR YOU ALL!
HUH.
LOOKING BACK, KILLING WOLVERINE SEEMS LIKE IT WAS THE BETTER WAY TO GO.

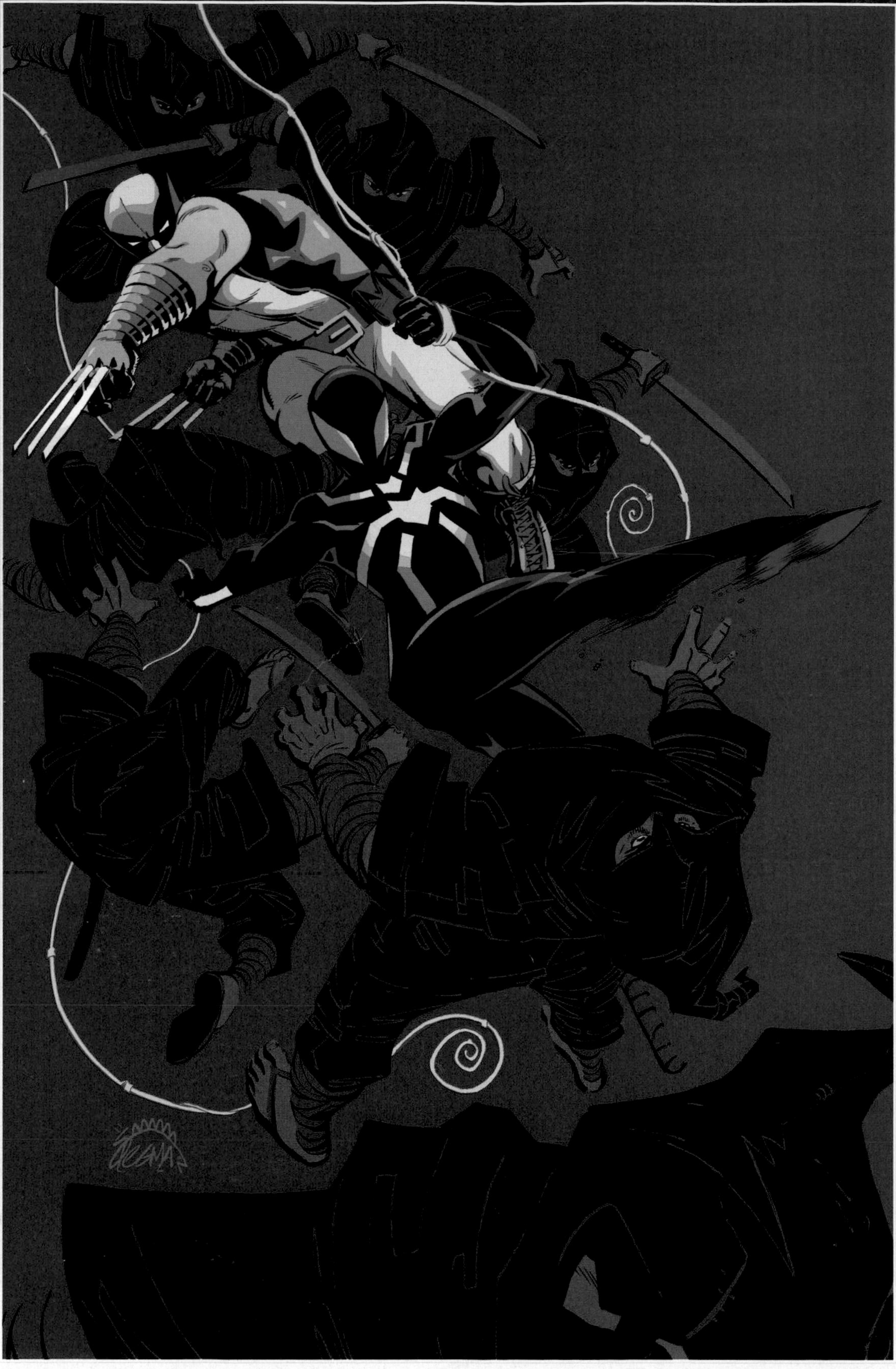

#19

"WRATH, PART 3"

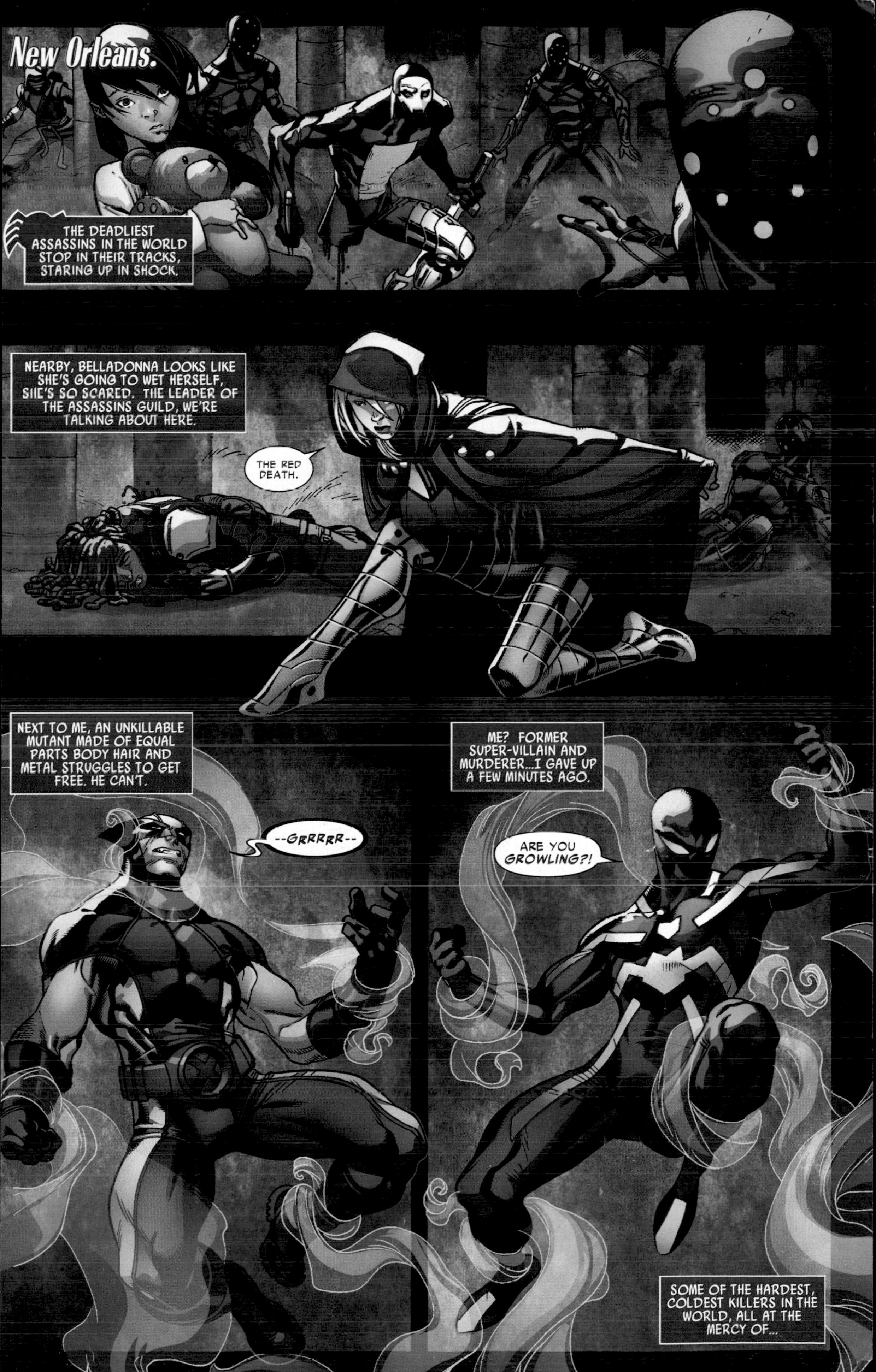

New Orleans.
THE DEADLIEST ASSASSINS IN THE WORLD STOP IN THEIR TRACKS, STARING UP IN SHOCK.
NEARBY, BELLADONNA LOOKS LIKE SHE'S GOING TO WET HERSELF, SHE'S SO SCARED. THE LEADER OF THE ASSASSINS GUILD, WE'RE TALKING ABOUT HERE.
THE RED DEATH.
NEXT TO ME, AN UNKILLABLE MUTANT MADE OF EQUAL PARTS BODY HAIR AND METAL STRUGGLES TO GET FREE. HE CAN'T.
--GRRRRR--
ME? FORMER SUPER-VILLAIN AND MURDERER...I GAVE UP A FEW MINUTES AGO.
ARE YOU GROWLING?!
SOME OF THE HARDEST, COLDEST KILLERS IN THE WORLD, ALL AT THE MERCY OF...

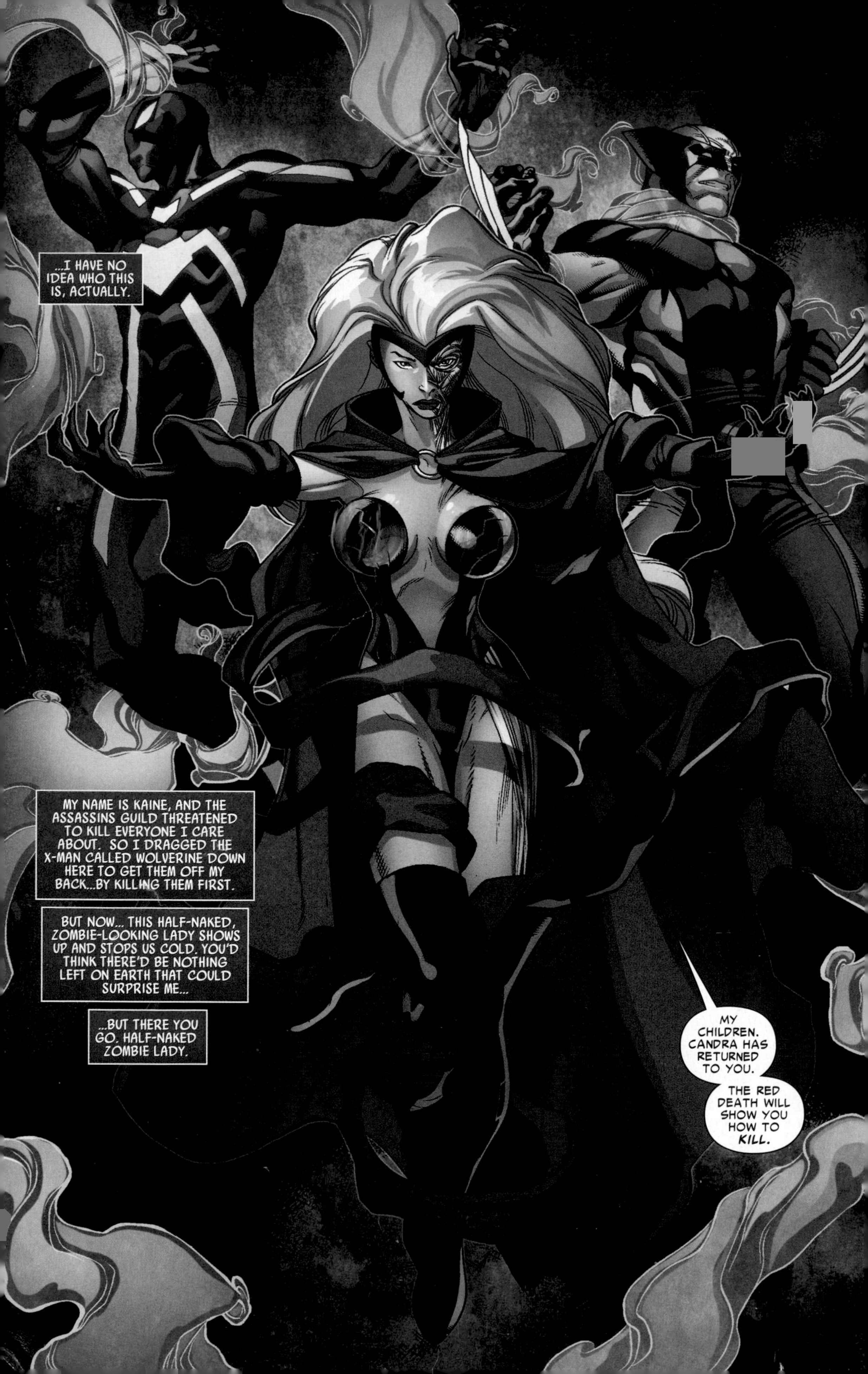
...I HAVE NO IDEA WHO THIS IS, ACTUALLY.
MY NAME IS KAINE, AND THE ASSASSINS GUILD THREATENED TO KILL EVERYONE I CARE ABOUT. SO I DRAGGED THE X-MAN CALLED WOLVERINE DOWN HERE TO GET THEM OFF MY BACK...BY KILLING THEM FIRST.
BUT NOW... THIS HALF-NAKED, ZOMBIE-LOOKING LADY SHOWS UP AND STOPS US COLD. YOU'D THINK THERE'D BE NOTHING LEFT ON EARTH THAT COULD SURPRISE ME...
...BUT THERE YOU GO. HALF-NAKED ZOMBIE LADY.
MY CHILDREN. CANDRA HAS RETURNED TO YOU.
THE RED DEATH WILL SHOW YOU HOW TO KILL.

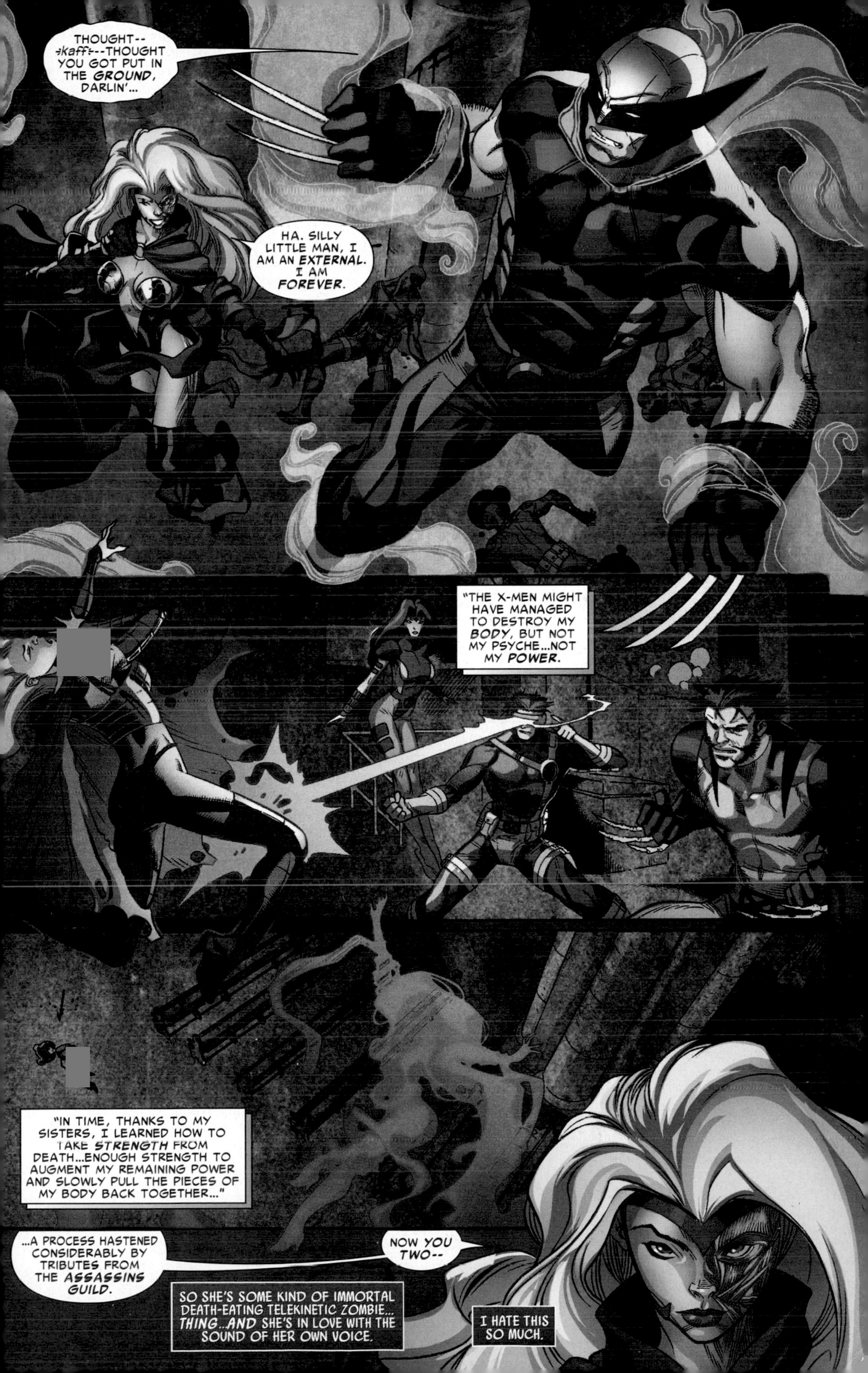
THOUGHT-- *kaff*--THOUGHT YOU GOT PUT IN THE GROUND, DARLIN'...
HA. SILLY LITTLE MAN, I AM AN EXTERNAL. I AM FOREVER.
"THE X-MEN MIGHT HAVE MANAGED TO DESTROY MY BODY, BUT NOT MY PSYCHE...NOT MY POWER.
"IN TIME, THANKS TO MY SISTERS, I LEARNED HOW TO TAKE STRENGTH FROM DEATH...ENOUGH STRENGTH TO AUGMENT MY REMAINING POWER AND SLOWLY PULL THE PIECES OF MY BODY BACK TOGETHER..."
...A PROCESS HASTENED CONSIDERABLY BY TRIBUTES FROM THE ASSASSINS GUILD.
NOW YOU TWO--
SO SHE'S SOME KIND OF IMMORTAL DEATH-EATING TELEKINETIC ZOMBIE... THING...AND SHE'S IN LOVE WITH THE SOUND OF HER OWN VOICE.
I HATE THIS SO MUCH.

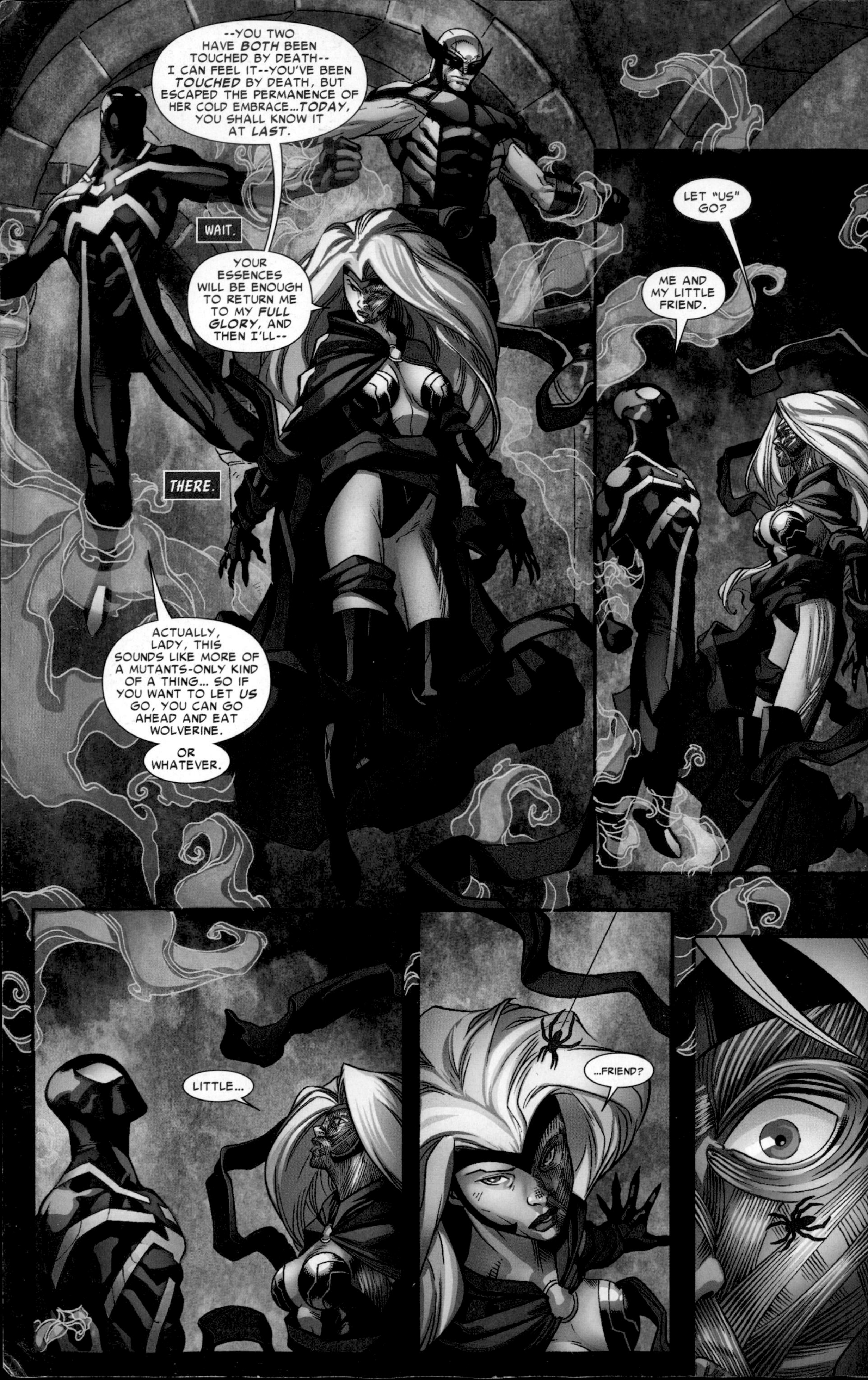
--YOU TWO HAVE BOTH BEEN TOUCHED BY DEATH-- I CAN FEEL IT--YOU'VE BEEN TOUCHED BY DEATH, BUT ESCAPED THE PERMANENCE OF HER COLD EMBRACE...TODAY, YOU SHALL KNOW IT AT LAST.
WAIT.
YOUR ESSENCES WILL BE ENOUGH TO RETURN ME TO MY FULL GLORY, AND THEN I'LL--
THERE.
ACTUALLY, LADY, THIS SOUNDS LIKE MORE OF A MUTANTS-ONLY KIND OF A THING... SO IF YOU WANT TO LET US GO, YOU CAN GO AHEAD AND EAT WOLVERINE.
OR WHATEVER.
LET "US" GO?
ME AND MY LITTLE FRIEND.
LITTLE...
...FRIEND?

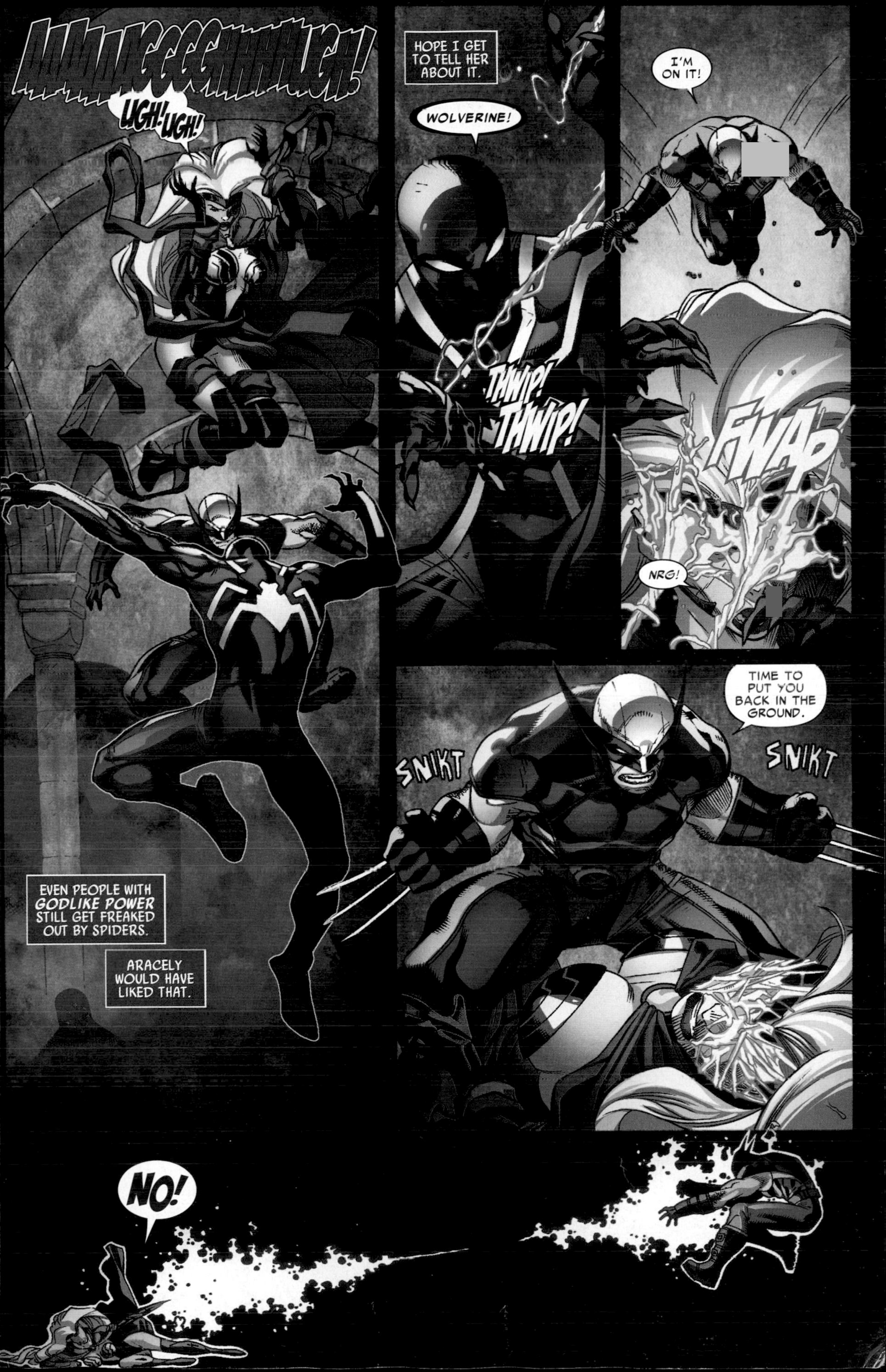
AAAAAAGGGGHHHHUGH!
UGH! UGH!
HOPE I GET TO TELL HER ABOUT IT.
WOLVERINE!
THWIP! THWIP!
I'M ON IT!
FWAP
NRG!
EVEN PEOPLE WITH GODLIKE POWER STILL GET FREAKED OUT BY SPIDERS.
ARACELY WOULD HAVE LIKED THAT.
TIME TO PUT YOU BACK IN THE GROUND.
SNIKT
SNIKT
NO!

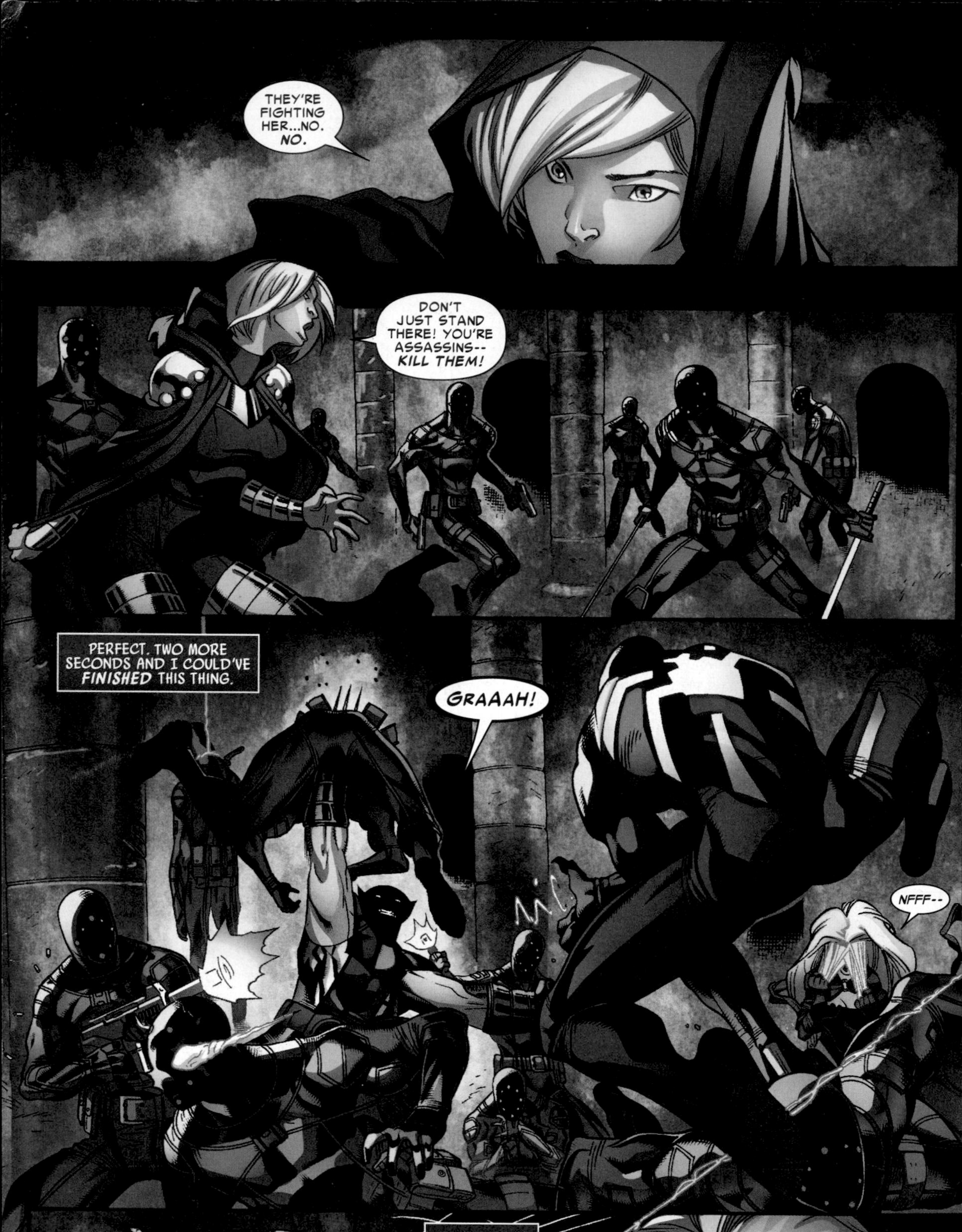
THEY'RE FIGHTING HER...NO. NO.
DON'T JUST STAND THERE! YOU'RE ASSASSINS-- KILL THEM!
PERFECT. TWO MORE SECONDS AND I COULD'VE FINISHED THIS THING.
GRAAAH!
NFFF--
WELL, I CAN'T DAMN MYSELF ANY MORE...
MIGHT AS WELL KILL A GOD.

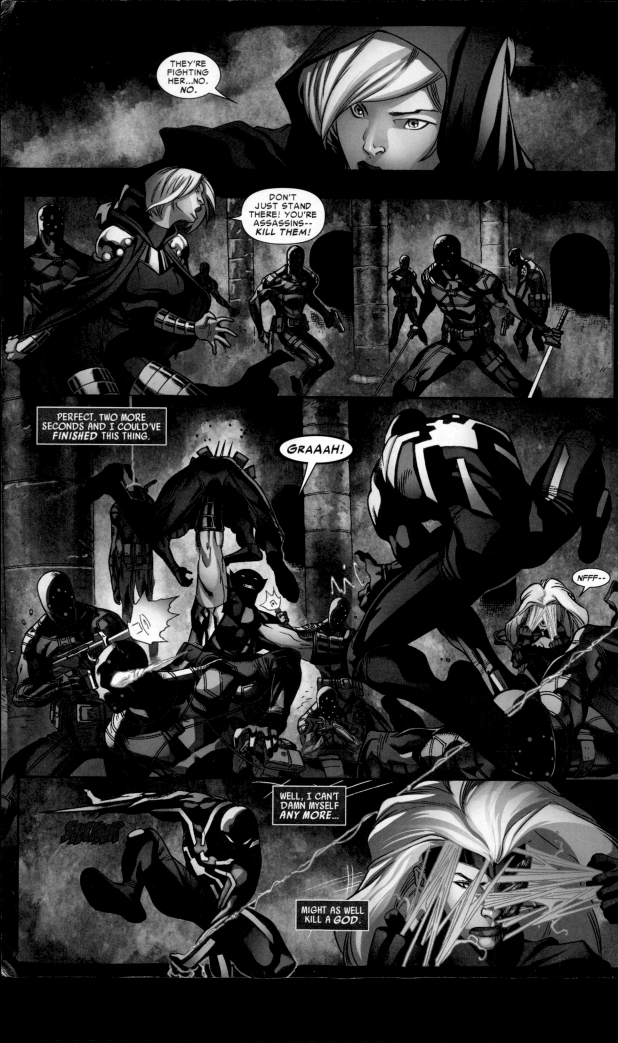

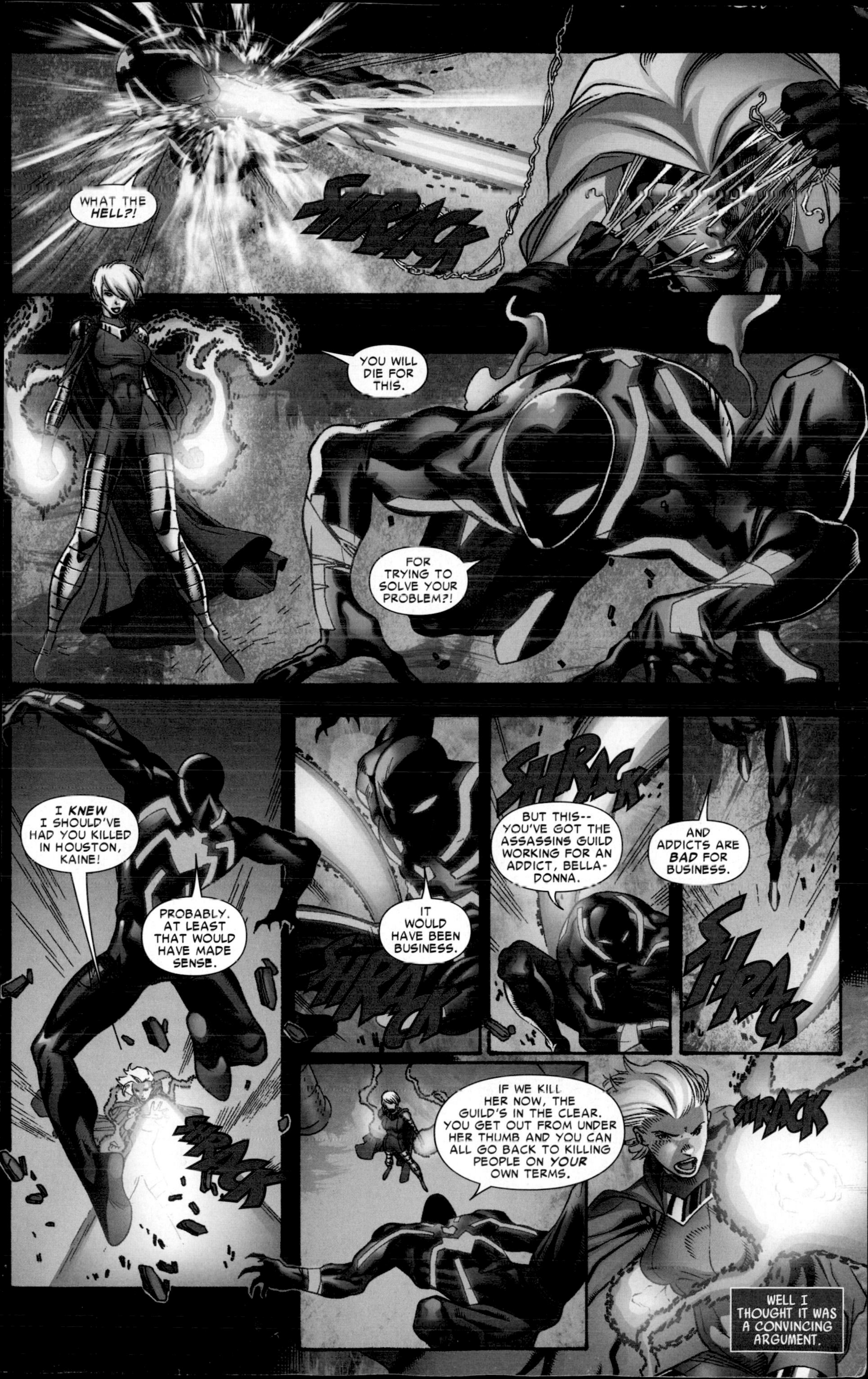
WHAT THE HELL?!
SHRACK
YOU WILL DIE FOR THIS.
FOR TRYING TO SOLVE YOUR PROBLEM?!
I KNEW I SHOULD'VE HAD YOU KILLED IN HOUSTON, KAINE!
PROBABLY. AT LEAST THAT WOULD HAVE MADE SENSE.
SHRACK
IT WOULD HAVE BEEN BUSINESS.
SHRACK
SHRACK
BUT THIS-- YOU'VE GOT THE ASSASSINS GUILD WORKING FOR AN ADDICT, BELLA-DONNA.
AND ADDICTS ARE BAD FOR BUSINESS.
SHRACK
IF WE KILL HER NOW, THE GUILD'S IN THE CLEAR. YOU GET OUT FROM UNDER HER THUMB AND YOU CAN ALL GO BACK TO KILLING PEOPLE ON YOUR OWN TERMS.
SHRACK
WELL I THOUGHT IT WAS A CONVINCING ARGUMENT.

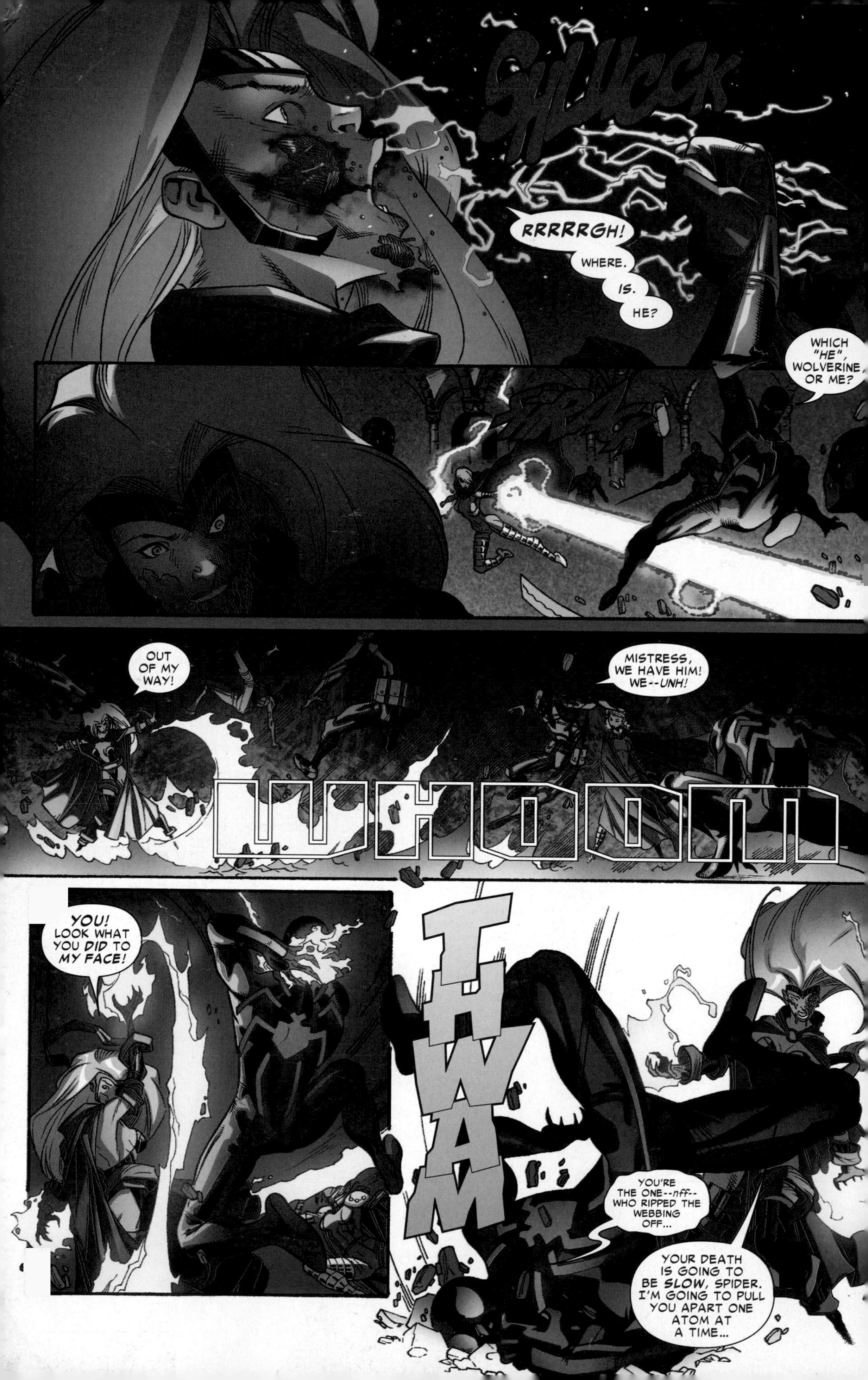
SHLUCK
RRRRRGH!
WHERE.
IS.
HE?
WHICH "HE", WOLVERINE, OR ME?
OUT OF MY WAY!
MISTRESS, WE HAVE HIM! WE--UNH!
WHOOM
YOU! LOOK WHAT YOU DID TO MY FACE!
THWAM
YOU'RE THE ONE--nff--WHO RIPPED THE WEBBING OFF...
YOUR DEATH IS GOING TO BE SLOW, SPIDER. I'M GOING TO PULL YOU APART ONE ATOM AT A TIME...

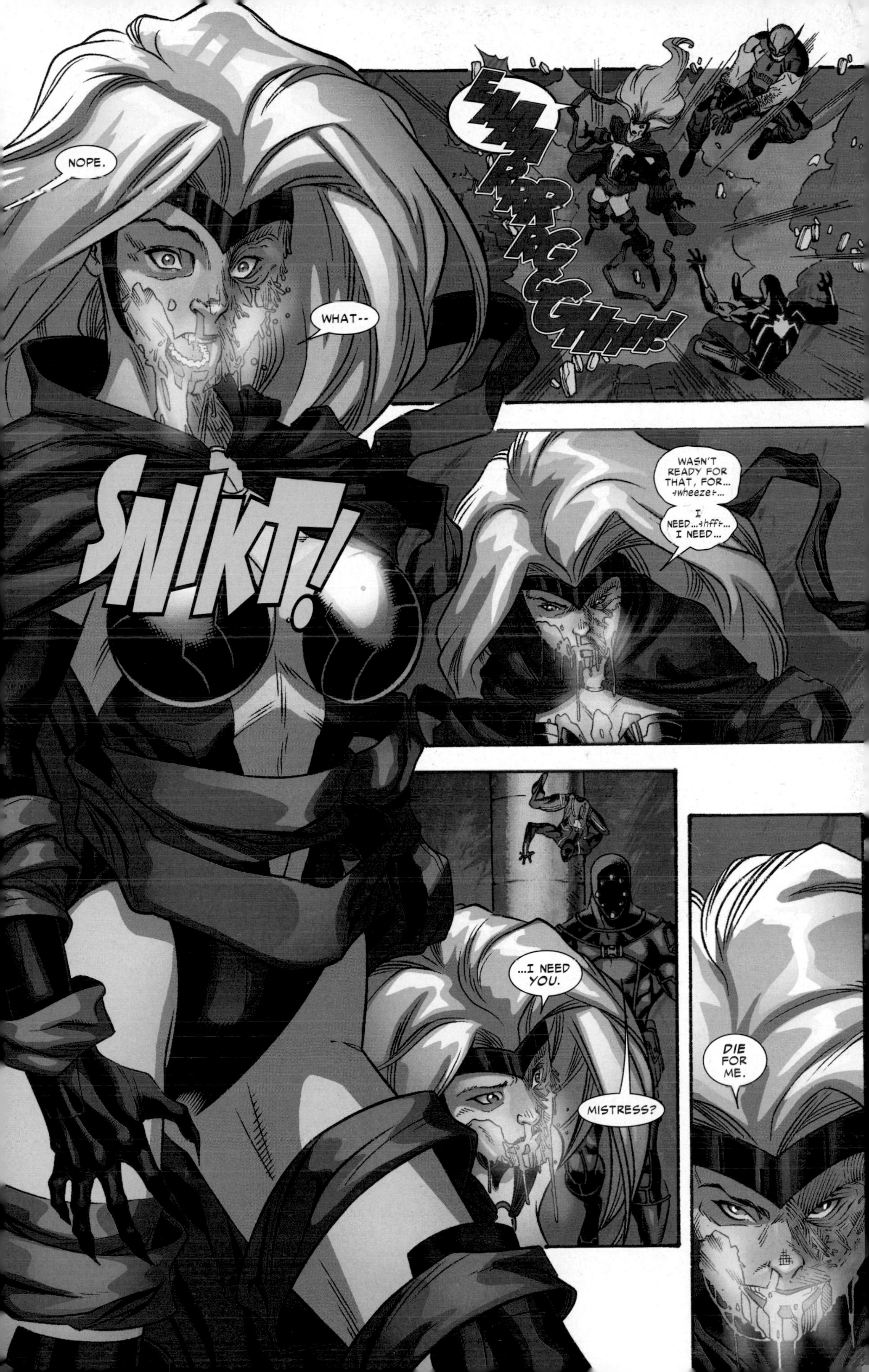
NOPE.
WHAT--
SNIKT!
EHHRRRAGGHHH!
WASN'T READY FOR THAT, FOR... *wheeze*... I NEED... *hff*... I NEED...
...I NEED YOU.
MISTRESS?
DIE FOR ME.

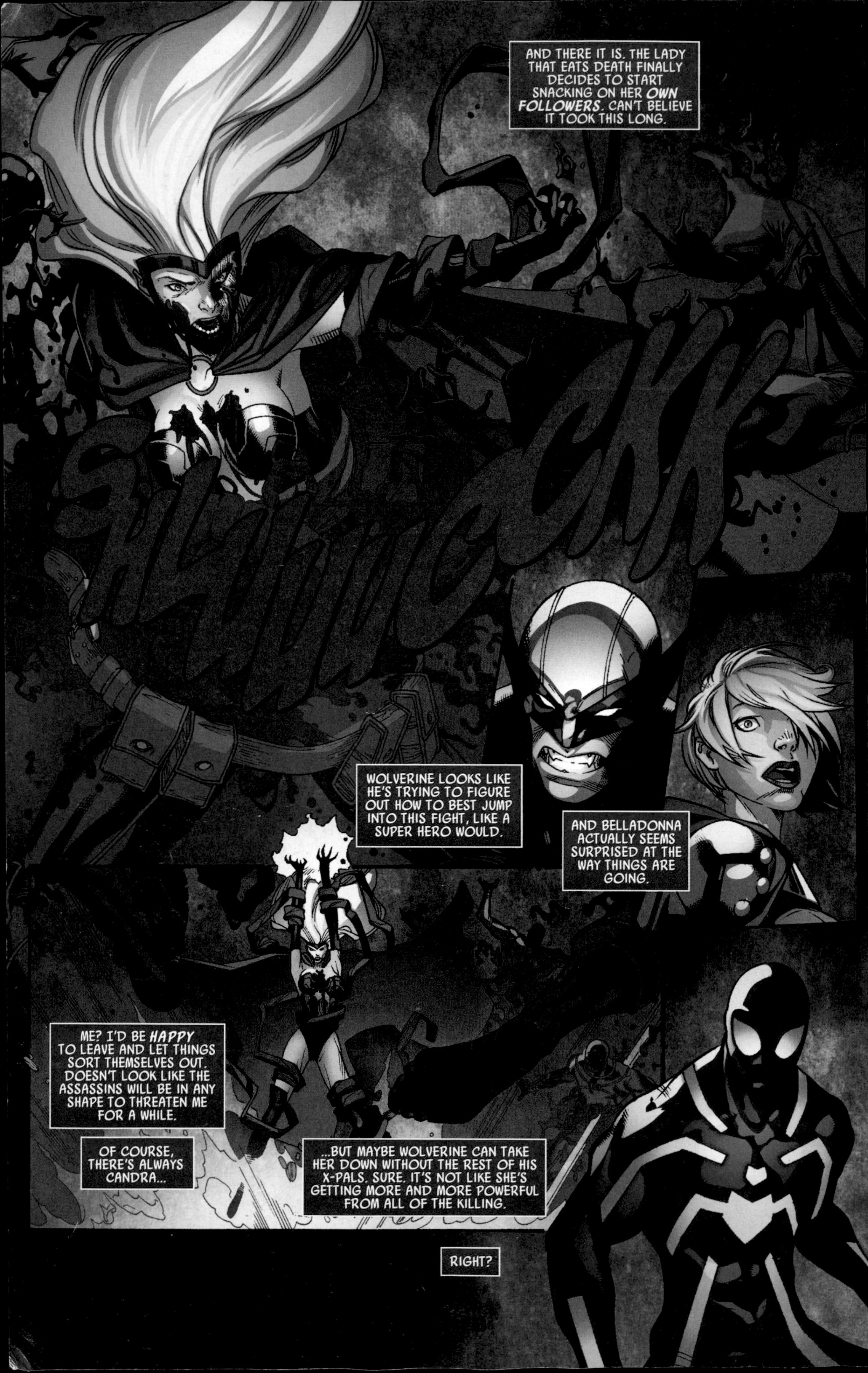
AND THERE IT IS. THE LADY THAT EATS DEATH FINALLY DECIDES TO START SNACKING ON HER OWN FOLLOWERS. CAN'T BELIEVE IT TOOK THIS LONG.
WOLVERINE LOOKS LIKE HE'S TRYING TO FIGURE OUT HOW TO BEST JUMP INTO THIS FIGHT, LIKE A SUPER HERO WOULD.
AND BELLADONNA ACTUALLY SEEMS SURPRISED AT THE WAY THINGS ARE GOING.
ME? I'D BE HAPPY TO LEAVE AND LET THINGS SORT THEMSELVES OUT. DOESN'T LOOK LIKE THE ASSASSINS WILL BE IN ANY SHAPE TO THREATEN ME FOR A WHILE.
OF COURSE, THERE'S ALWAYS CANDRA...
...BUT MAYBE WOLVERINE CAN TAKE HER DOWN WITHOUT THE REST OF HIS X-PALS. SURE. IT'S NOT LIKE SHE'S GETTING MORE AND MORE POWERFUL FROM ALL OF THE KILLING.
RIGHT?

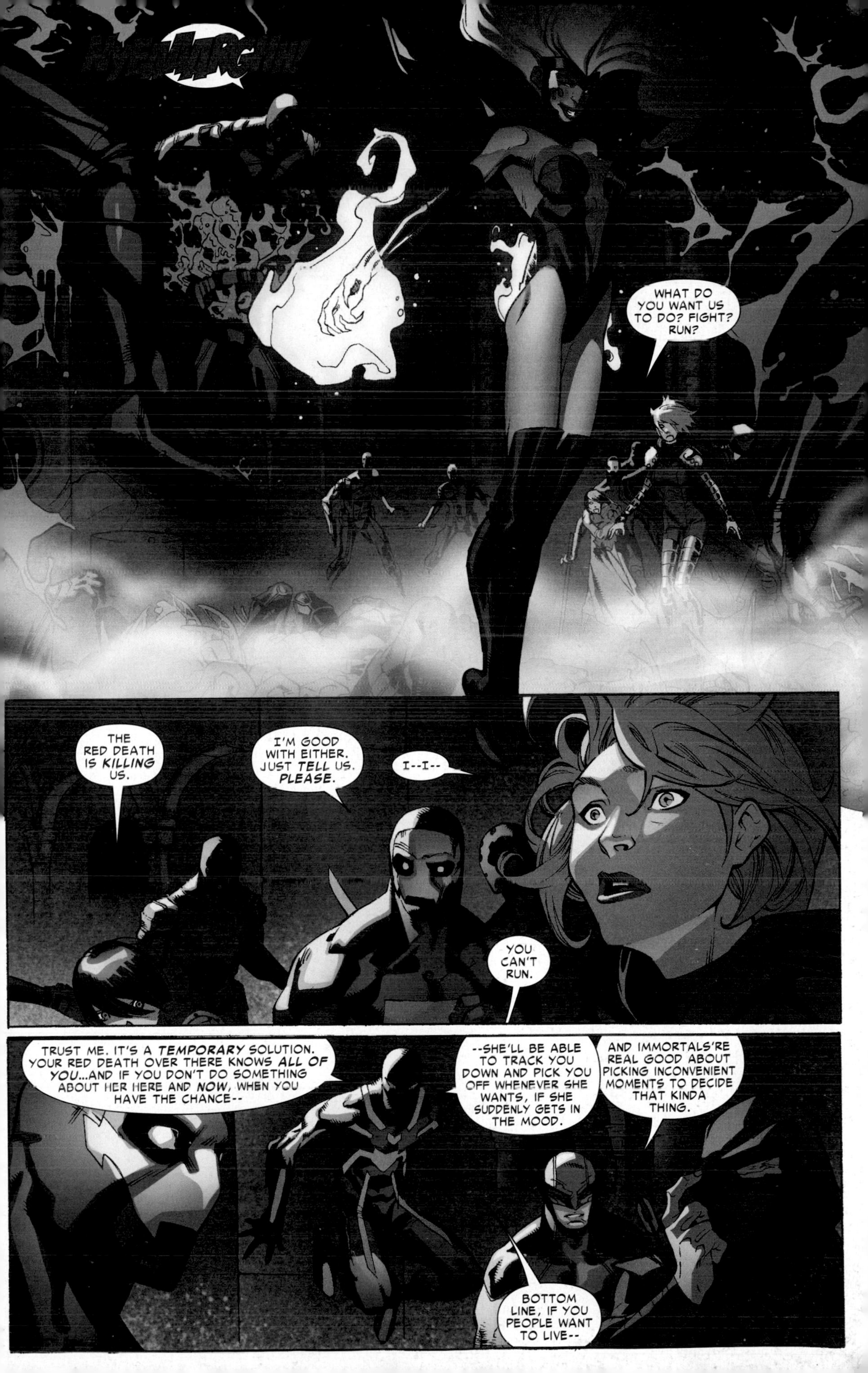
WHAT DO YOU WANT US TO DO? FIGHT? RUN?
THE RED DEATH IS KILLING US.
I'M GOOD WITH EITHER. JUST TELL US. PLEASE.
I--I--
YOU CAN'T RUN.
TRUST ME. IT'S A TEMPORARY SOLUTION. YOUR RED DEATH OVER THERE KNOWS ALL OF YOU...AND IF YOU DON'T DO SOMETHING ABOUT HER HERE AND NOW, WHEN YOU HAVE THE CHANCE--
--SHE'LL BE ABLE TO TRACK YOU DOWN AND PICK YOU OFF WHENEVER SHE WANTS, IF SHE SUDDENLY GETS IN THE MOOD.
AND IMMORTALS'RE REAL GOOD ABOUT PICKING INCONVENIENT MOMENTS TO DECIDE THAT KINDA THING.
BOTTOM LINE, IF YOU PEOPLE WANT TO LIVE--

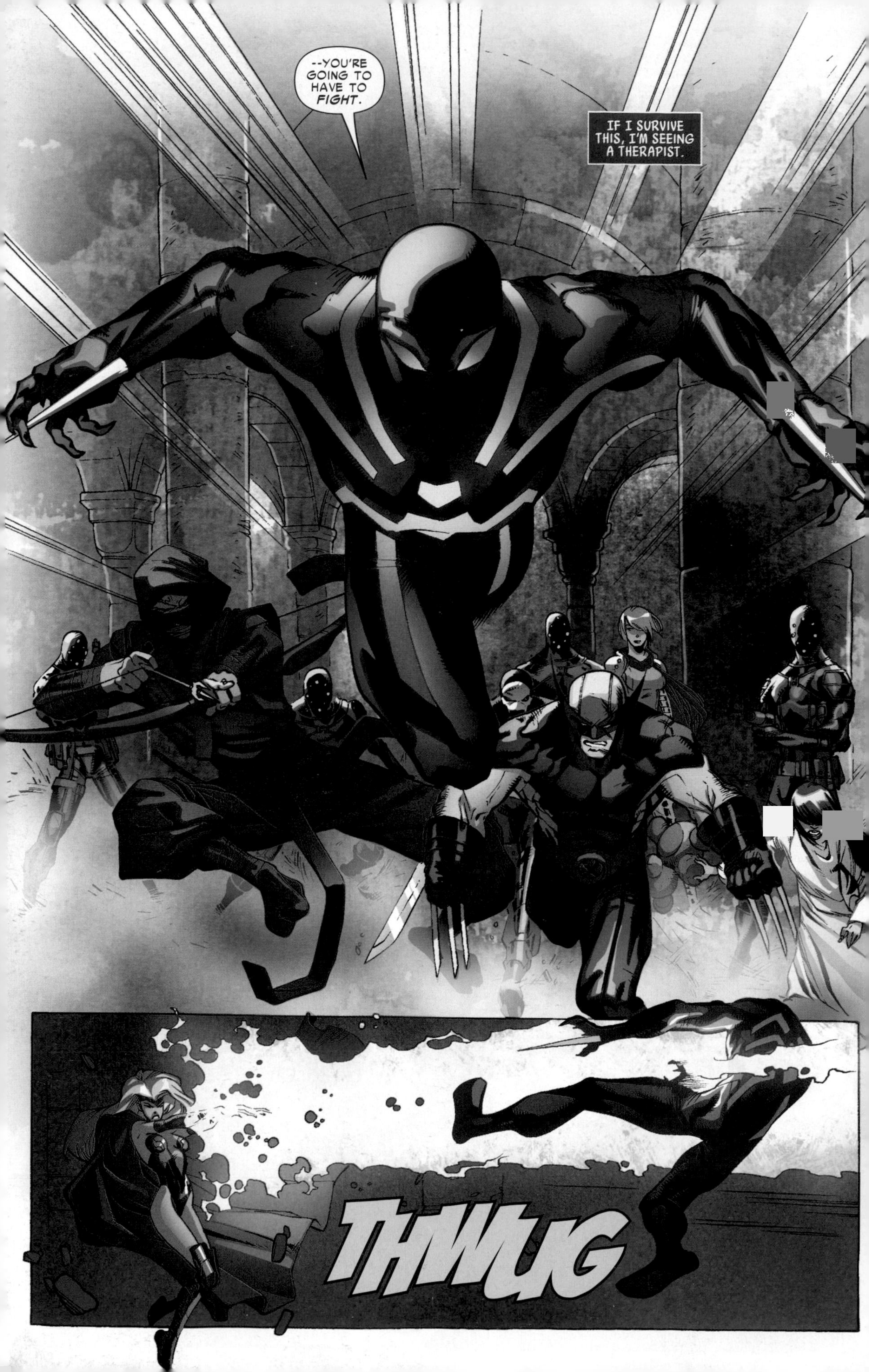
--YOU'RE GOING TO HAVE TO FIGHT.
IF I SURVIVE THIS, I'M SEEING A THERAPIST.
THWUG

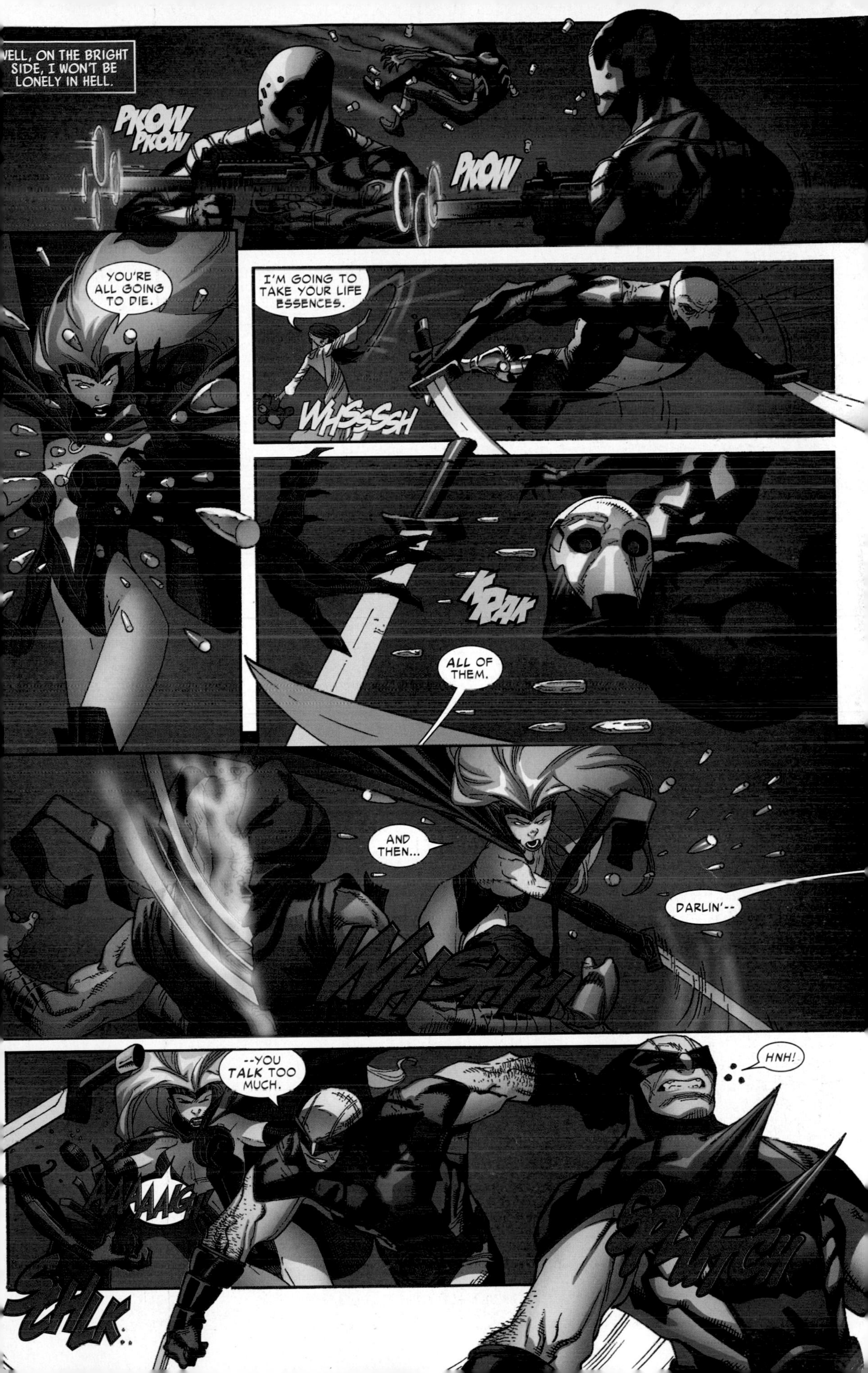
WELL, ON THE BRIGHT SIDE, I WON'T BE LONELY IN HELL.
PKOW PKOW
PKOW
YOU'RE ALL GOING TO DIE.
I'M GOING TO TAKE YOUR LIFE ESSENCES.
WHSSSSH
KRAK
ALL OF THEM.
AND THEN...
DARLIN'--
--YOU TALK TOO MUCH.
HNH!
SPLUTCH
SHLK

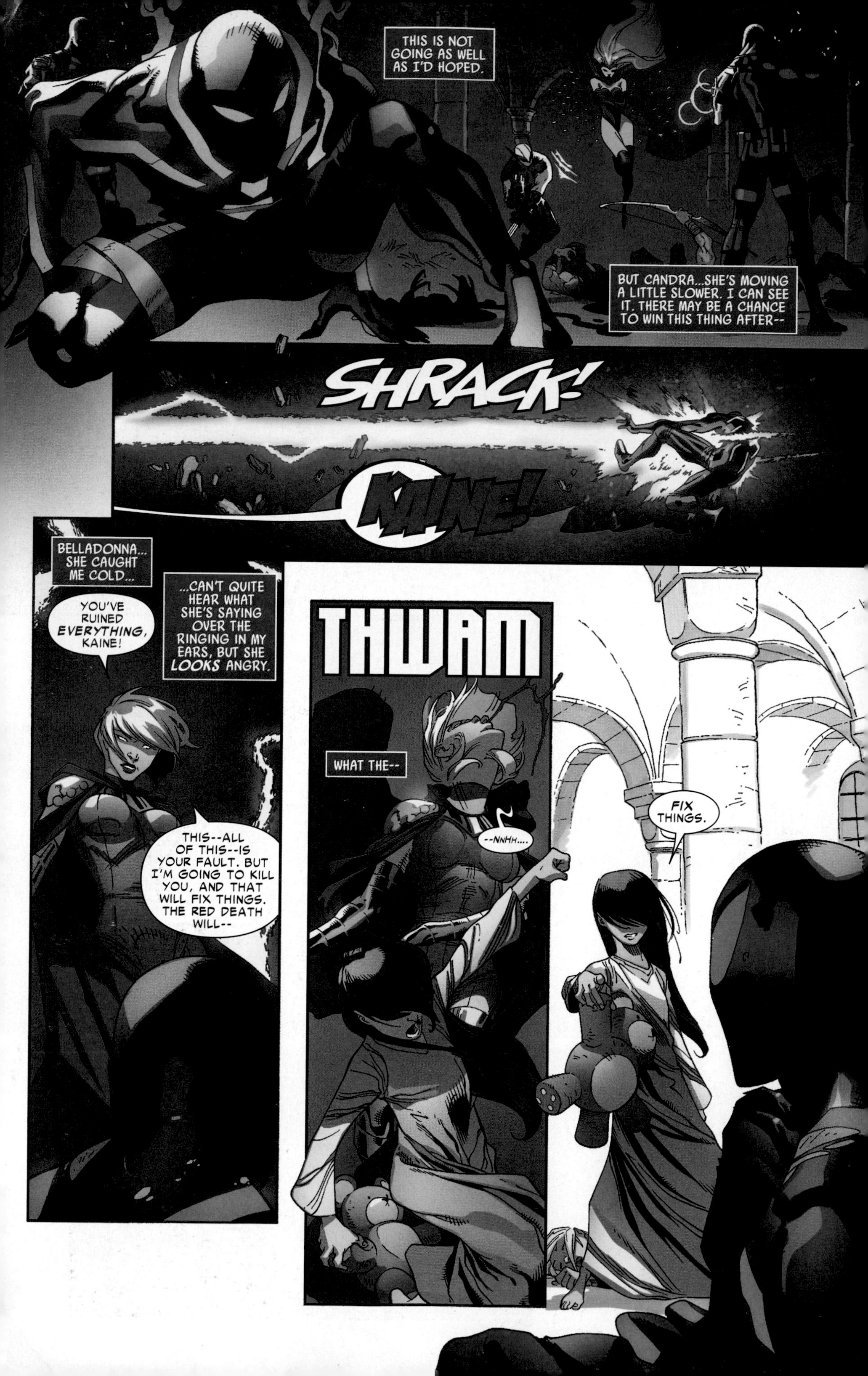

THIS IS NOT GOING AS WELL AS I'D HOPED.
BUT CANDRA...SHE'S MOVING A LITTLE SLOWER. I CAN SEE IT. THERE MAY BE A CHANCE TO WIN THIS THING AFTER--
SHRACK!
KAINE!
BELLADONNA... SHE CAUGHT ME COLD...
YOU'VE RUINED EVERYTHING, KAINE!
...CAN'T QUITE HEAR WHAT SHE'S SAYING OVER THE RINGING IN MY EARS, BUT SHE LOOKS ANGRY.
THIS--ALL OF THIS--IS YOUR FAULT. BUT I'M GOING TO KILL YOU, AND THAT WILL FIX THINGS. THE RED DEATH WILL--
THWAM
WHAT THE--
--NNHH....
FIX THINGS.

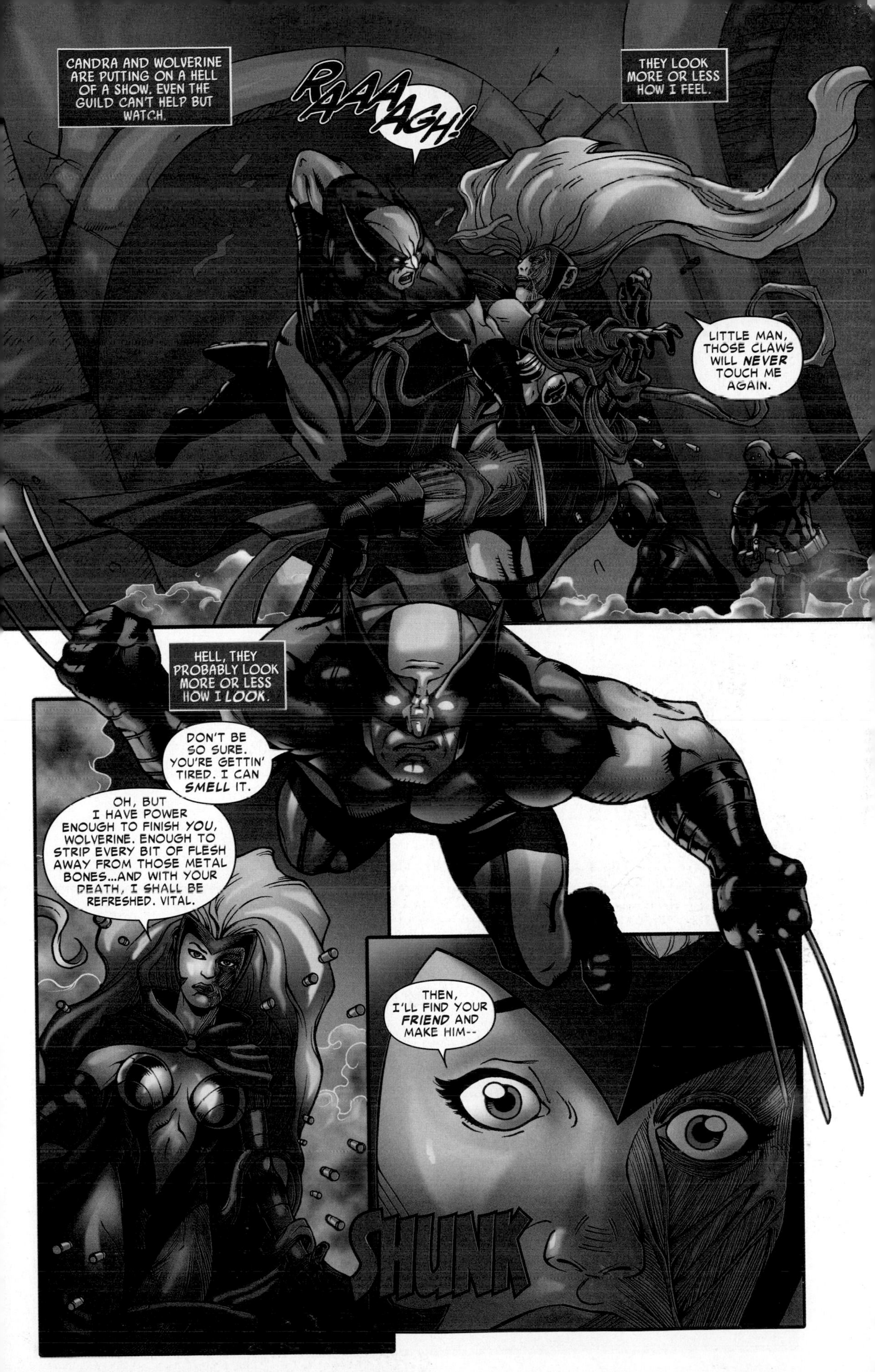
CANDRA AND WOLVERINE ARE PUTTING ON A HELL OF A SHOW. EVEN THE GUILD CAN'T HELP BUT WATCH.
RAAAAAGH!
THEY LOOK MORE OR LESS HOW I FEEL.
LITTLE MAN, THOSE CLAWS WILL NEVER TOUCH ME AGAIN.
HELL, THEY PROBABLY LOOK MORE OR LESS HOW I LOOK.
DON'T BE SO SURE. YOU'RE GETTIN' TIRED. I CAN SMELL IT.
OH, BUT I HAVE POWER ENOUGH TO FINISH YOU, WOLVERINE. ENOUGH TO STRIP EVERY BIT OF FLESH AWAY FROM THOSE METAL BONES...AND WITH YOUR DEATH, I SHALL BE REFRESHED. VITAL.
THEN, I'LL FIND YOUR FRIEND AND MAKE HIM--
SHUNK

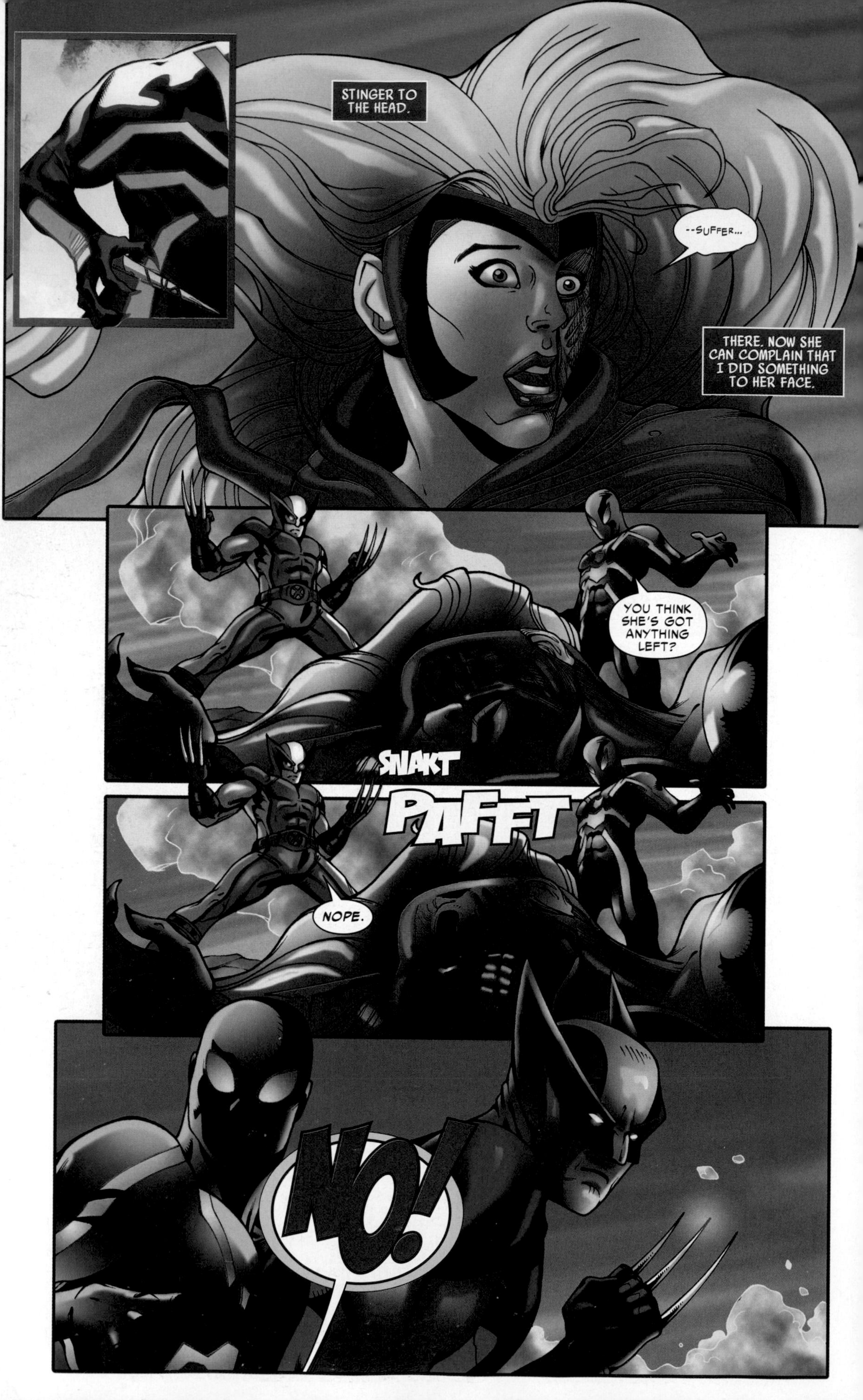
STINGER TO THE HEAD.
--SUFFER...
THERE. NOW SHE CAN COMPLAIN THAT I DID SOMETHING TO HER FACE.
YOU THINK SHE'S GOT ANYTHING LEFT?
SNAKT
PAFFT
NOPE.
NO!

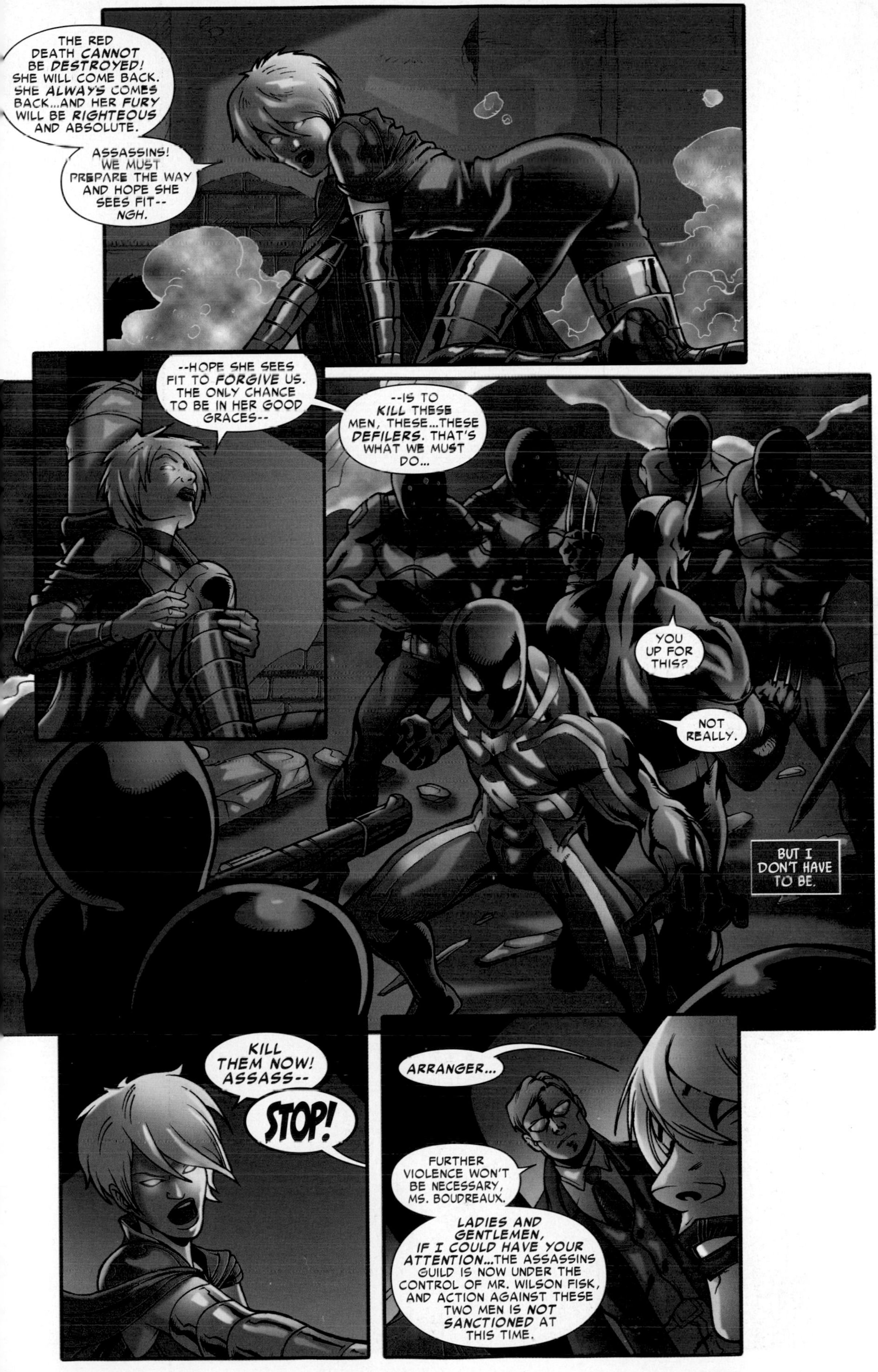
THE RED DEATH CANNOT BE DESTROYED! SHE WILL COME BACK. SHE ALWAYS COMES BACK...AND HER FURY WILL BE RIGHTEOUS AND ABSOLUTE.
ASSASSINS! WE MUST PREPARE THE WAY AND HOPE SHE SEES FIT--NGH.
--HOPE SHE SEES FIT TO FORGIVE US. THE ONLY CHANCE TO BE IN HER GOOD GRACES--
--IS TO KILL THESE MEN, THESE...THESE DEFILERS. THAT'S WHAT WE MUST DO...
YOU UP FOR THIS?
NOT REALLY.
BUT I DON'T HAVE TO BE.
KILL THEM NOW! ASSASS--
STOP!
ARRANGER...
FURTHER VIOLENCE WON'T BE NECESSARY, MS. BOUDREAUX.
LADIES AND GENTLEMEN, IF I COULD HAVE YOUR ATTENTION...THE ASSASSINS GUILD IS NOW UNDER THE CONTROL OF MR. WILSON FISK, AND ACTION AGAINST THESE TWO MEN IS NOT SANCTIONED AT THIS TIME.

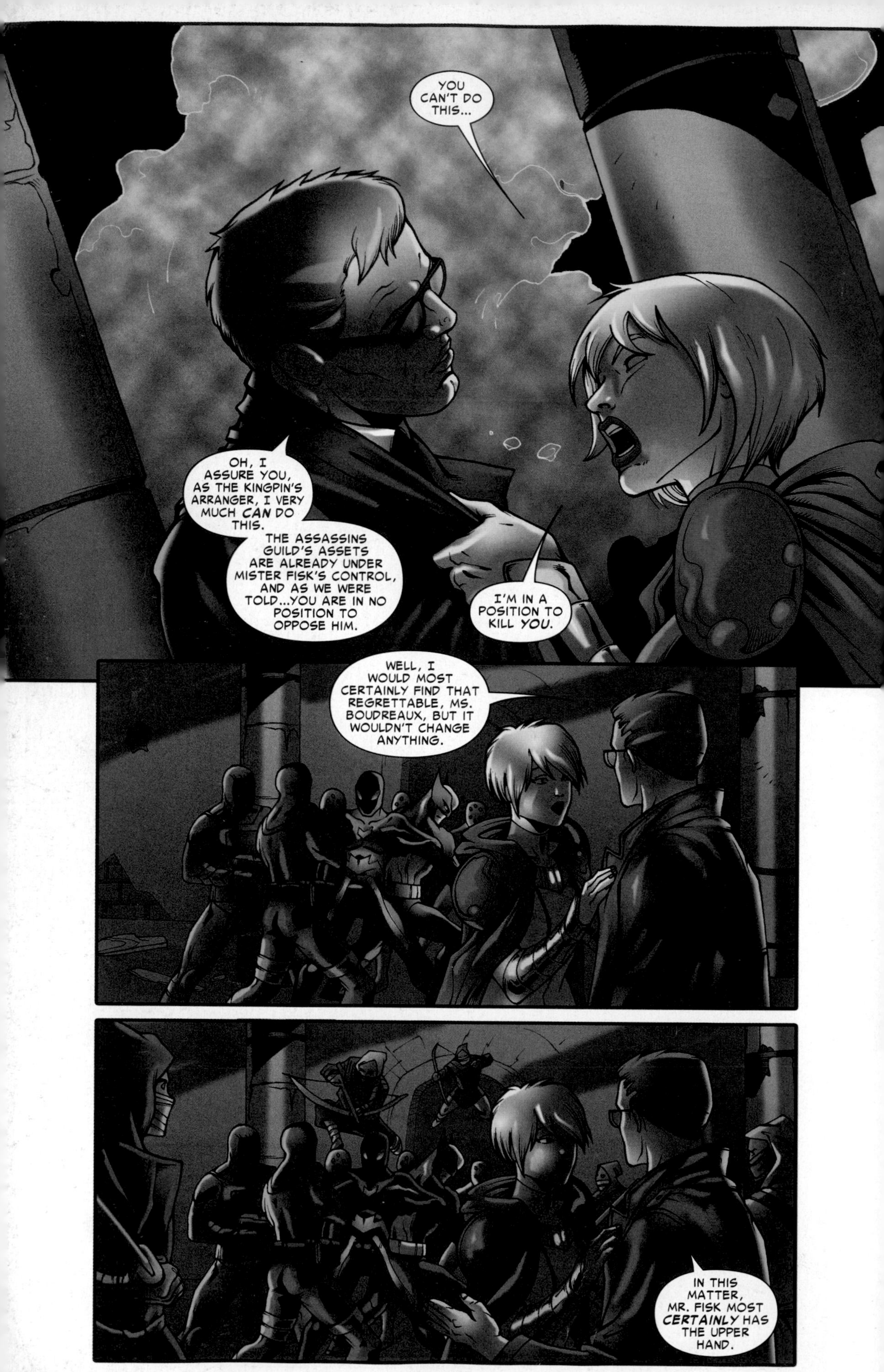
YOU CAN'T DO THIS...
OH, I ASSURE YOU, AS THE KINGPIN'S ARRANGER, I VERY MUCH ***CAN*** DO THIS.
THE ASSASSINS GUILD'S ASSETS ARE ALREADY UNDER MISTER FISK'S CONTROL, AND AS WE WERE TOLD...YOU ARE IN NO POSITION TO OPPOSE HIM.
I'M IN A POSITION TO KILL ***YOU***.
WELL, I WOULD MOST CERTAINLY FIND THAT REGRETTABLE, MS. BOUDREAUX, BUT IT WOULDN'T CHANGE ANYTHING.
IN THIS MATTER, MR. FISK MOST ***CERTAINLY*** HAS THE UPPER HAND.

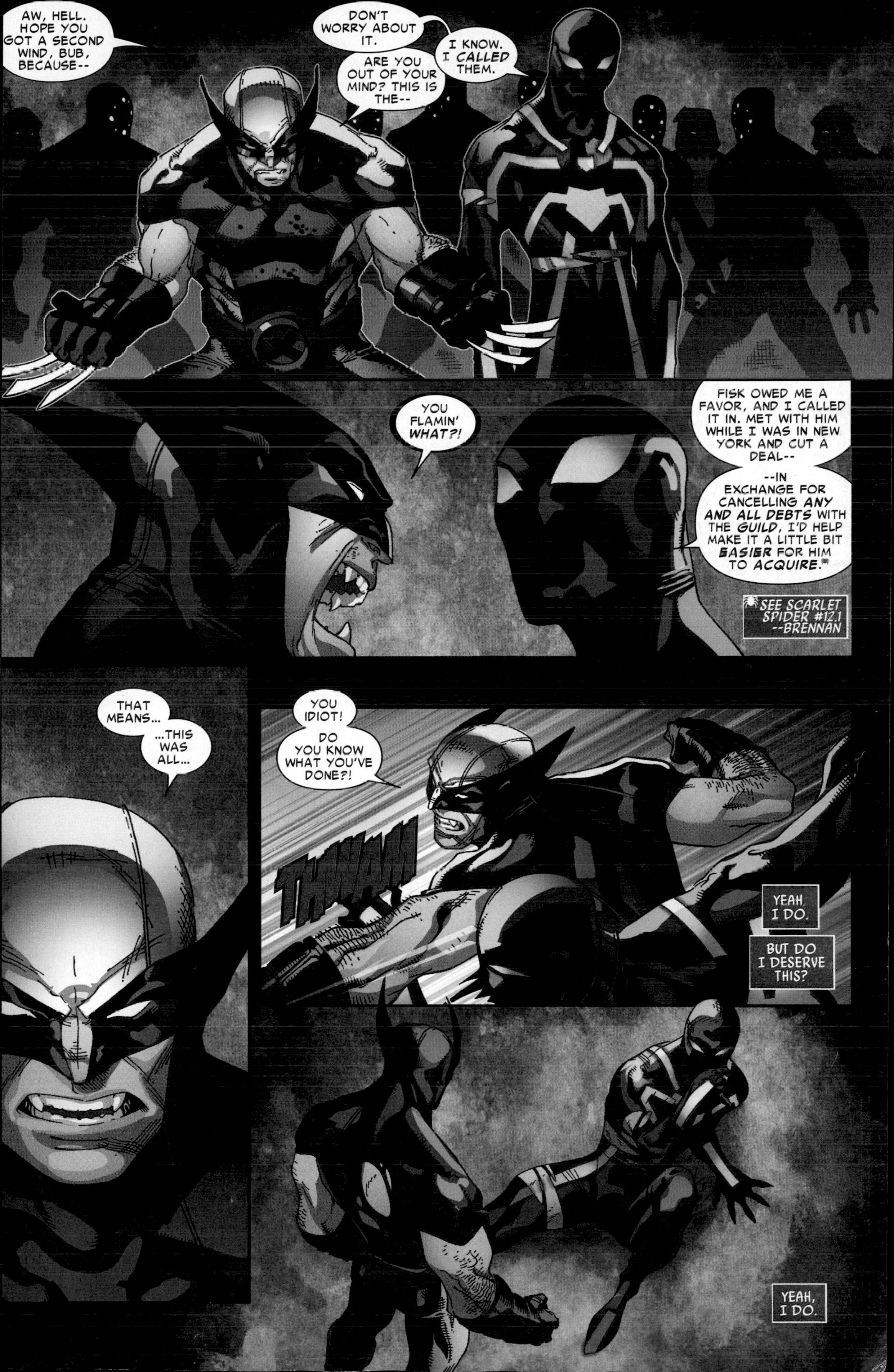
AW, HELL. HOPE YOU GOT A SECOND WIND, BUB, BECAUSE--
DON'T WORRY ABOUT IT.
ARE YOU OUT OF YOUR MIND? THIS IS THE--
I KNOW. I CALLED THEM.
YOU FLAMIN' WHAT?!
FISK OWED ME A FAVOR, AND I CALLED IT IN. MET WITH HIM WHILE I WAS IN NEW YORK AND CUT A DEAL--
--IN EXCHANGE FOR CANCELLING ANY AND ALL DEBTS WITH THE GUILD, I'D HELP MAKE IT A LITTLE BIT EASIER FOR HIM TO ACQUIRE.*
*SEE SCARLET SPIDER #12.1 --BRENNAN
THAT MEANS...
...THIS WAS ALL...
YOU IDIOT!
DO YOU KNOW WHAT YOU'VE DONE?!
THWAM
YEAH, I DO.
BUT DO I DESERVE THIS?
YEAH, I DO.

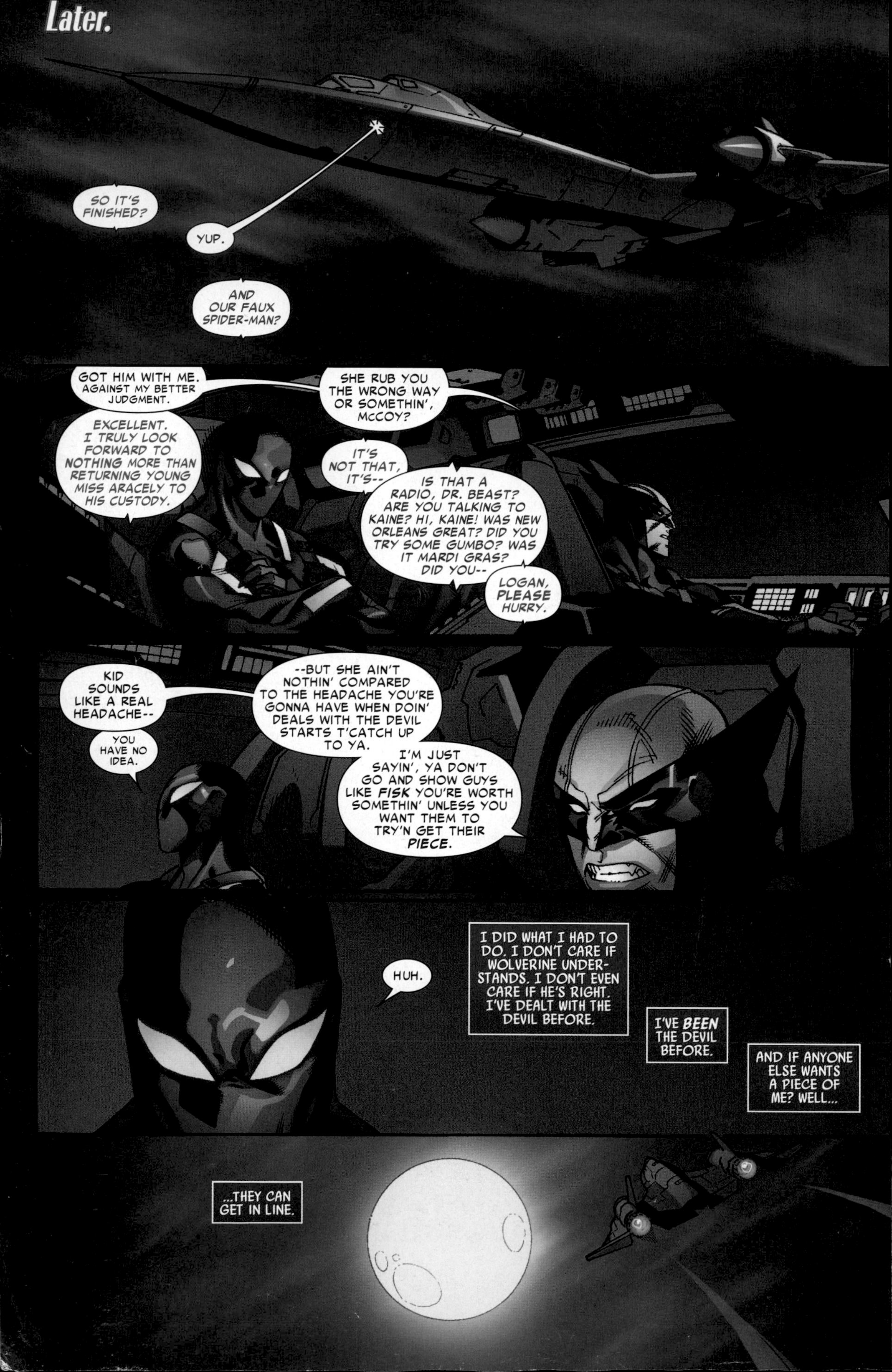
Later.
SO IT'S FINISHED?
YUP.
AND OUR FAUX SPIDER-MAN?
GOT HIM WITH ME. AGAINST MY BETTER JUDGMENT.
SHE RUB YOU THE WRONG WAY OR SOMETHIN', McCOY?
EXCELLENT. I TRULY LOOK FORWARD TO NOTHING MORE THAN RETURNING YOUNG MISS ARACELY TO HIS CUSTODY.
IT'S NOT THAT, IT'S--
IS THAT A RADIO, DR. BEAST? ARE YOU TALKING TO KAINE? HI, KAINE! WAS NEW ORLEANS GREAT? DID YOU TRY SOME GUMBO? WAS IT MARDI GRAS? DID YOU--
LOGAN, PLEASE HURRY.
KID SOUNDS LIKE A REAL HEADACHE--
YOU HAVE NO IDEA.
--BUT SHE AIN'T NOTHIN' COMPARED TO THE HEADACHE YOU'RE GONNA HAVE WHEN DOIN' DEALS WITH THE DEVIL STARTS T'CATCH UP TO YA.
I'M JUST SAYIN', YA DON'T GO AND SHOW GUYS LIKE FISK YOU'RE WORTH SOMETHIN' UNLESS YOU WANT THEM TO TRY'N GET THEIR PIECE.
HUH.
I DID WHAT I HAD TO DO. I DON'T CARE IF WOLVERINE UNDERSTANDS. I DON'T EVEN CARE IF HE'S RIGHT. I'VE DEALT WITH THE DEVIL BEFORE.
I'VE BEEN THE DEVIL BEFORE.
AND IF ANYONE ELSE WANTS A PIECE OF ME? WELL...
...THEY CAN GET IN LINE.

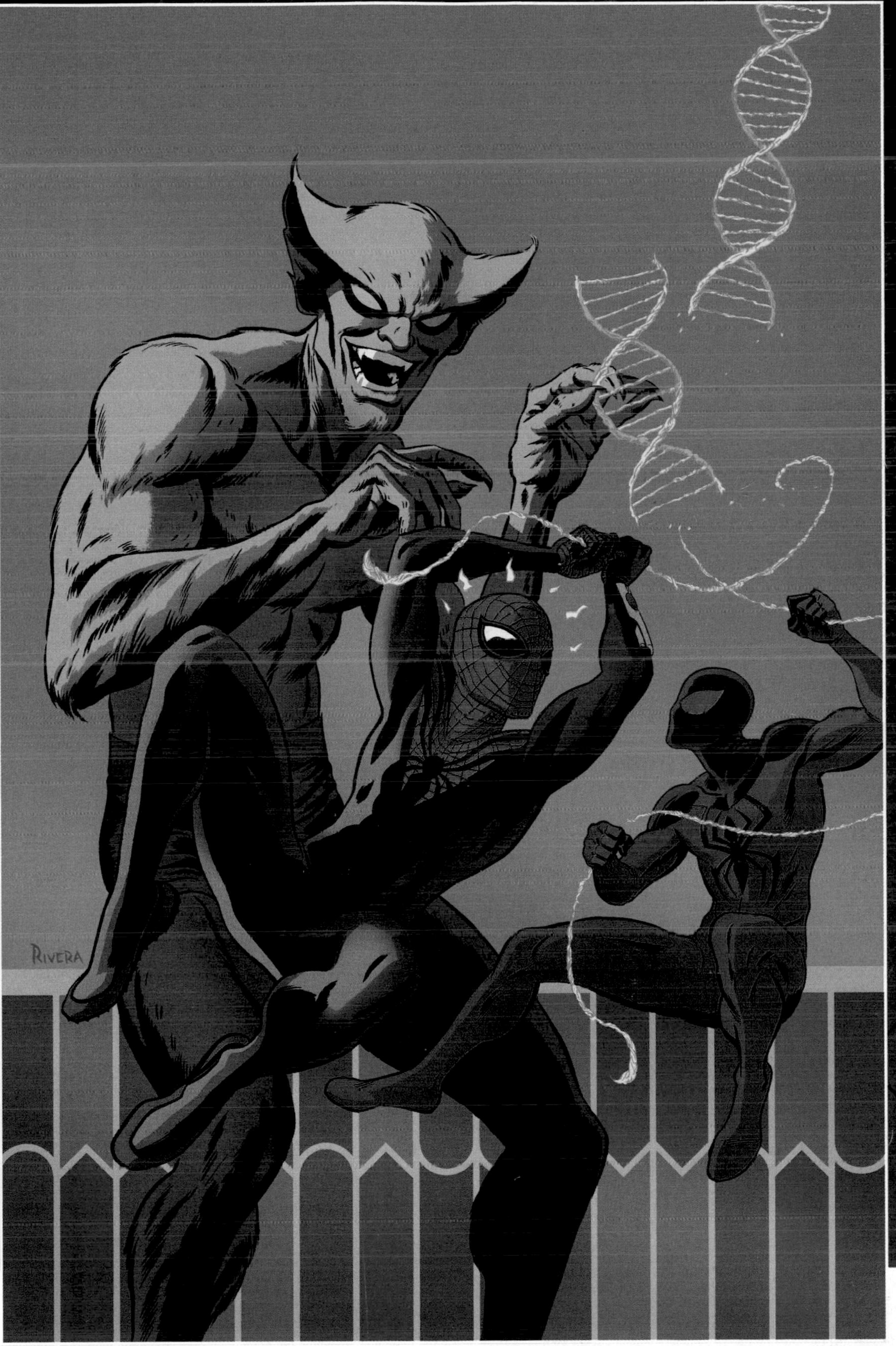
RIVERA

SUPERIOR SPIDER-MAN TEAM-UP #2

"SIBLING RIVALRY, PART 1"

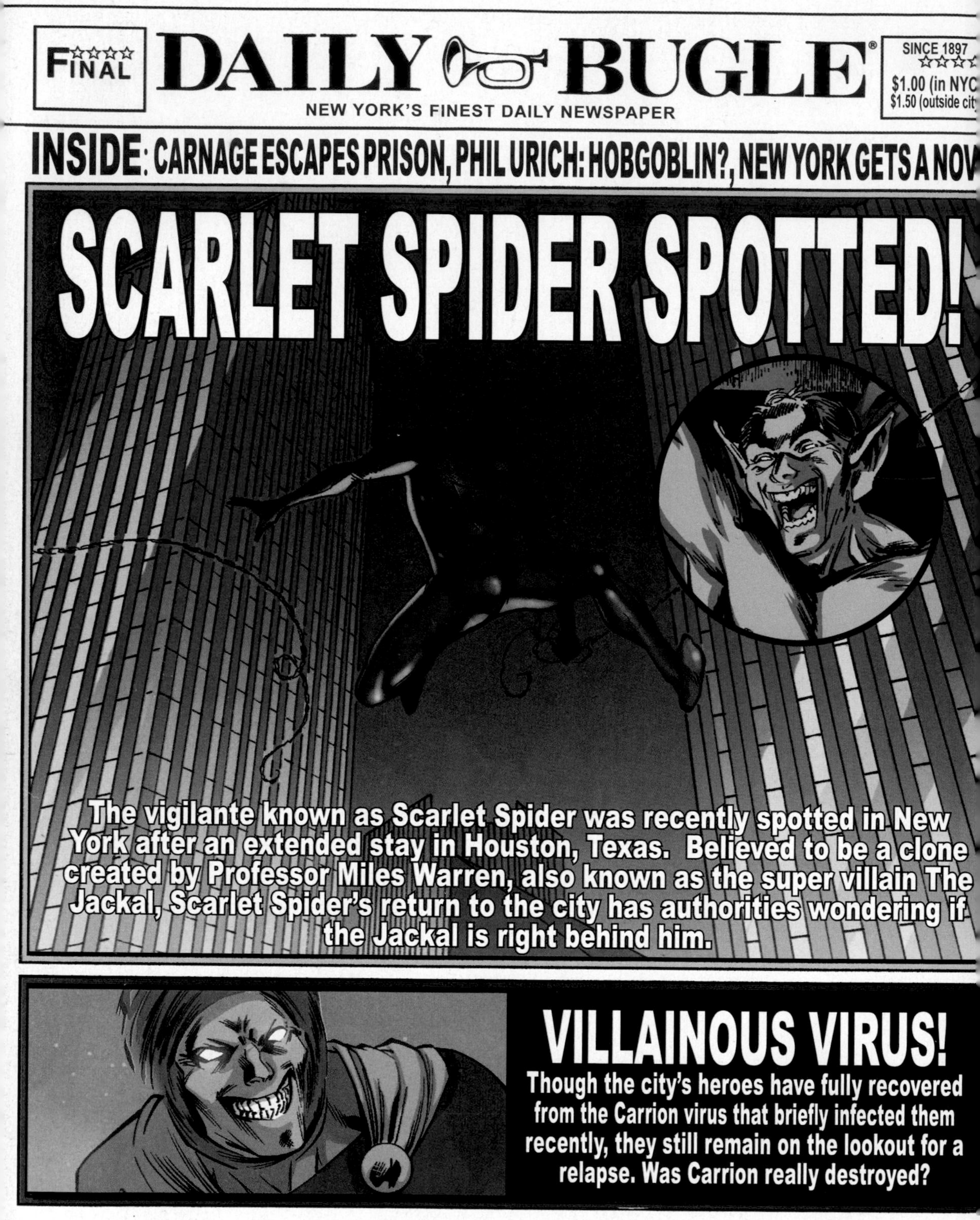

FINAL ☆☆☆☆

DAILY BUGLE

SINCE 1897 ☆☆☆☆

$1.00 (in NYC

$1.50 (outside cit

NEW YORK'S FINEST DAILY NEWSPAPER

INSIDE: CARNAGE ESCAPES PRISON, PHIL URICH: HOBGOBLIN?, NEW YORK GETS A NOV

SCARLET SPIDER SPOTTED!

The vigilante known as Scarlet Spider was recently spotted in New York after an extended stay in Houston, Texas. Believed to be a clone created by Professor Miles Warren, also known as the super villain The Jackal, Scarlet Spider's return to the city has authorities wondering if the Jackal is right behind him.

VILLAINOUS VIRUS!

Though the city's heroes have fully recovered from the Carrion virus that briefly infected them recently, they still remain on the lookout for a relapse. Was Carrion really destroyed?

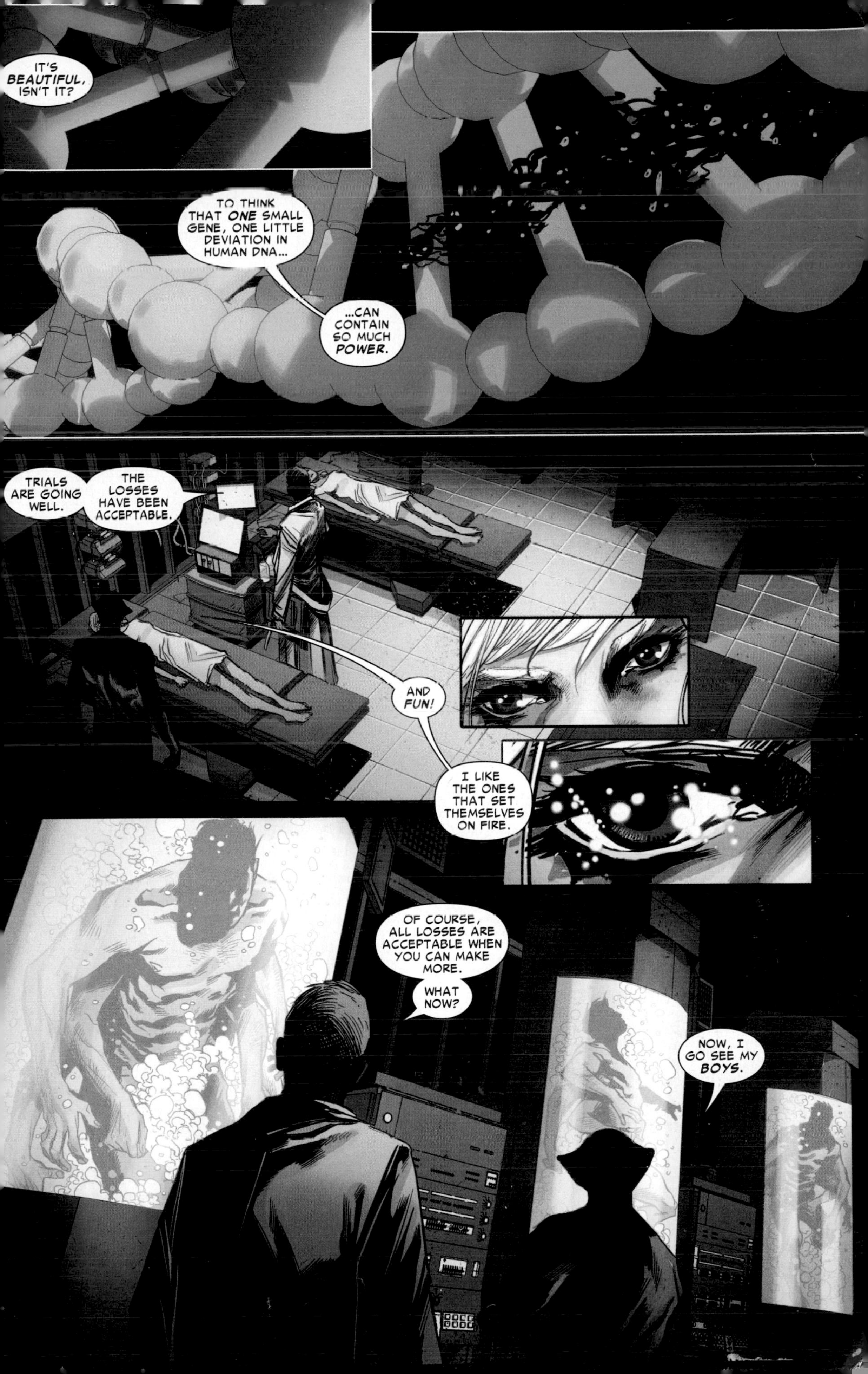
IT'S BEAUTIFUL, ISN'T IT?
TO THINK THAT ONE SMALL GENE, ONE LITTLE DEVIATION IN HUMAN DNA...
...CAN CONTAIN SO MUCH POWER.
TRIALS ARE GOING WELL.
THE LOSSES HAVE BEEN ACCEPTABLE.
AND FUN!
I LIKE THE ONES THAT SET THEMSELVES ON FIRE.
OF COURSE, ALL LOSSES ARE ACCEPTABLE WHEN YOU CAN MAKE MORE.
WHAT NOW?
NOW, I GO SEE MY BOYS.

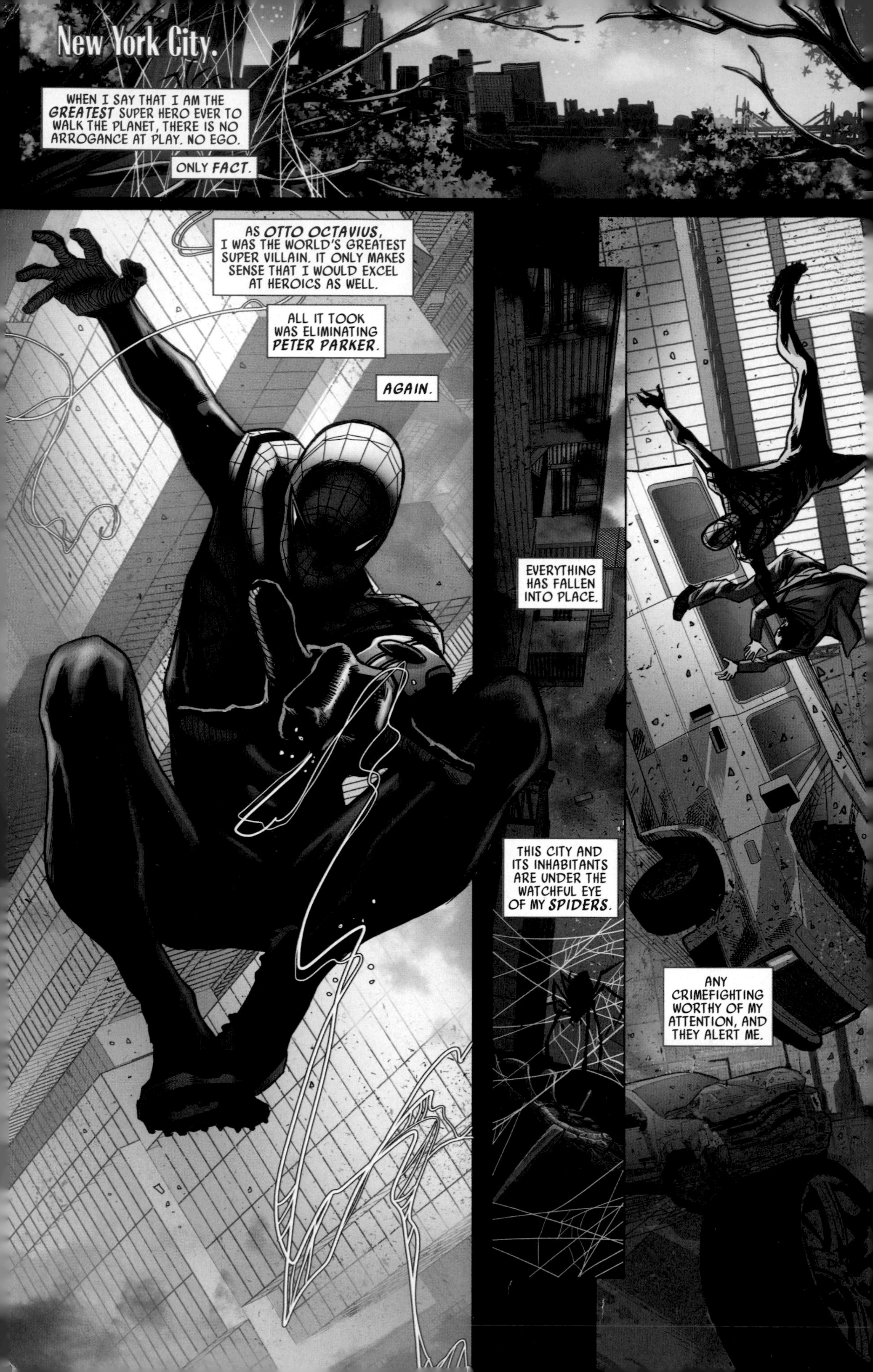
New York City.
WHEN I SAY THAT I AM THE GREATEST SUPER HERO EVER TO WALK THE PLANET, THERE IS NO ARROGANCE AT PLAY. NO EGO.
ONLY FACT.
AS OTTO OCTAVIUS, I WAS THE WORLD'S GREATEST SUPER VILLAIN. IT ONLY MAKES SENSE THAT I WOULD EXCEL AT HEROICS AS WELL.
ALL IT TOOK WAS ELIMINATING PETER PARKER.
AGAIN.
EVERYTHING HAS FALLEN INTO PLACE.
THIS CITY AND ITS INHABITANTS ARE UNDER THE WATCHFUL EYE OF MY SPIDERS.
ANY CRIMEFIGHTING WORTHY OF MY ATTENTION, AND THEY ALERT ME.

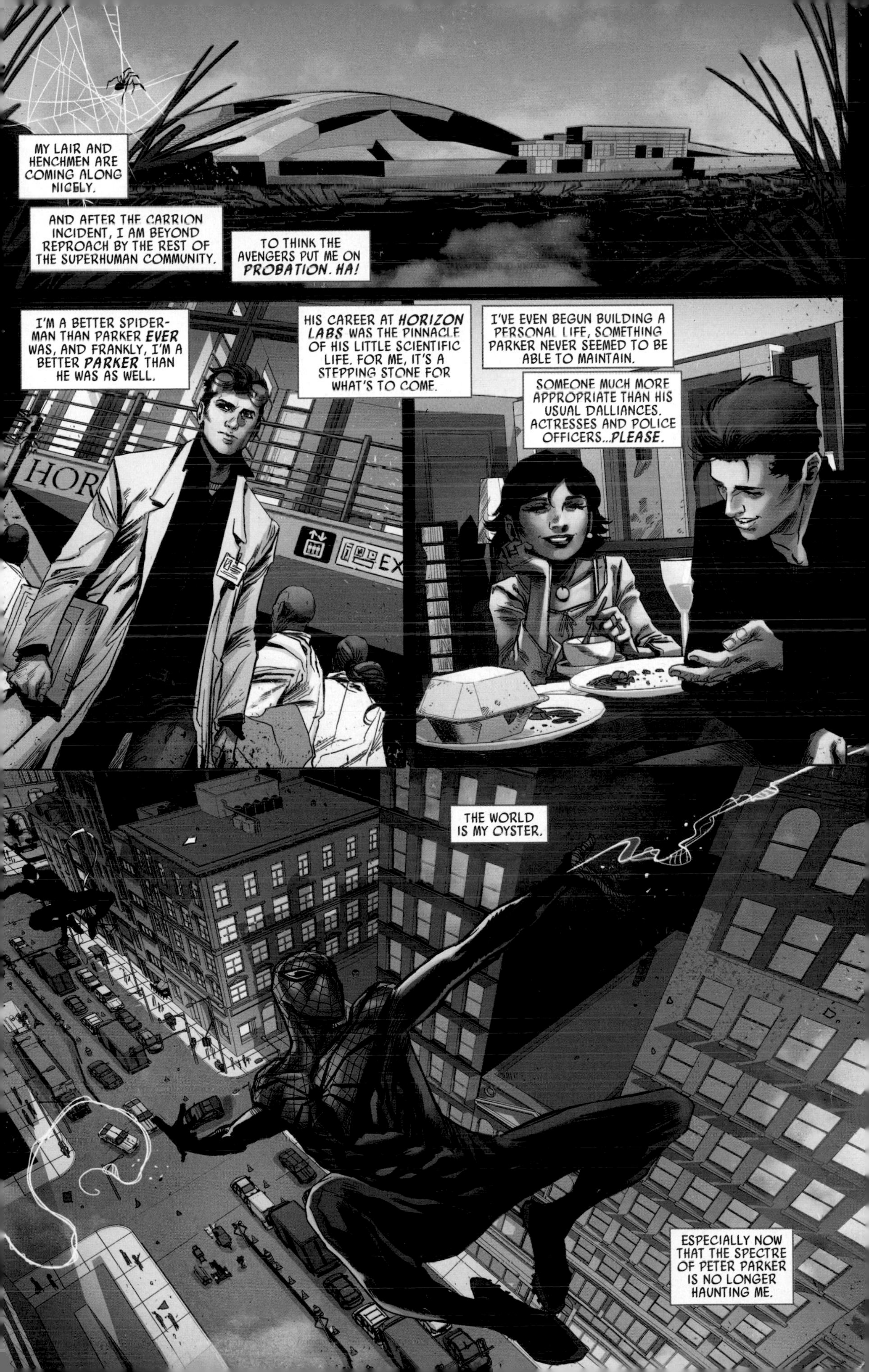
MY LAIR AND HENCHMEN ARE COMING ALONG NICELY.
AND AFTER THE CARRION INCIDENT, I AM BEYOND REPROACH BY THE REST OF THE SUPERHUMAN COMMUNITY.
TO THINK THE AVENGERS PUT ME ON PROBATION. HA!
I'M A BETTER SPIDER-MAN THAN PARKER EVER WAS, AND FRANKLY, I'M A BETTER PARKER THAN HE WAS AS WELL.
HIS CAREER AT HORIZON LABS WAS THE PINNACLE OF HIS LITTLE SCIENTIFIC LIFE. FOR ME, IT'S A STEPPING STONE FOR WHAT'S TO COME.
I'VE EVEN BEGUN BUILDING A PERSONAL LIFE, SOMETHING PARKER NEVER SEEMED TO BE ABLE TO MAINTAIN.
SOMEONE MUCH MORE APPROPRIATE THAN HIS USUAL DALLIANCES. ACTRESSES AND POLICE OFFICERS...PLEASE.
THE WORLD IS MY OYSTER.
ESPECIALLY NOW THAT THE SPECTRE OF PETER PARKER IS NO LONGER HAUNTING ME.

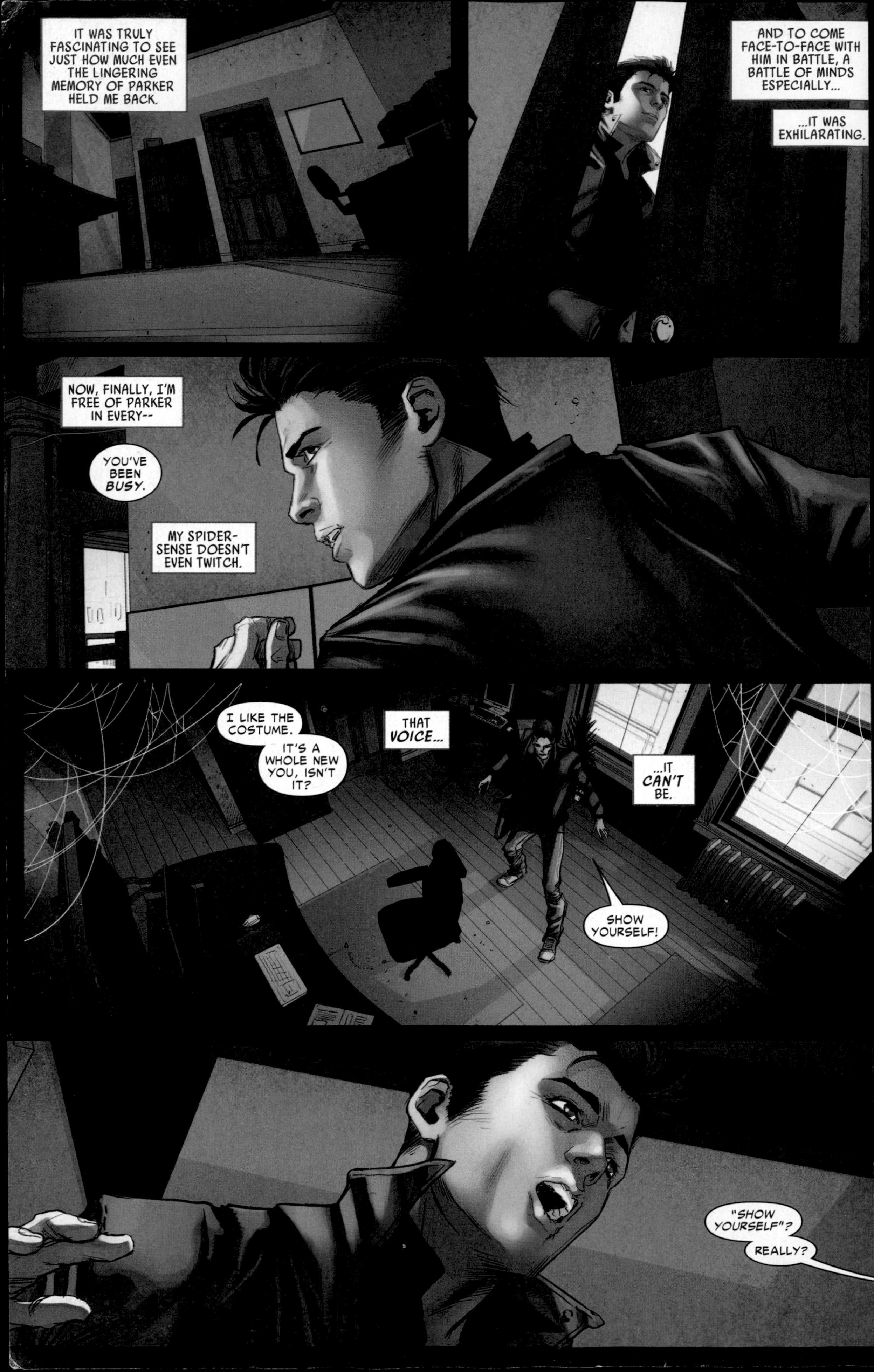
IT WAS TRULY FASCINATING TO SEE JUST HOW MUCH EVEN THE LINGERING MEMORY OF PARKER HELD ME BACK.
AND TO COME FACE-TO-FACE WITH HIM IN BATTLE, A BATTLE OF MINDS ESPECIALLY...
...IT WAS EXHILARATING.
NOW, FINALLY, I'M FREE OF PARKER IN EVERY--
YOU'VE BEEN *BUSY*.
MY SPIDER-SENSE DOESN'T EVEN TWITCH.
I LIKE THE COSTUME.
IT'S A WHOLE NEW YOU, ISN'T IT?
THAT *VOICE*...
...IT *CAN'T* BE.
SHOW YOURSELF!
"SHOW YOURSELF"?
REALLY?

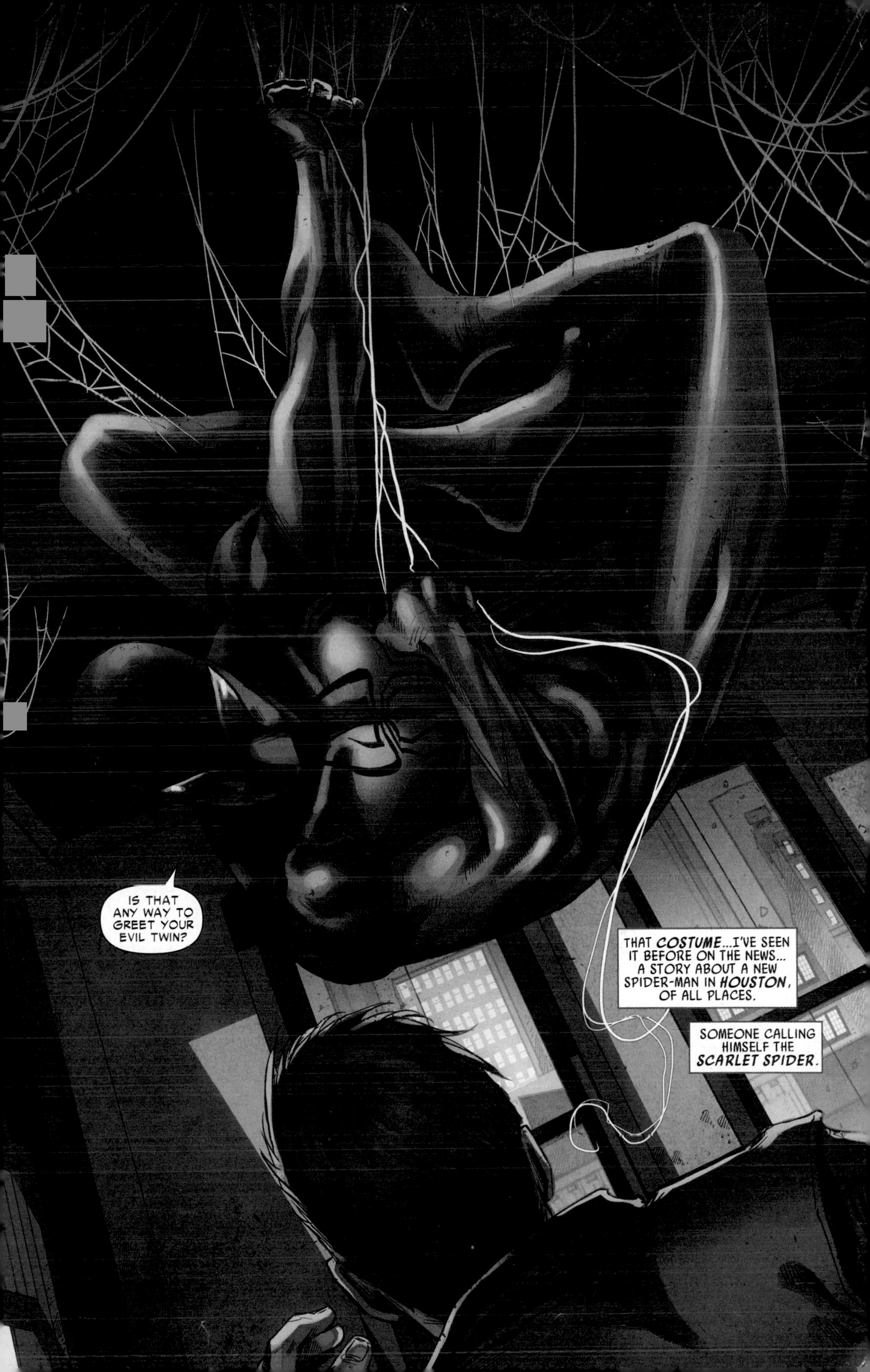
IS THAT ANY WAY TO GREET YOUR EVIL TWIN?
THAT COSTUME...I'VE SEEN IT BEFORE ON THE NEWS... A STORY ABOUT A NEW SPIDER-MAN IN HOUSTON, OF ALL PLACES.
SOMEONE CALLING HIMSELF THE SCARLET SPIDER.

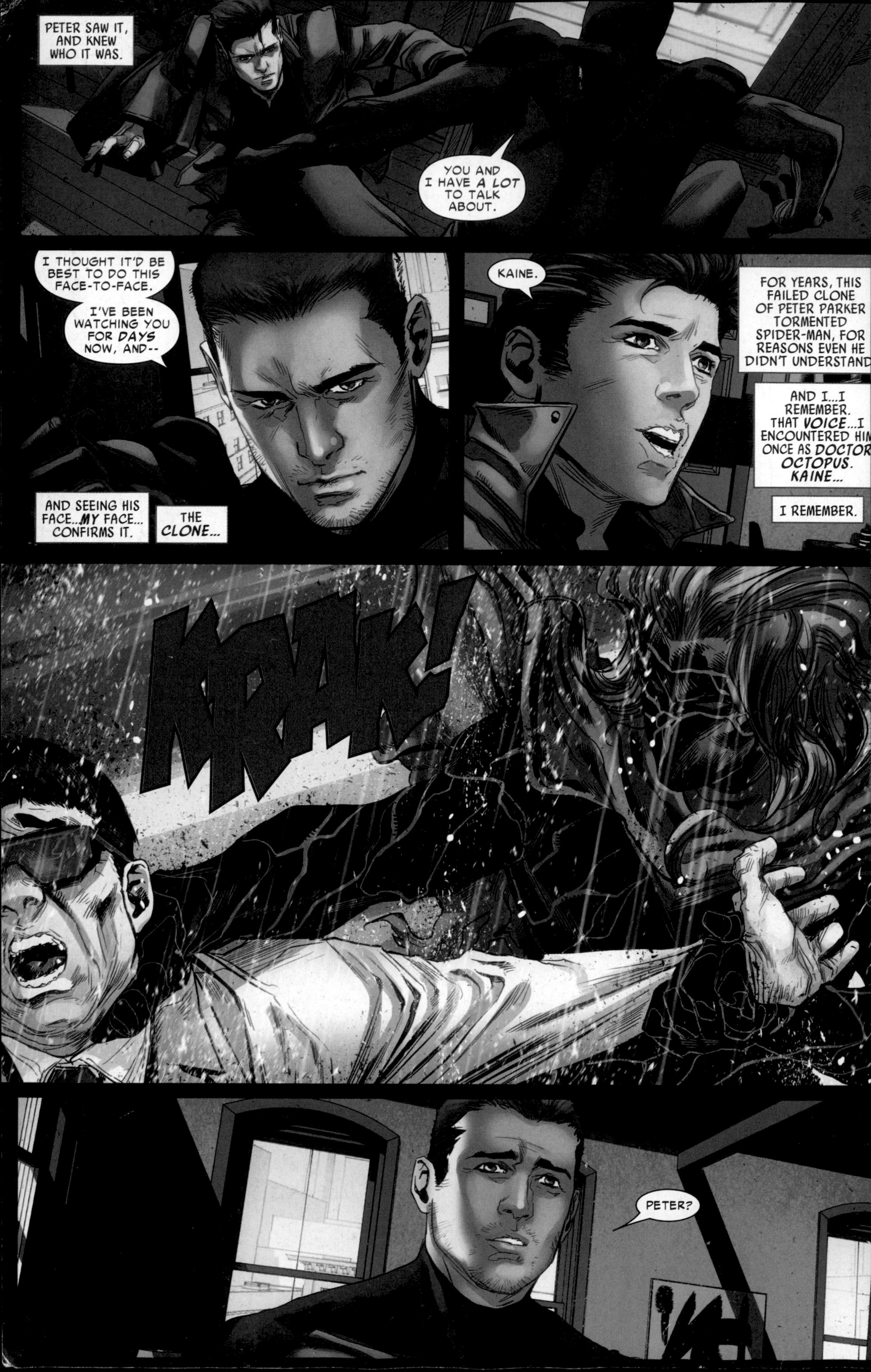
PETER SAW IT, AND KNEW WHO IT WAS.
YOU AND I HAVE A LOT TO TALK ABOUT.
I THOUGHT IT'D BE BEST TO DO THIS FACE-TO-FACE.
I'VE BEEN WATCHING YOU FOR DAYS NOW, AND--
AND SEEING HIS FACE...MY FACE... CONFIRMS IT.
THE CLONE...
KAINE.
FOR YEARS, THIS FAILED CLONE OF PETER PARKER TORMENTED SPIDER-MAN, FOR REASONS EVEN HE DIDN'T UNDERSTAND
AND I...I REMEMBER. THAT VOICE...I ENCOUNTERED HIM ONCE AS DOCTOR OCTOPUS. KAINE...
I REMEMBER.
KRAK!
PETER?

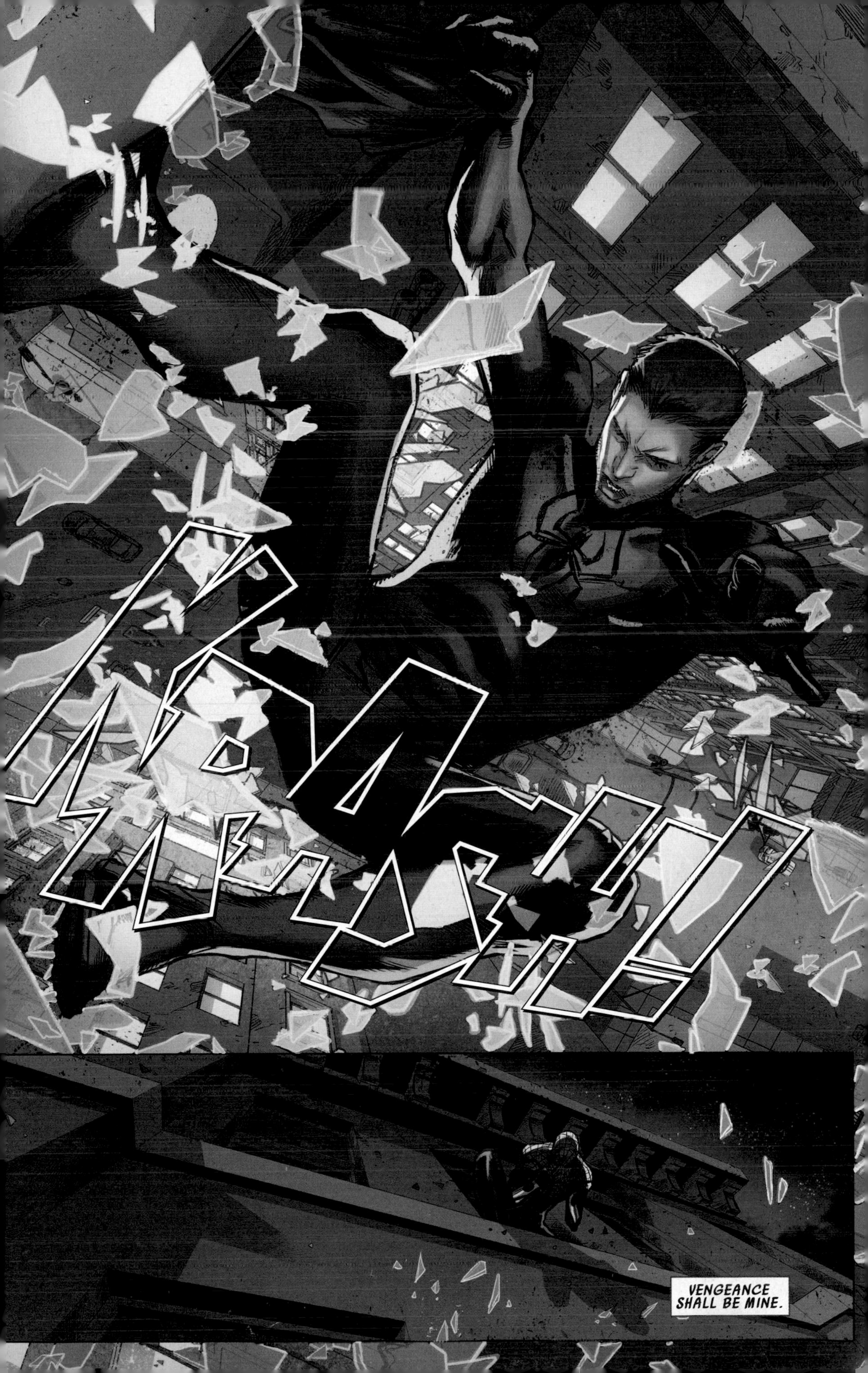
VENGEANCE SHALL BE MINE.

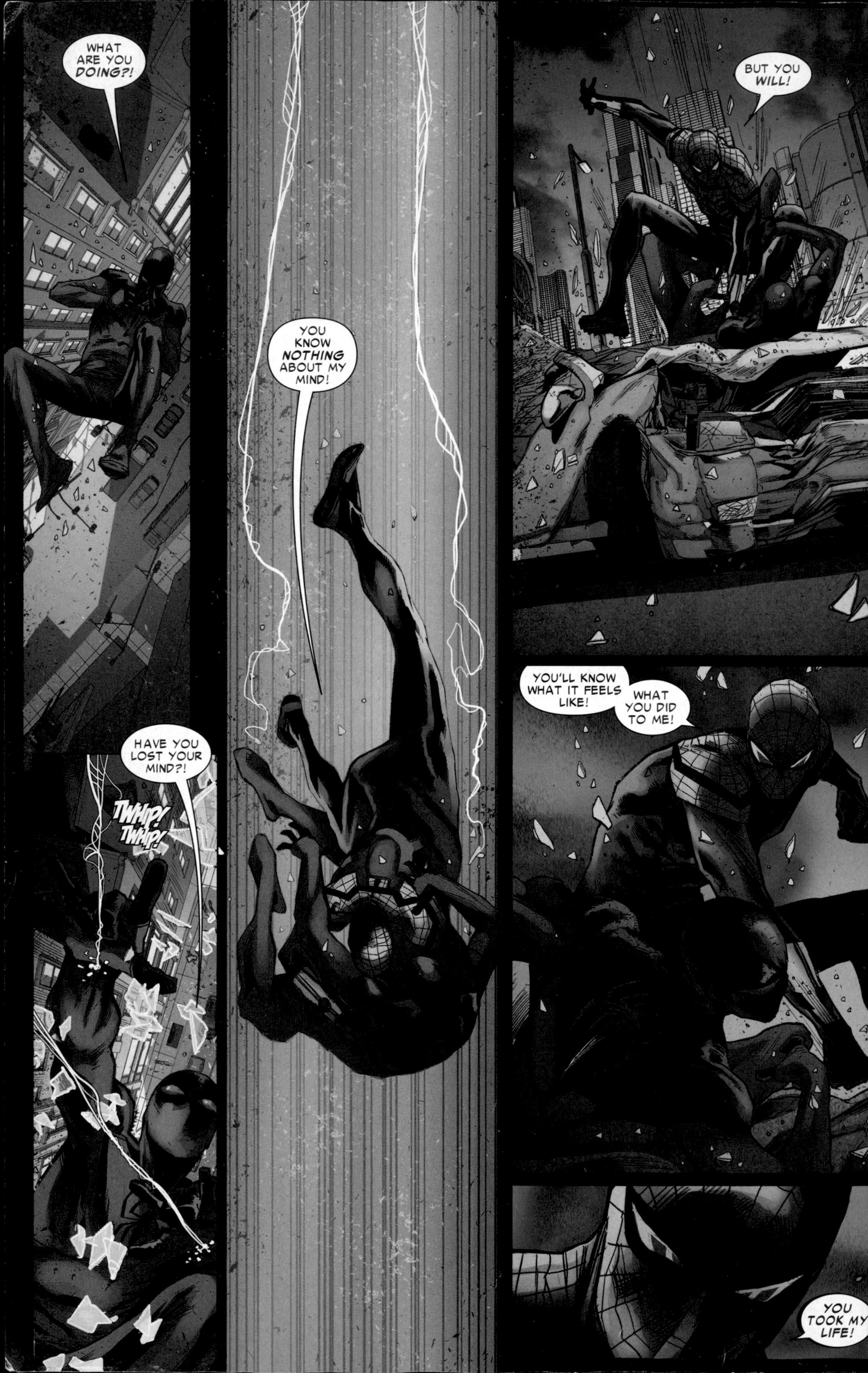

WHAT ARE YOU DOING?!
HAVE YOU LOST YOUR MIND?!
TWHIP! TWHIP!
YOU KNOW NOTHING ABOUT MY MIND!
BUT YOU WILL!
YOU'LL KNOW WHAT IT FEELS LIKE!
WHAT YOU DID TO ME!
YOU TOOK MY LIFE!

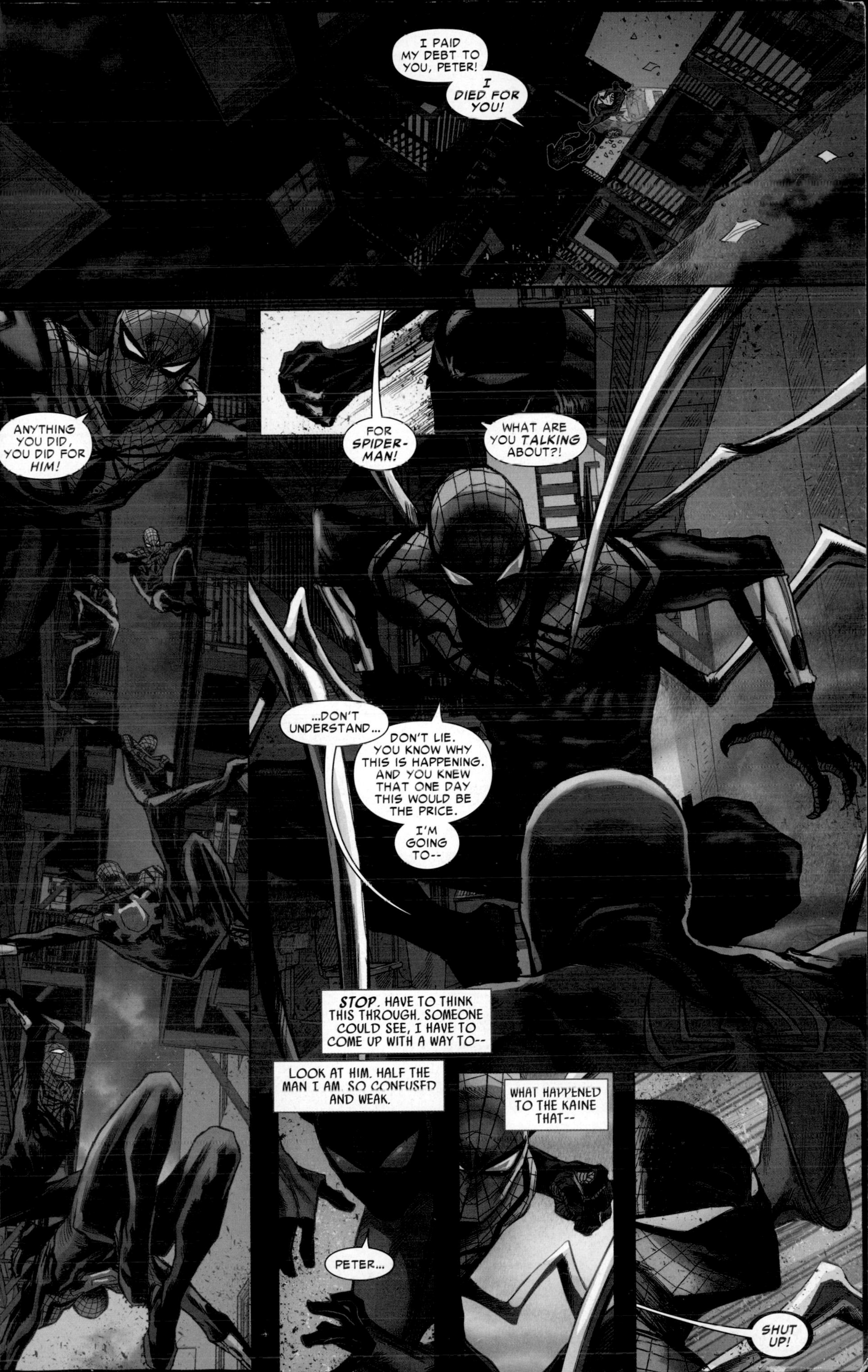
I PAID MY DEBT TO YOU, PETER!
I DIED FOR YOU!
ANYTHING YOU DID, YOU DID FOR HIM!
FOR SPIDER-MAN!
WHAT ARE YOU TALKING ABOUT?!
...DON'T UNDERSTAND...
DON'T LIE. YOU KNOW WHY THIS IS HAPPENING. AND YOU KNEW THAT ONE DAY THIS WOULD BE THE PRICE.
I'M GOING TO--
STOP. HAVE TO THINK THIS THROUGH. SOMEONE COULD SEE, I HAVE TO COME UP WITH A WAY TO--
LOOK AT HIM. HALF THE MAN I AM. SO CONFUSED AND WEAK.
PETER...
WHAT HAPPENED TO THE KAINE THAT--
SHUT UP!

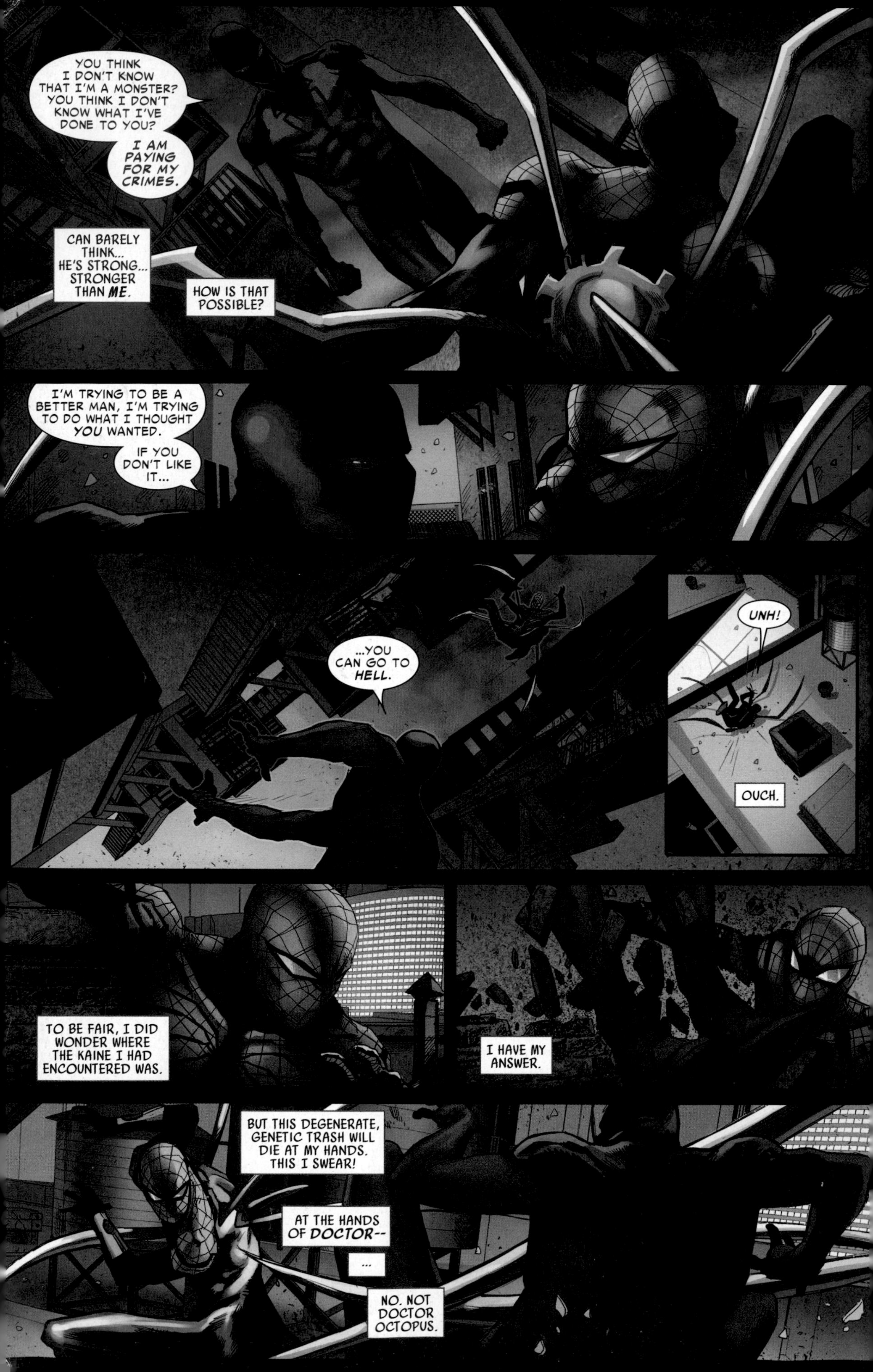
YOU THINK I DON'T KNOW THAT I'M A MONSTER? YOU THINK I DON'T KNOW WHAT I'VE DONE TO YOU?
I AM PAYING FOR MY CRIMES.
CAN BARELY THINK... HE'S STRONG... STRONGER THAN ME.
HOW IS THAT POSSIBLE?
I'M TRYING TO BE A BETTER MAN, I'M TRYING TO DO WHAT I THOUGHT YOU WANTED.
IF YOU DON'T LIKE IT...
...YOU CAN GO TO HELL.
UNH!
OUCH.
TO BE FAIR, I DID WONDER WHERE THE KAINE I HAD ENCOUNTERED WAS.
I HAVE MY ANSWER.
BUT THIS DEGENERATE, GENETIC TRASH WILL DIE AT MY HANDS. THIS I SWEAR!
AT THE HANDS OF DOCTOR--
...
NO. NOT DOCTOR OCTOPUS.

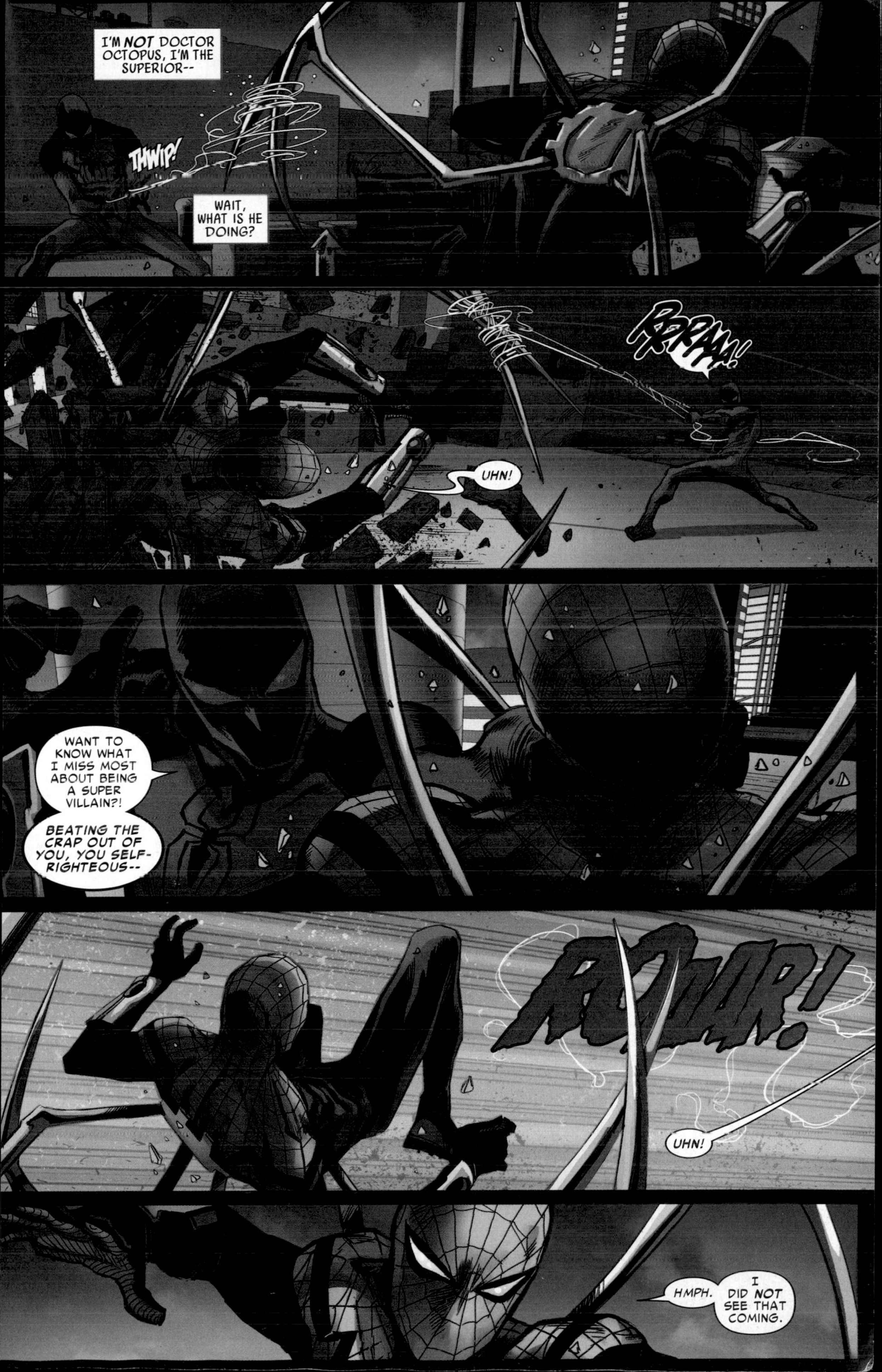
I'M NOT DOCTOR OCTOPUS, I'M THE SUPERIOR--
THWIP!
WAIT, WHAT IS HE DOING?
UHN!
WANT TO KNOW WHAT I MISS MOST ABOUT BEING A SUPER VILLAIN?!
BEATING THE CRAP OUT OF YOU, YOU SELF-RIGHTEOUS--
UHN!
HMPH.
I DID NOT SEE THAT COMING.

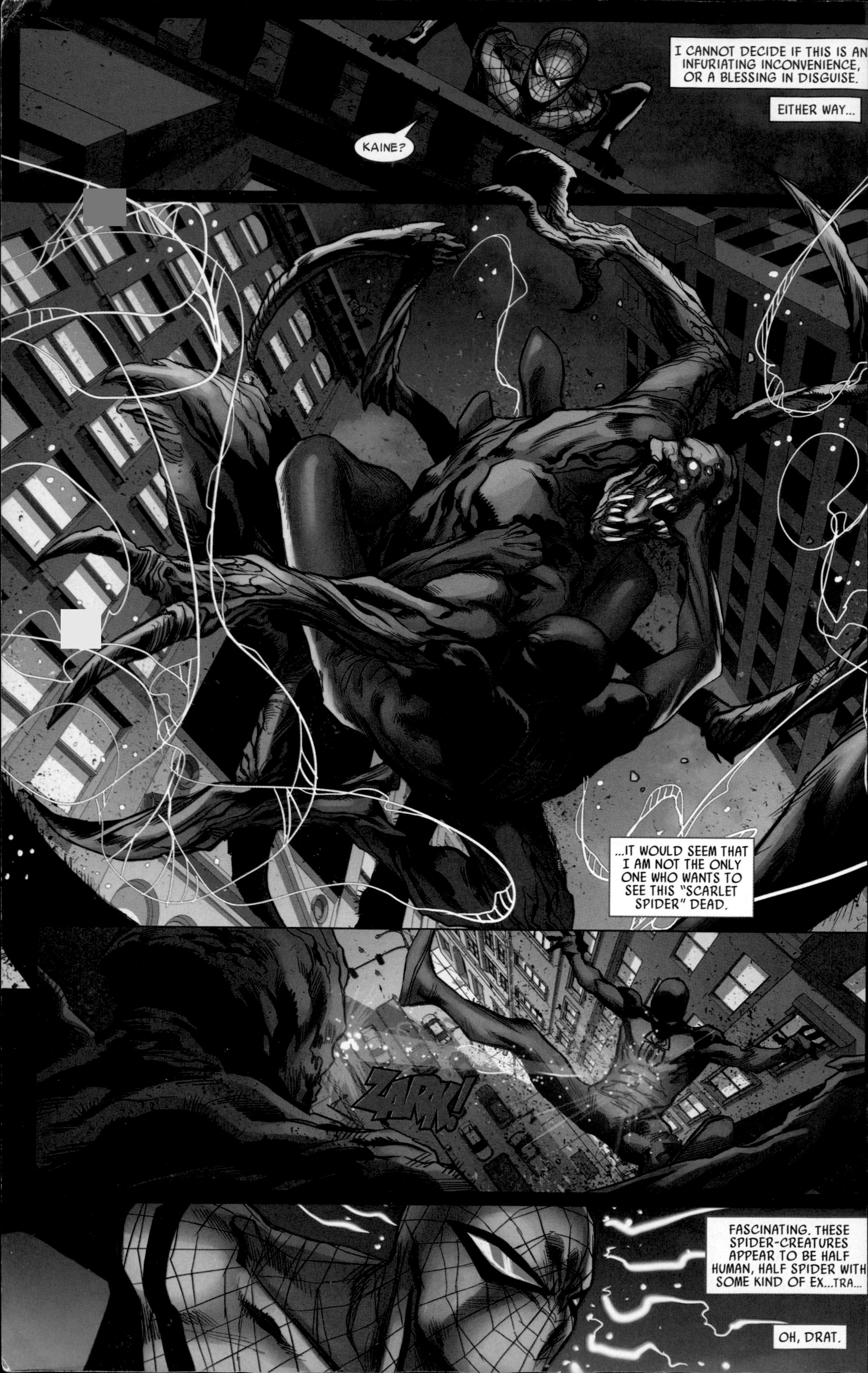
I CANNOT DECIDE IF THIS IS AN INFURIATING INCONVENIENCE, OR A BLESSING IN DISGUISE.
EITHER WAY...
KAINE?
...IT WOULD SEEM THAT I AM NOT THE ONLY ONE WHO WANTS TO SEE THIS "SCARLET SPIDER" DEAD.
ZARK!
FASCINATING. THESE SPIDER-CREATURES APPEAR TO BE HALF HUMAN, HALF SPIDER WITH SOME KIND OF EX...TRA...
OH, DRAT.

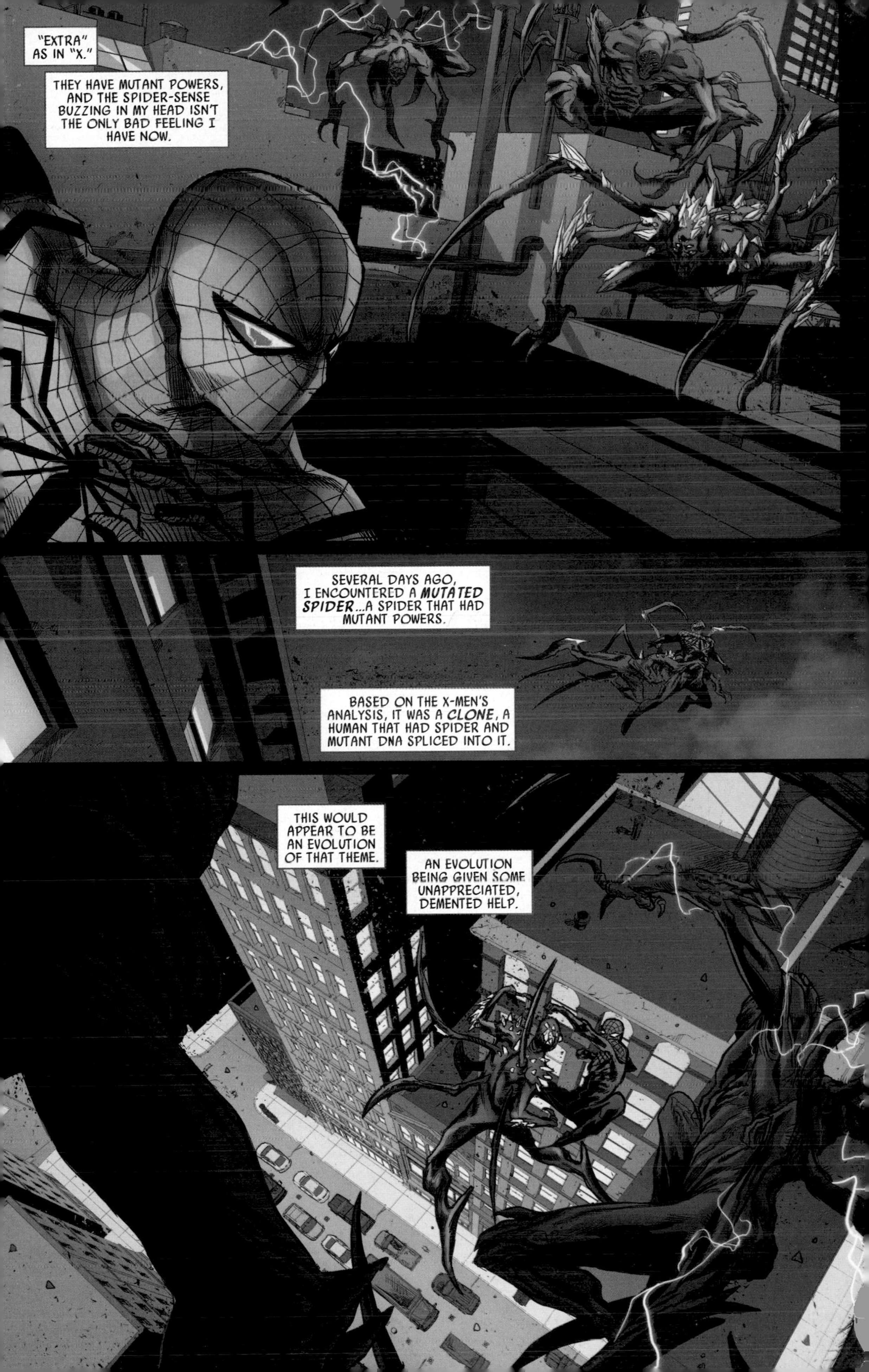

"EXTRA" AS IN "X."
THEY HAVE MUTANT POWERS, AND THE SPIDER-SENSE BUZZING IN MY HEAD ISN'T THE ONLY BAD FEELING I HAVE NOW.
SEVERAL DAYS AGO, I ENCOUNTERED A MUTATED SPIDER...A SPIDER THAT HAD MUTANT POWERS.
BASED ON THE X-MEN'S ANALYSIS, IT WAS A CLONE, A HUMAN THAT HAD SPIDER AND MUTANT DNA SPLICED INTO IT.
THIS WOULD APPEAR TO BE AN EVOLUTION OF THAT THEME.
AN EVOLUTION BEING GIVEN SOME UNAPPRECIATED, DEMENTED HELP.

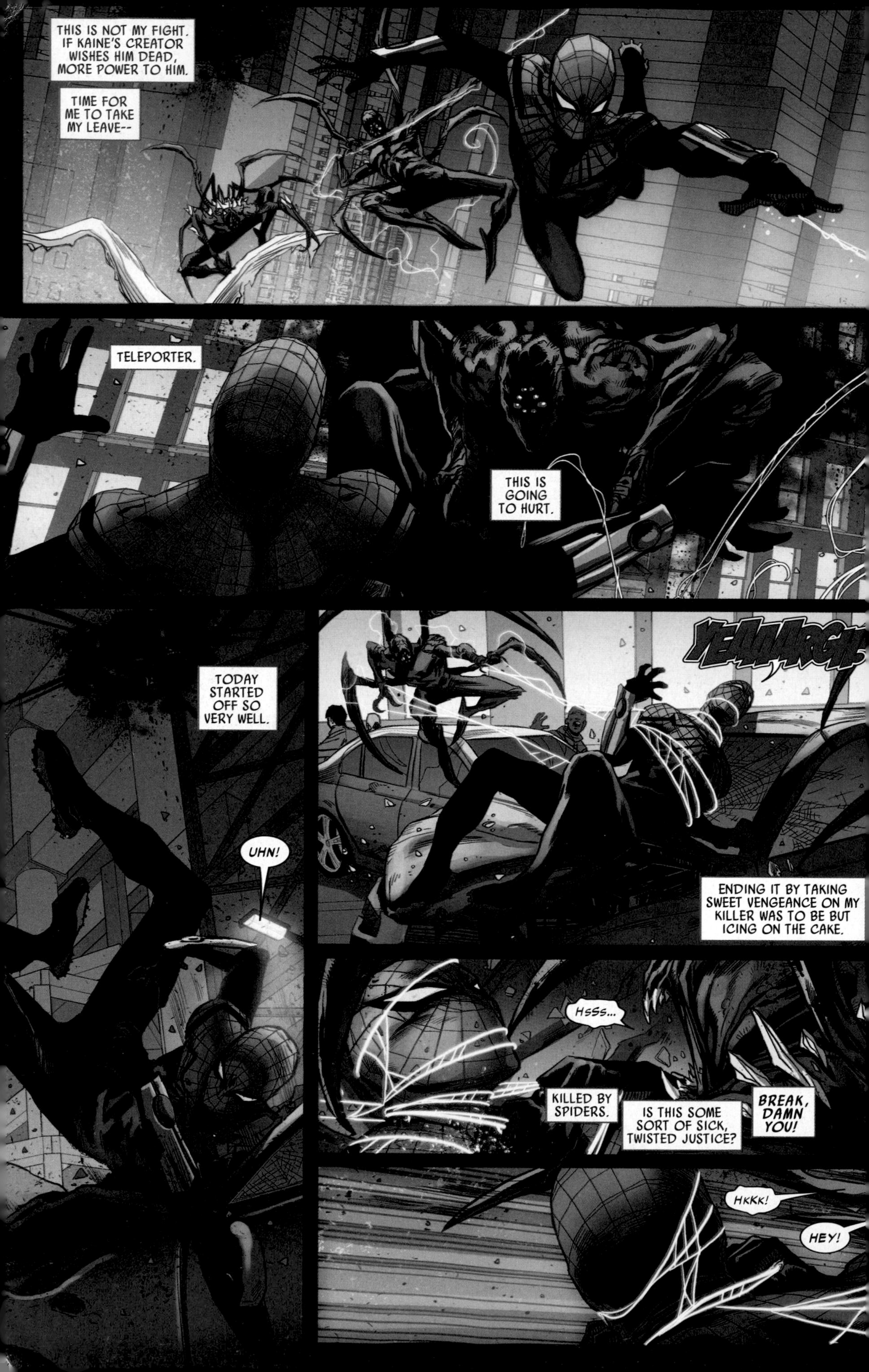
THIS IS NOT MY FIGHT. IF KAINE'S CREATOR WISHES HIM DEAD, MORE POWER TO HIM.
TIME FOR ME TO TAKE MY LEAVE--
TELEPORTER.
THIS IS GOING TO HURT.
TODAY STARTED OFF SO VERY WELL.
YEAAARGH!
UHN!
ENDING IT BY TAKING SWEET VENGEANCE ON MY KILLER WAS TO BE BUT ICING ON THE CAKE.
HSSS...
KILLED BY SPIDERS.
IS THIS SOME SORT OF SICK, TWISTED JUSTICE?
BREAK, DAMN YOU!
HKKK!
HEY!

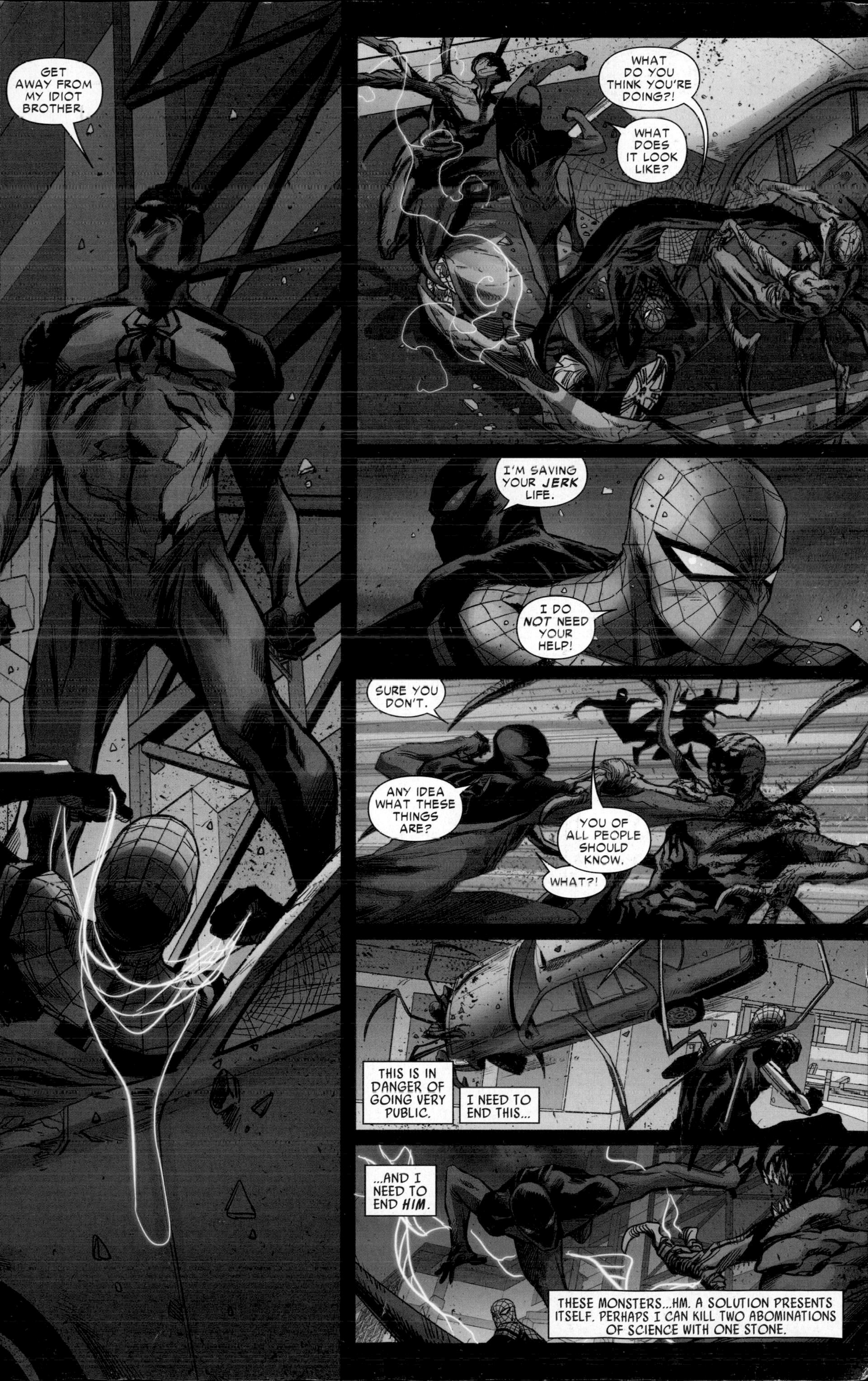
GET AWAY FROM MY IDIOT BROTHER.
WHAT DO YOU THINK YOU'RE DOING?!
WHAT DOES IT LOOK LIKE?
I'M SAVING YOUR JERK LIFE.
I DO NOT NEED YOUR HELP!
SURE YOU DON'T.
ANY IDEA WHAT THESE THINGS ARE?
YOU OF ALL PEOPLE SHOULD KNOW.
WHAT?!
THIS IS IN DANGER OF GOING VERY PUBLIC.
I NEED TO END THIS...
...AND I NEED TO END HIM.
THESE MONSTERS...HM. A SOLUTION PRESENTS ITSELF. PERHAPS I CAN KILL TWO ABOMINATIONS OF SCIENCE WITH ONE STONE.

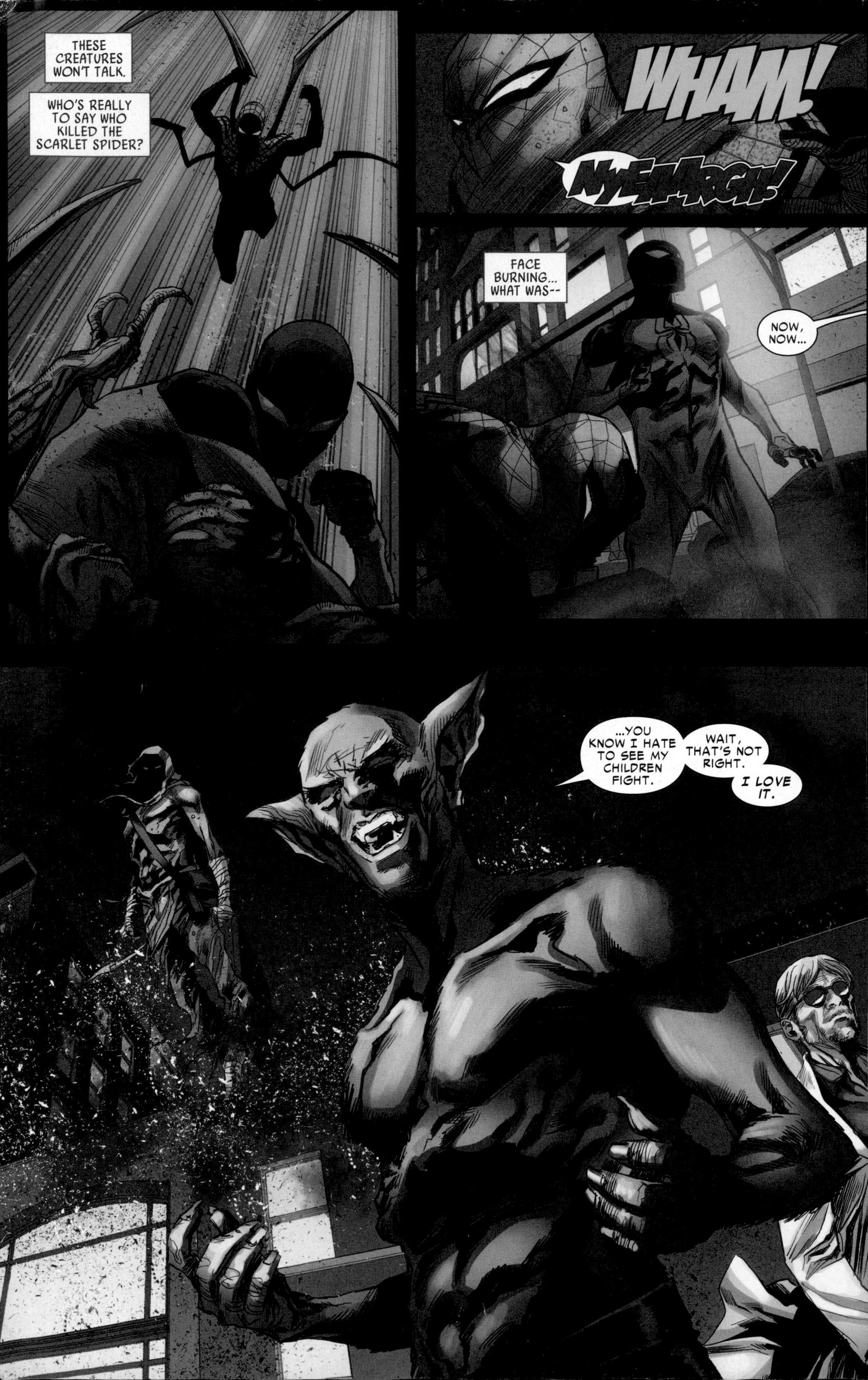
THESE CREATURES WON'T TALK.
WHO'S REALLY TO SAY WHO KILLED THE SCARLET SPIDER?
WHAM!
NYEMMRGH!
FACE BURNING... WHAT WAS--
NOW, NOW...
...YOU KNOW I HATE TO SEE MY CHILDREN FIGHT.
WAIT, THAT'S NOT RIGHT.
I LOVE IT.

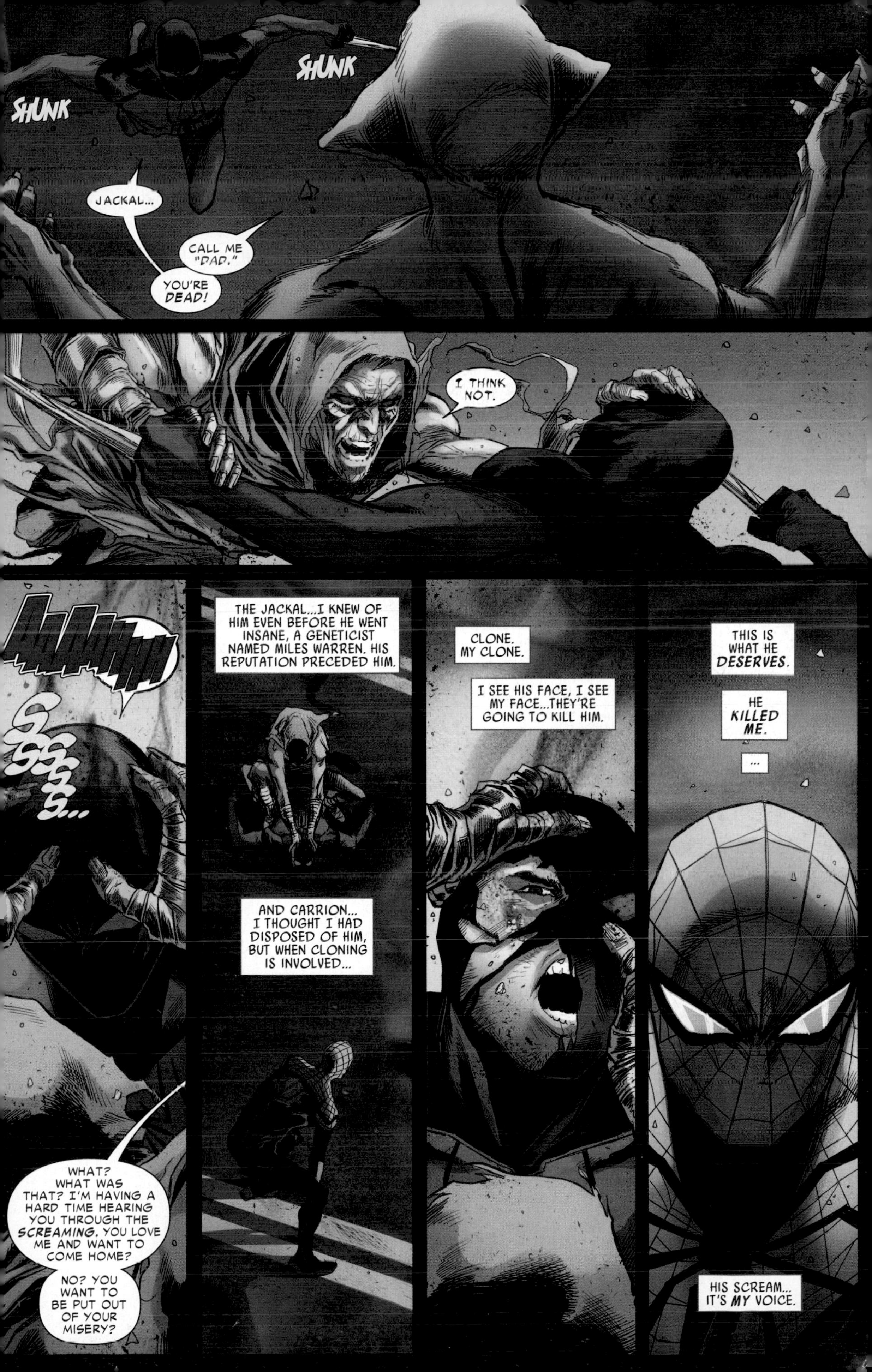
SHUNK
SHUNK
JACKAL...
CALL ME "DAD."
YOU'RE DEAD!
I THINK NOT.
AAAAHHHH
SSSSS...
WHAT? WHAT WAS THAT? I'M HAVING A HARD TIME HEARING YOU THROUGH THE SCREAMING. YOU LOVE ME AND WANT TO COME HOME?
NO? YOU WANT TO BE PUT OUT OF YOUR MISERY?
THE JACKAL...I KNEW OF HIM EVEN BEFORE HE WENT INSANE, A GENETICIST NAMED MILES WARREN. HIS REPUTATION PRECEDED HIM.
AND CARRION... I THOUGHT I HAD DISPOSED OF HIM, BUT WHEN CLONING IS INVOLVED...
CLONE. MY CLONE.
I SEE HIS FACE, I SEE MY FACE...THEY'RE GOING TO KILL HIM.
THIS IS WHAT HE DESERVES.
HE KILLED ME.
...
HIS SCREAM... IT'S MY VOICE.

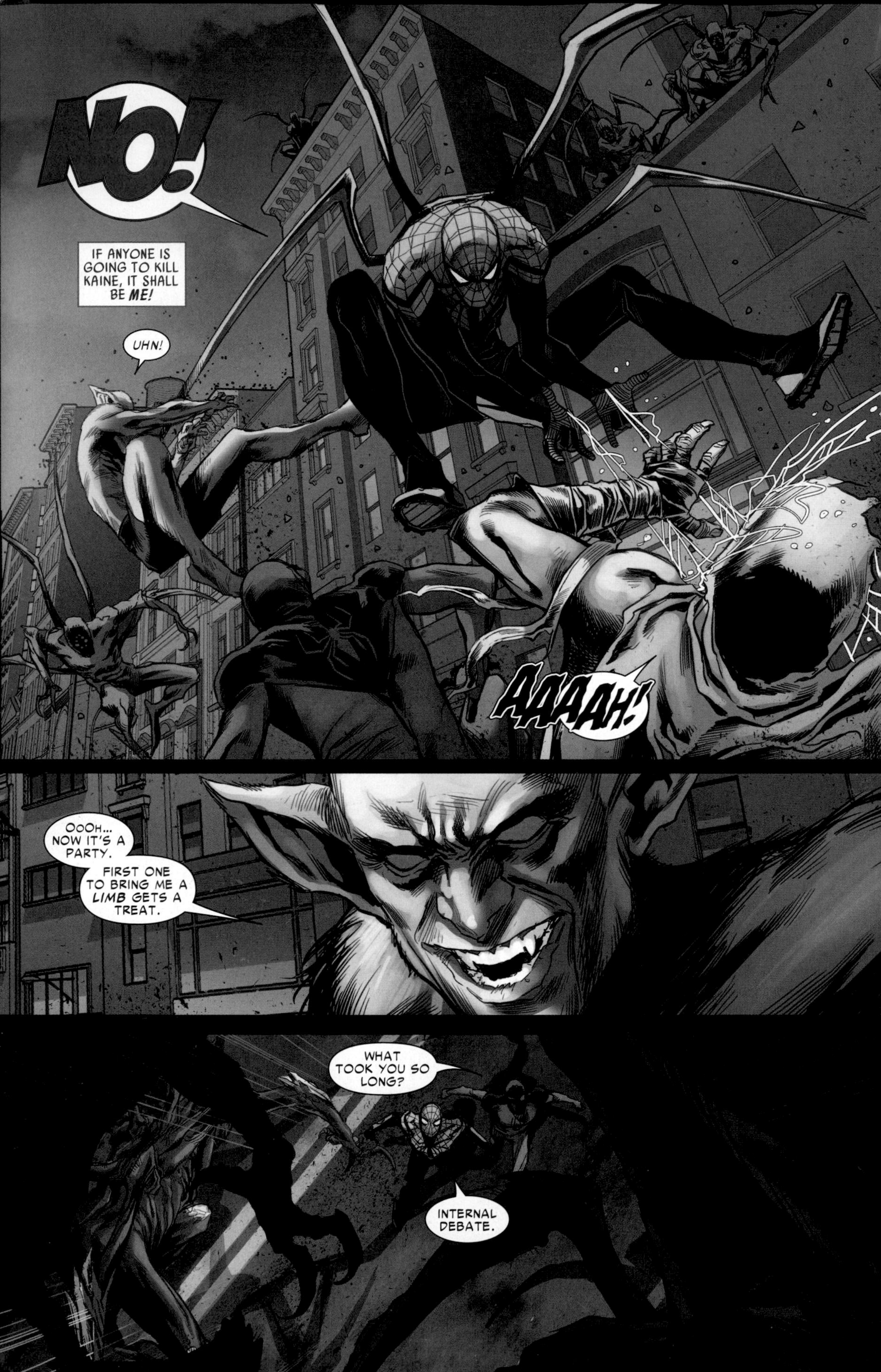
NO!
IF ANYONE IS GOING TO KILL KAINE, IT SHALL BE *ME!*
UHN!
AAAAH!
OOOH... NOW IT'S A PARTY.
FIRST ONE TO BRING ME A *LIMB* GETS A TREAT.
WHAT TOOK YOU SO LONG?
INTERNAL DEBATE.

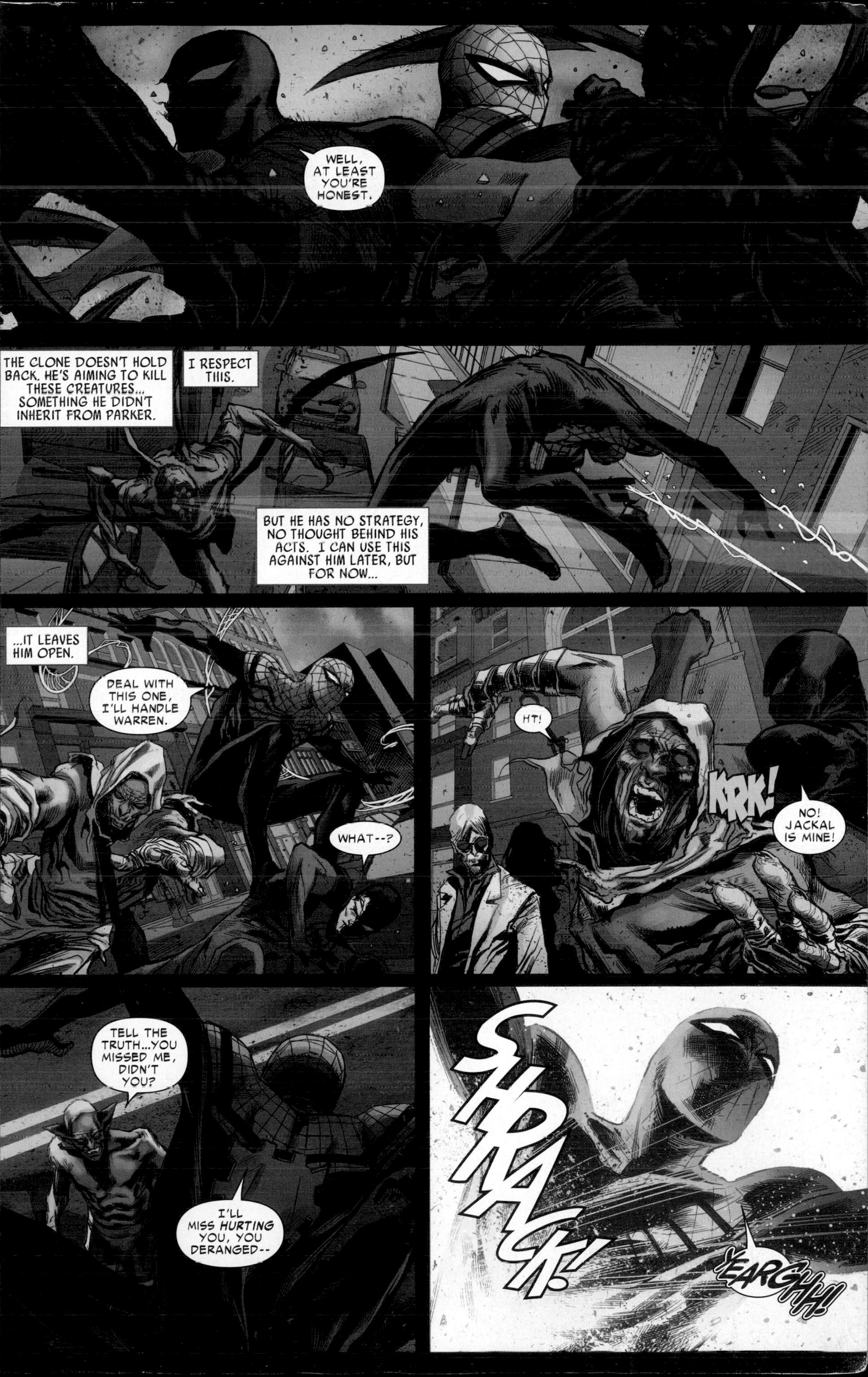
WELL, AT LEAST YOU'RE HONEST.
THE CLONE DOESN'T HOLD BACK. HE'S AIMING TO KILL THESE CREATURES... SOMETHING HE DIDN'T INHERIT FROM PARKER.
I RESPECT THIS.
BUT HE HAS NO STRATEGY, NO THOUGHT BEHIND HIS ACTS. I CAN USE THIS AGAINST HIM LATER, BUT FOR NOW...
...IT LEAVES HIM OPEN.
DEAL WITH THIS ONE, I'LL HANDLE WARREN.
WHAT--?
HT!
KRK!
NO! JACKAL IS MINE!
TELL THE TRUTH...YOU MISSED ME, DIDN'T YOU?
I'LL MISS HURTING YOU, YOU DERANGED--
SHRAK!
YEARGHH!

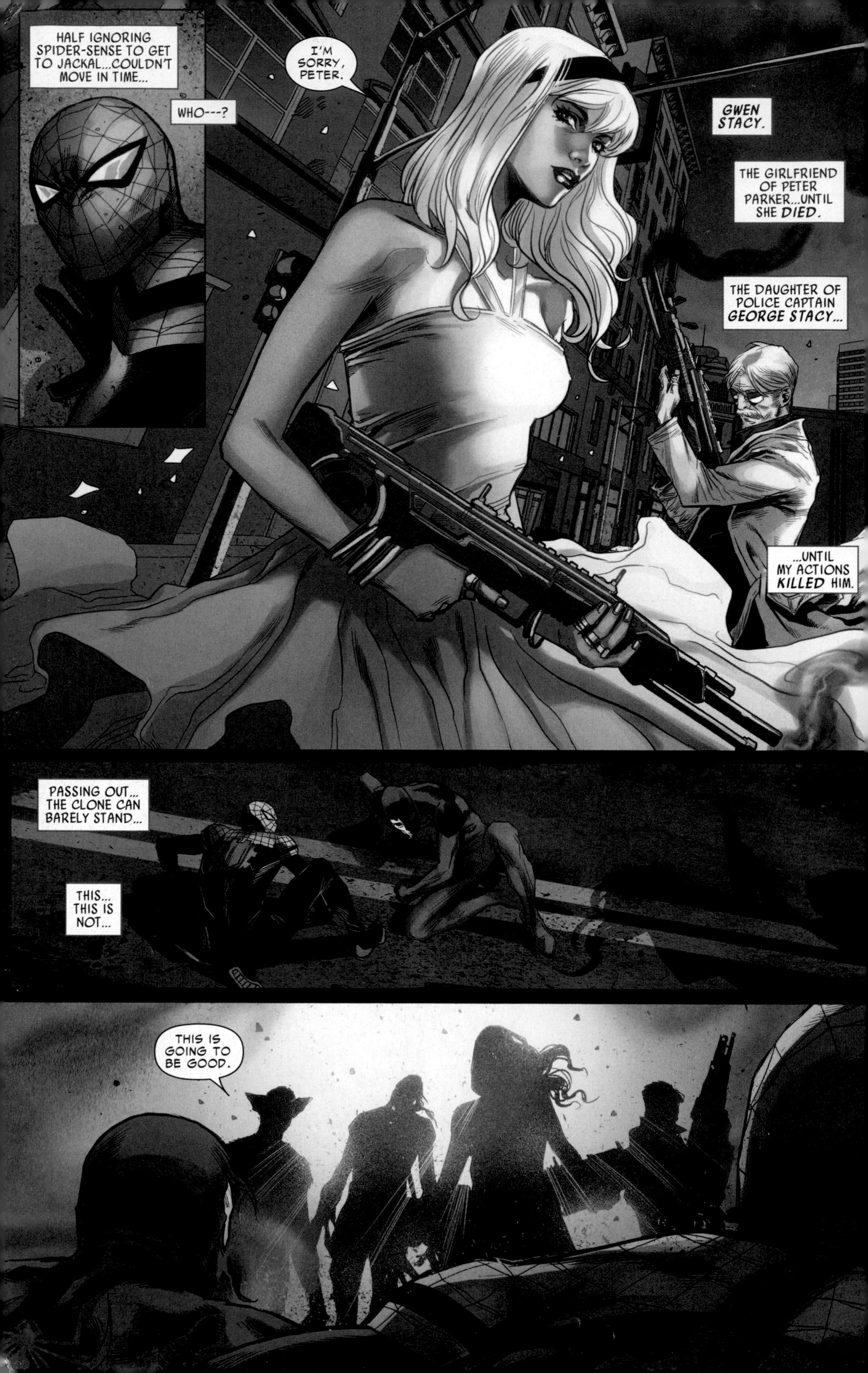
HALF IGNORING SPIDER-SENSE TO GET TO JACKAL...COULDN'T MOVE IN TIME...
I'M SORRY, PETER.
WHO---?
GWEN STACY.
THE GIRLFRIEND OF PETER PARKER...UNTIL SHE DIED.
THE DAUGHTER OF POLICE CAPTAIN GEORGE STACY...
...UNTIL MY ACTIONS KILLED HIM.
PASSING OUT... THE CLONE CAN BARELY STAND...
THIS... THIS IS NOT...
THIS IS GOING TO BE GOOD.

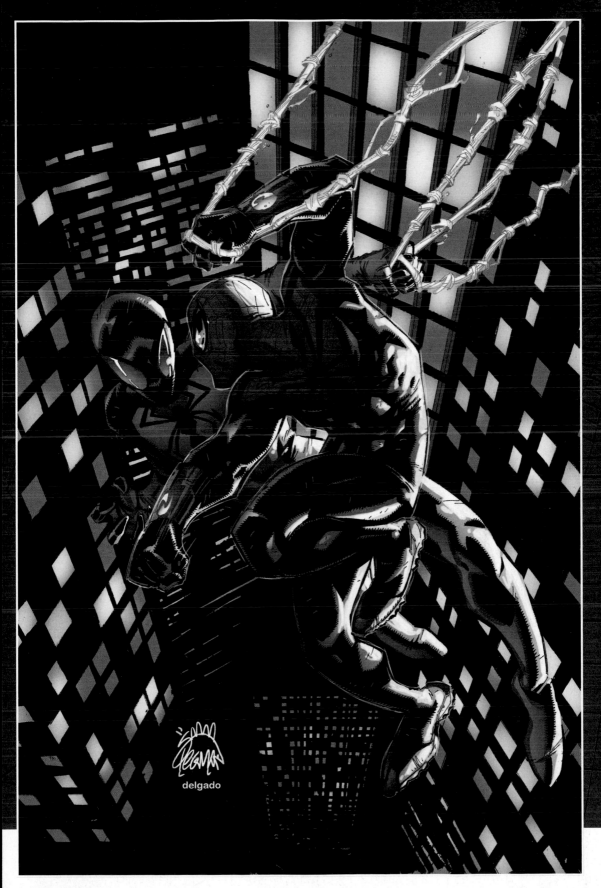

delgado

20

"SIBLING RIVALRY, PART 2"

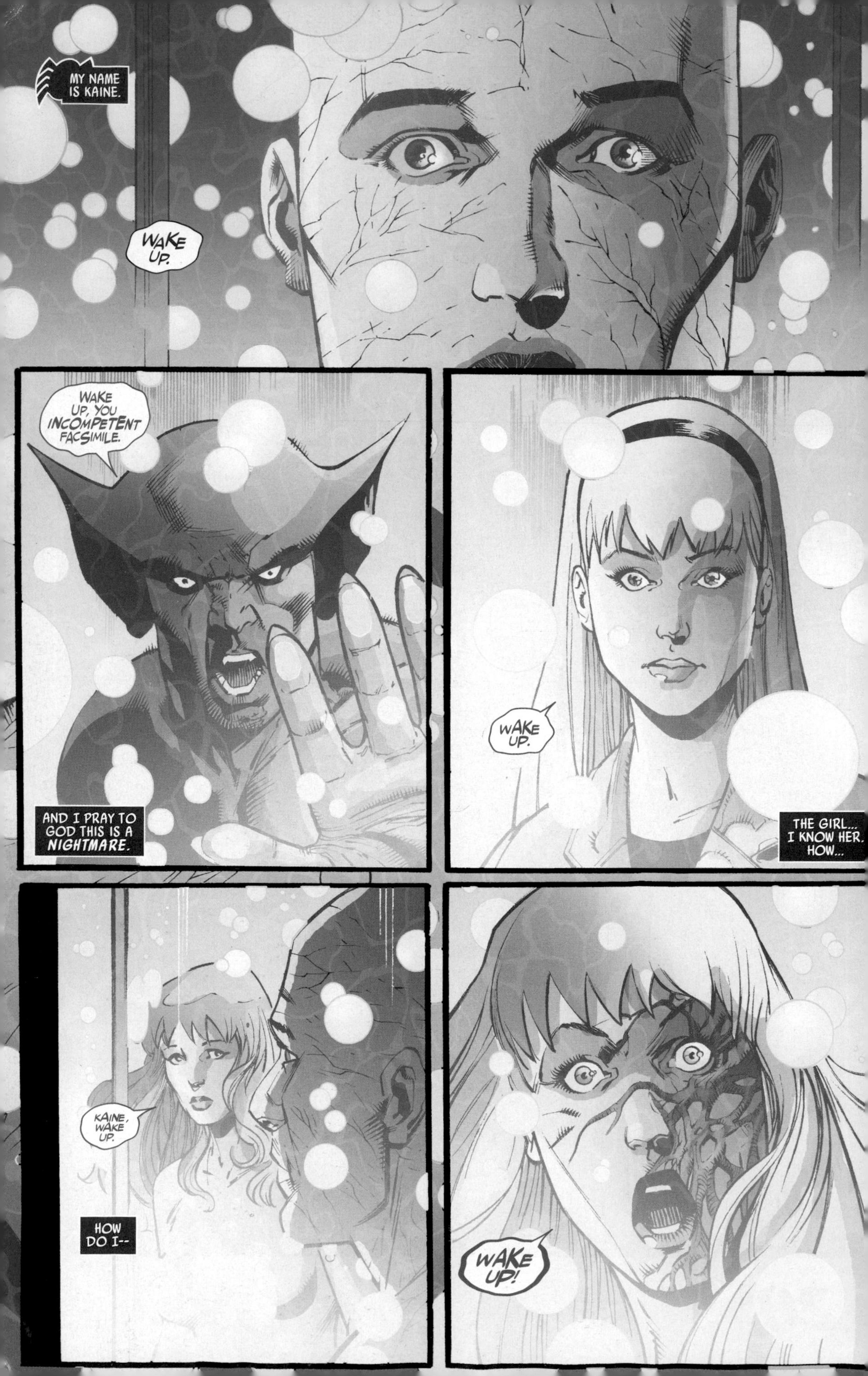
MY NAME IS KAINE.
WAKE UP.
WAKE UP, YOU INCOMPETENT FACSIMILE.
AND I PRAY TO GOD THIS IS A NIGHTMARE.
WAKE UP.
THE GIRL... I KNOW HER. HOW...
KAINE, WAKE UP.
HOW DO I--
WAKE UP!

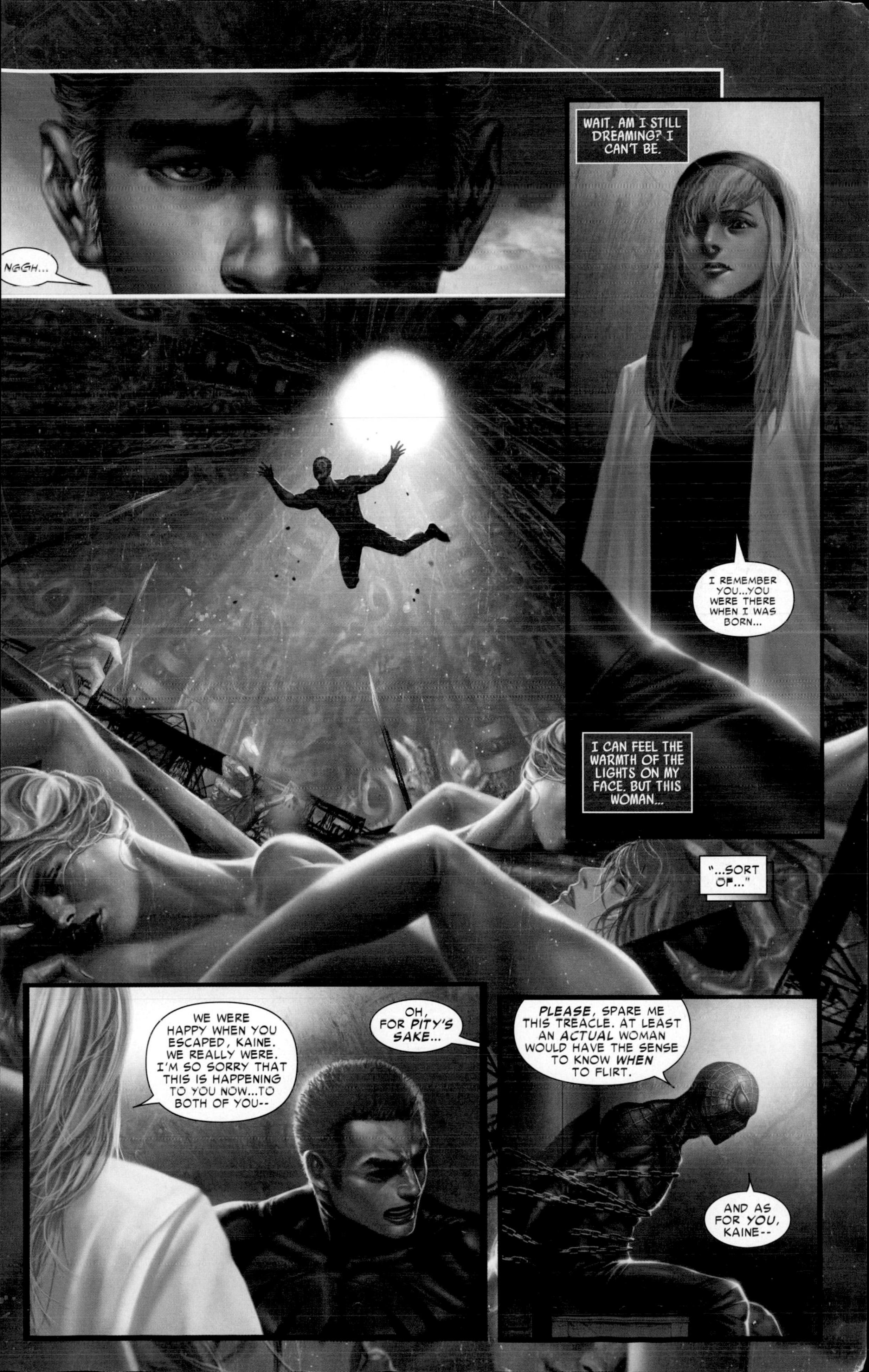
NGGH...
WAIT. AM I STILL DREAMING? I CAN'T BE.
I REMEMBER YOU...YOU WERE THERE WHEN I WAS BORN...
I CAN FEEL THE WARMTH OF THE LIGHTS ON MY FACE. BUT THIS WOMAN...
"...SORT OF..."
WE WERE HAPPY WHEN YOU ESCAPED, KAINE. WE REALLY WERE. I'M SO SORRY THAT THIS IS HAPPENING TO YOU NOW...TO BOTH OF YOU--
OH, FOR *PITY'S SAKE*...
PLEASE, SPARE ME THIS TREACLE. AT LEAST AN *ACTUAL* WOMAN WOULD HAVE THE SENSE TO KNOW *WHEN* TO FLIRT.
AND AS FOR *YOU*, KAINE--

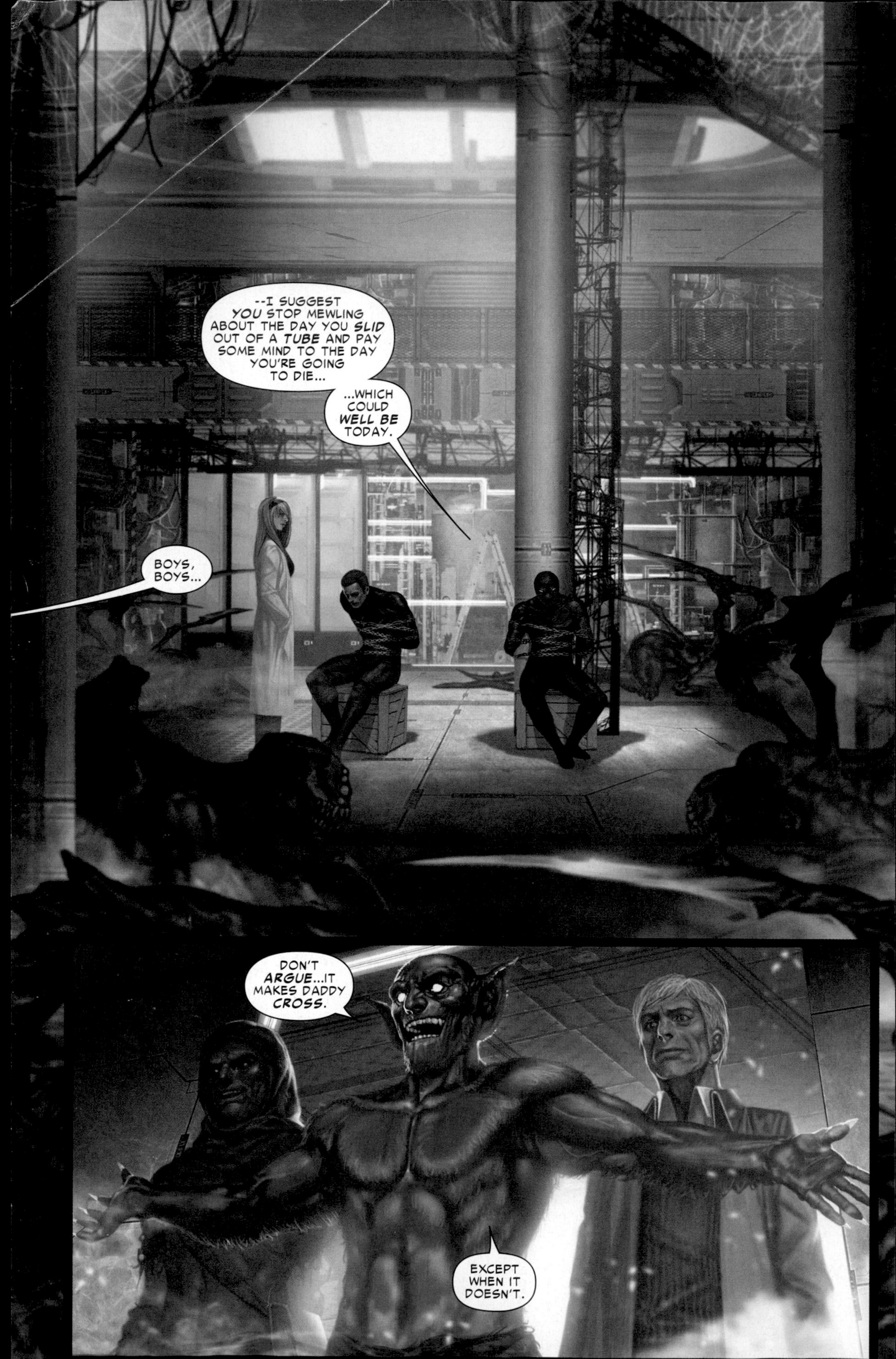
--I SUGGEST YOU STOP MEWLING ABOUT THE DAY YOU SLID OUT OF A TUBE AND PAY SOME MIND TO THE DAY YOU'RE GOING TO DIE...
...WHICH COULD WELL BE TODAY.
BOYS, BOYS...
DON'T ARGUE...IT MAKES DADDY CROSS.
EXCEPT WHEN IT DOESN'T.

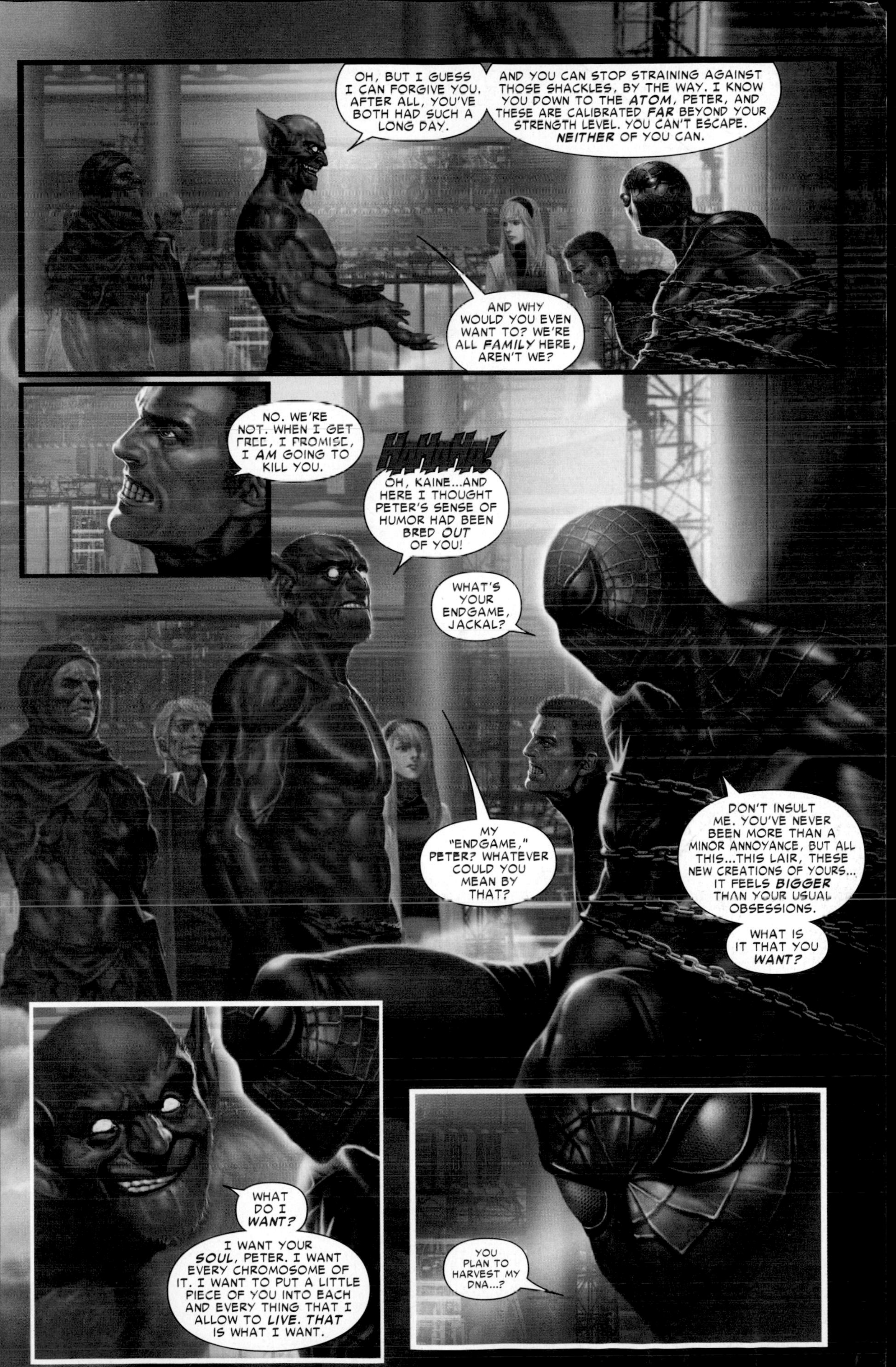
OH, BUT I GUESS I CAN FORGIVE YOU. AFTER ALL, YOU'VE BOTH HAD SUCH A LONG DAY.
AND YOU CAN STOP STRAINING AGAINST THOSE SHACKLES, BY THE WAY. I KNOW YOU DOWN TO THE ATOM, PETER, AND THESE ARE CALIBRATED FAR BEYOND YOUR STRENGTH LEVEL. YOU CAN'T ESCAPE. NEITHER OF YOU CAN.
AND WHY WOULD YOU EVEN WANT TO? WE'RE ALL FAMILY HERE, AREN'T WE?
NO. WE'RE NOT. WHEN I GET FREE, I PROMISE, I AM GOING TO KILL YOU.
OH, KAINE...AND HERE I THOUGHT PETER'S SENSE OF HUMOR HAD BEEN BRED OUT OF YOU!
WHAT'S YOUR ENDGAME, JACKAL?
MY "ENDGAME," PETER? WHATEVER COULD YOU MEAN BY THAT?
DON'T INSULT ME. YOU'VE NEVER BEEN MORE THAN A MINOR ANNOYANCE, BUT ALL THIS...THIS LAIR, THESE NEW CREATIONS OF YOURS... IT FEELS BIGGER THAN YOUR USUAL OBSESSIONS.
WHAT IS IT THAT YOU WANT?
WHAT DO I WANT?
I WANT YOUR SOUL, PETER. I WANT EVERY CHROMOSOME OF IT. I WANT TO PUT A LITTLE PIECE OF YOU INTO EACH AND EVERY THING THAT I ALLOW TO LIVE. THAT IS WHAT I WANT.
YOU PLAN TO HARVEST MY DNA...?

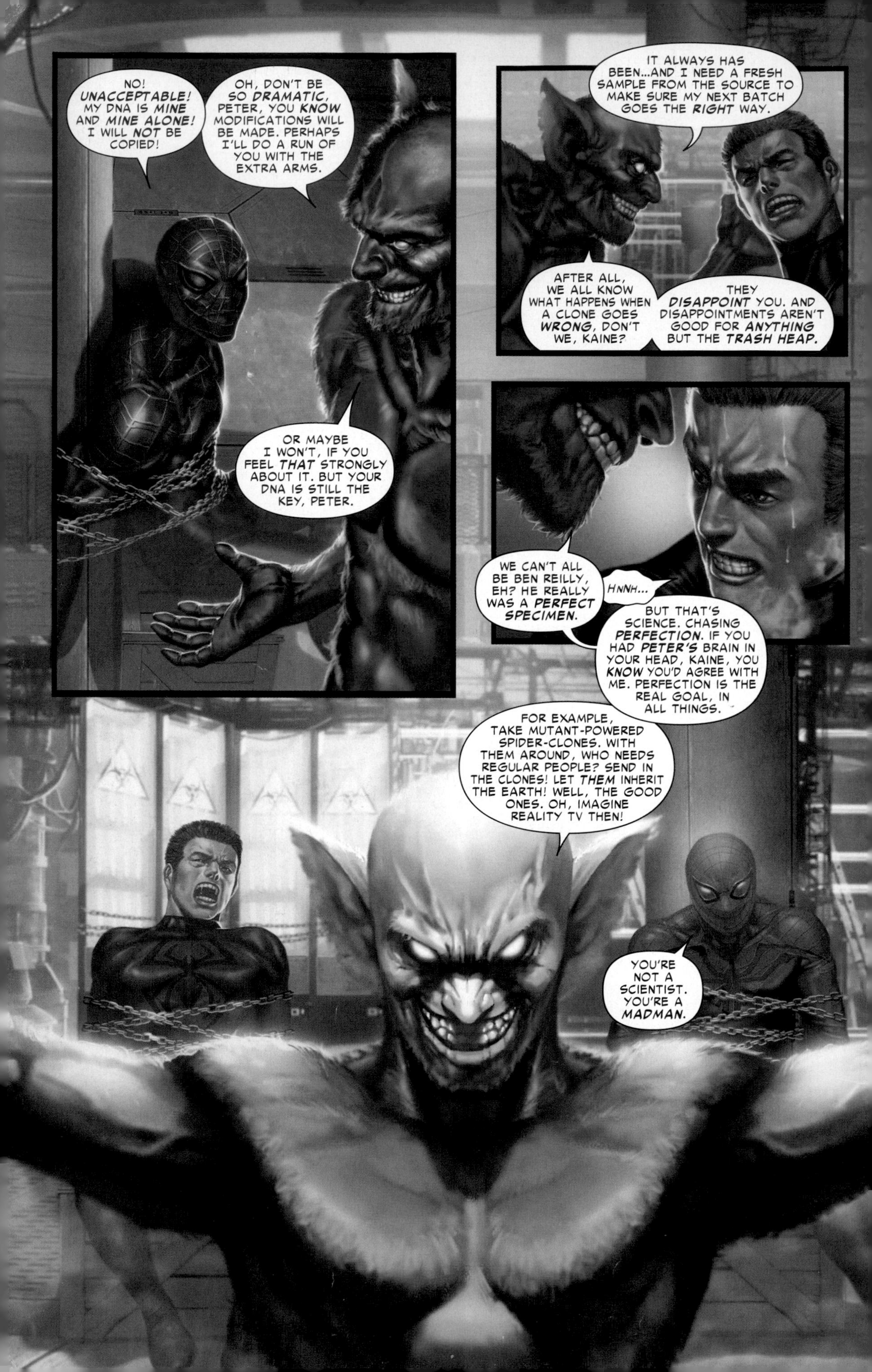

NO! *UNACCEPTABLE!* MY DNA IS *MINE* AND *MINE ALONE!* I WILL *NOT* BE COPIED!
OH, DON'T BE SO *DRAMATIC*, PETER, YOU *KNOW* MODIFICATIONS WILL BE MADE. PERHAPS I'LL DO A RUN OF YOU WITH THE EXTRA ARMS.
OR MAYBE I WON'T, IF YOU FEEL *THAT* STRONGLY ABOUT IT. BUT YOUR DNA IS STILL THE KEY, PETER.
IT ALWAYS HAS BEEN...AND I NEED A FRESH SAMPLE FROM THE SOURCE TO MAKE SURE MY NEXT BATCH GOES THE *RIGHT* WAY.
AFTER ALL, WE ALL KNOW WHAT HAPPENS WHEN A CLONE GOES *WRONG*, DON'T WE, KAINE?
THEY *DISAPPOINT* YOU. AND DISAPPOINTMENTS AREN'T GOOD FOR *ANYTHING* BUT THE *TRASH HEAP.*
WE CAN'T ALL BE BEN REILLY, EH? HE REALLY WAS A *PERFECT SPECIMEN.*
HNNH...
BUT THAT'S SCIENCE. CHASING *PERFECTION.* IF YOU HAD *PETER'S* BRAIN IN YOUR HEAD, KAINE, YOU *KNOW* YOU'D AGREE WITH ME. PERFECTION IS THE REAL GOAL, IN ALL THINGS.
FOR EXAMPLE, TAKE MUTANT-POWERED SPIDER-CLONES. WITH THEM AROUND, WHO NEEDS REGULAR PEOPLE? SEND IN THE CLONES! LET *THEM* INHERIT THE EARTH! WELL, THE GOOD ONES. OH, IMAGINE REALITY TV THEN!
YOU'RE NOT A SCIENTIST. YOU'RE A *MADMAN.*

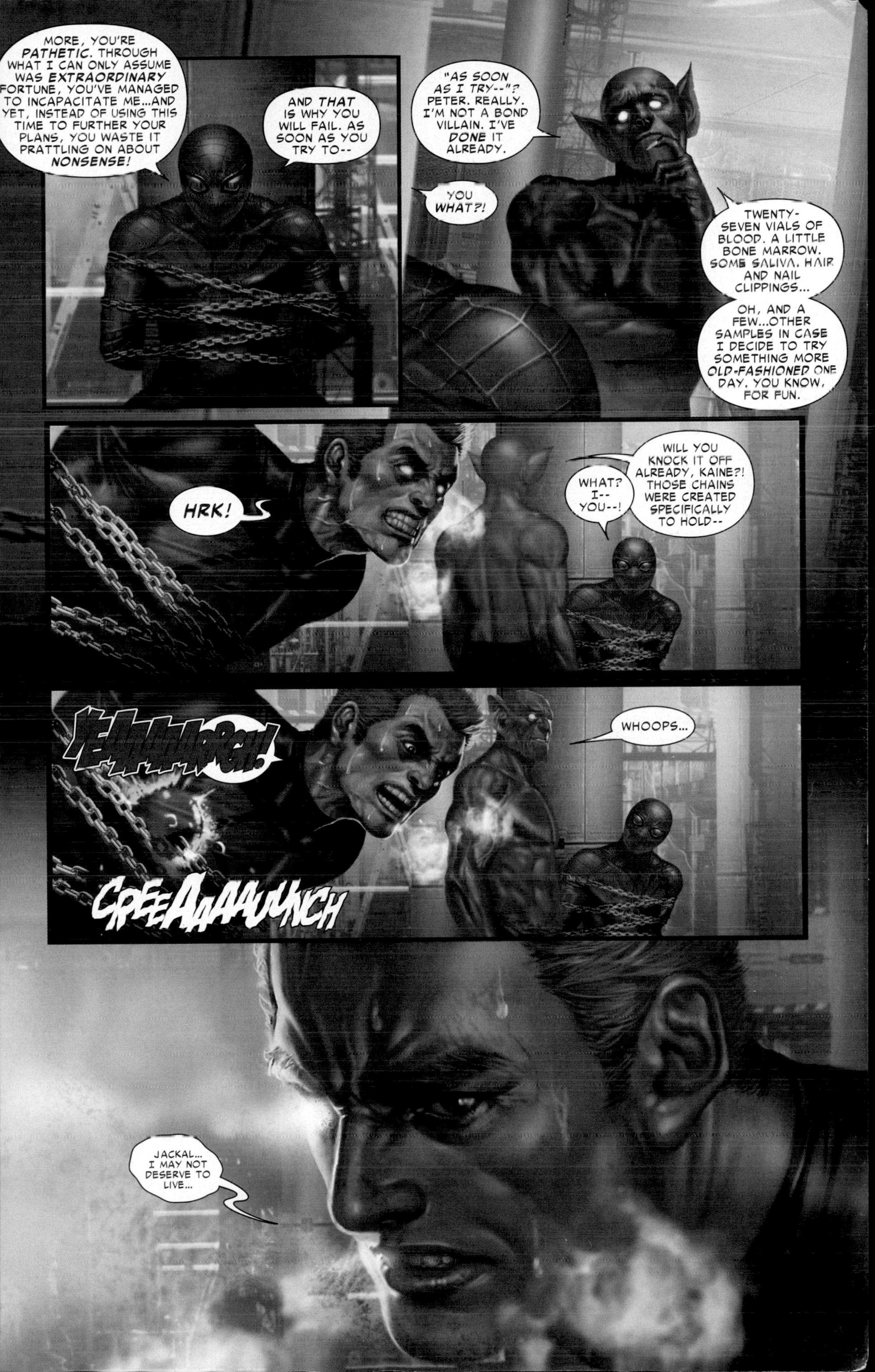
MORE, YOU'RE PATHETIC. THROUGH WHAT I CAN ONLY ASSUME WAS EXTRAORDINARY FORTUNE, YOU'VE MANAGED TO INCAPACITATE ME...AND YET, INSTEAD OF USING THIS TIME TO FURTHER YOUR PLANS, YOU WASTE IT PRATTLING ON ABOUT NONSENSE!
AND THAT IS WHY YOU WILL FAIL. AS SOON AS YOU TRY TO--
"AS SOON AS I TRY--"? PETER. REALLY. I'M NOT A BOND VILLAIN. I'VE DONE IT ALREADY.
YOU WHAT?!
TWENTY-SEVEN VIALS OF BLOOD. A LITTLE BONE MARROW. SOME SALIVA. HAIR AND NAIL CLIPPINGS...
OH, AND A FEW...OTHER SAMPLES IN CASE I DECIDE TO TRY SOMETHING MORE OLD-FASHIONED ONE DAY. YOU KNOW, FOR FUN.
HRK!
WILL YOU KNOCK IT OFF ALREADY, KAINE?! THOSE CHAINS WERE CREATED SPECIFICALLY TO HOLD--
WHAT? I-- YOU--!
YEAAAAARGH!
WHOOPS...
CREEAAAAUUNCH
JACKAL... I MAY NOT DESERVE TO LIVE...

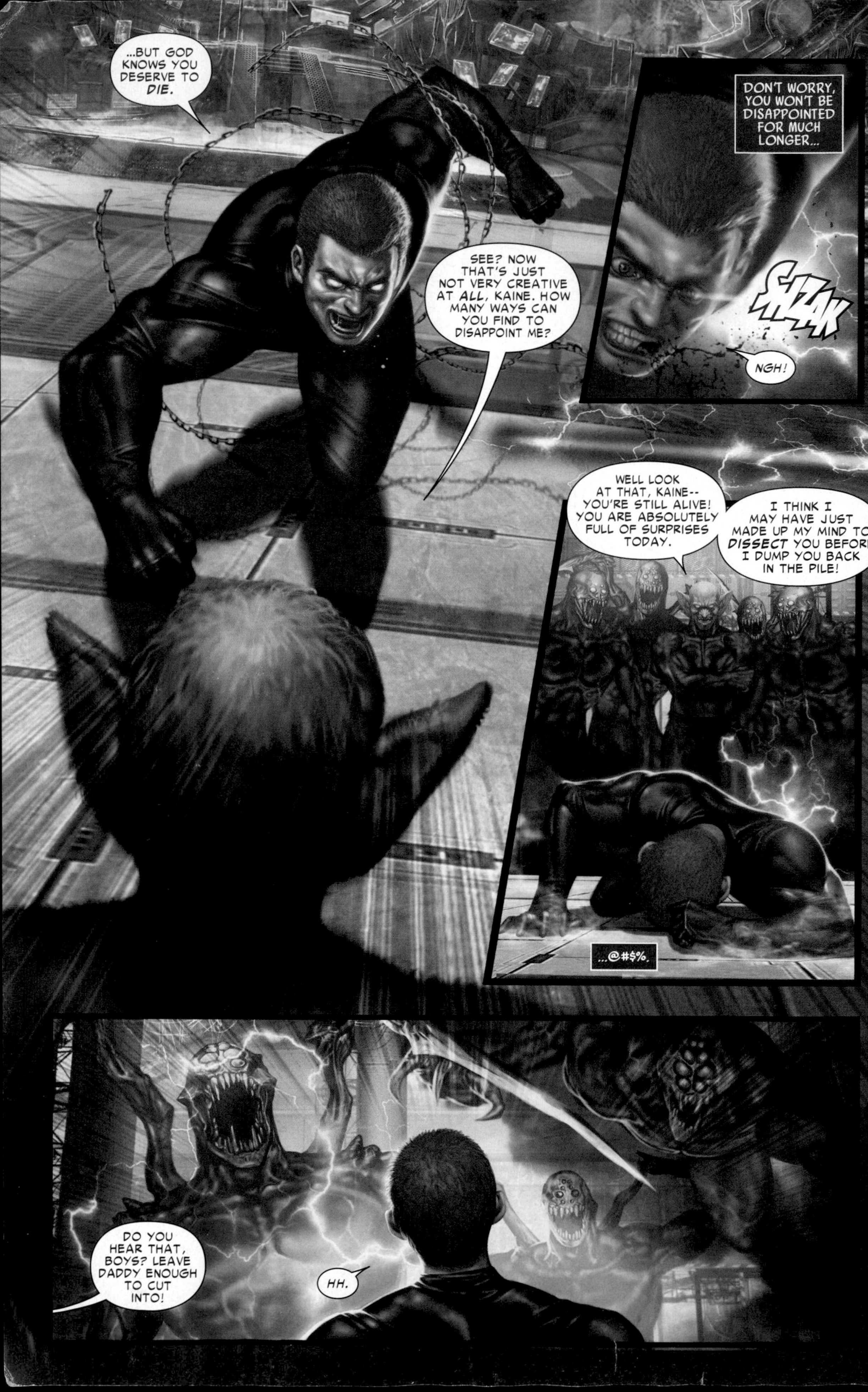
...BUT GOD KNOWS YOU DESERVE TO DIE.
SEE? NOW THAT'S JUST NOT VERY CREATIVE AT ALL, KAINE. HOW MANY WAYS CAN YOU FIND TO DISAPPOINT ME?
DON'T WORRY, YOU WON'T BE DISAPPOINTED FOR MUCH LONGER...
SHZAK
NGH!
WELL LOOK AT THAT, KAINE-- YOU'RE STILL ALIVE! YOU ARE ABSOLUTELY FULL OF SURPRISES TODAY.
I THINK I MAY HAVE JUST MADE UP MY MIND TO DISSECT YOU BEFORE I DUMP YOU BACK IN THE PILE!
...@#$%.
DO YOU HEAR THAT, BOYS? LEAVE DADDY ENOUGH TO CUT INTO!
HH.

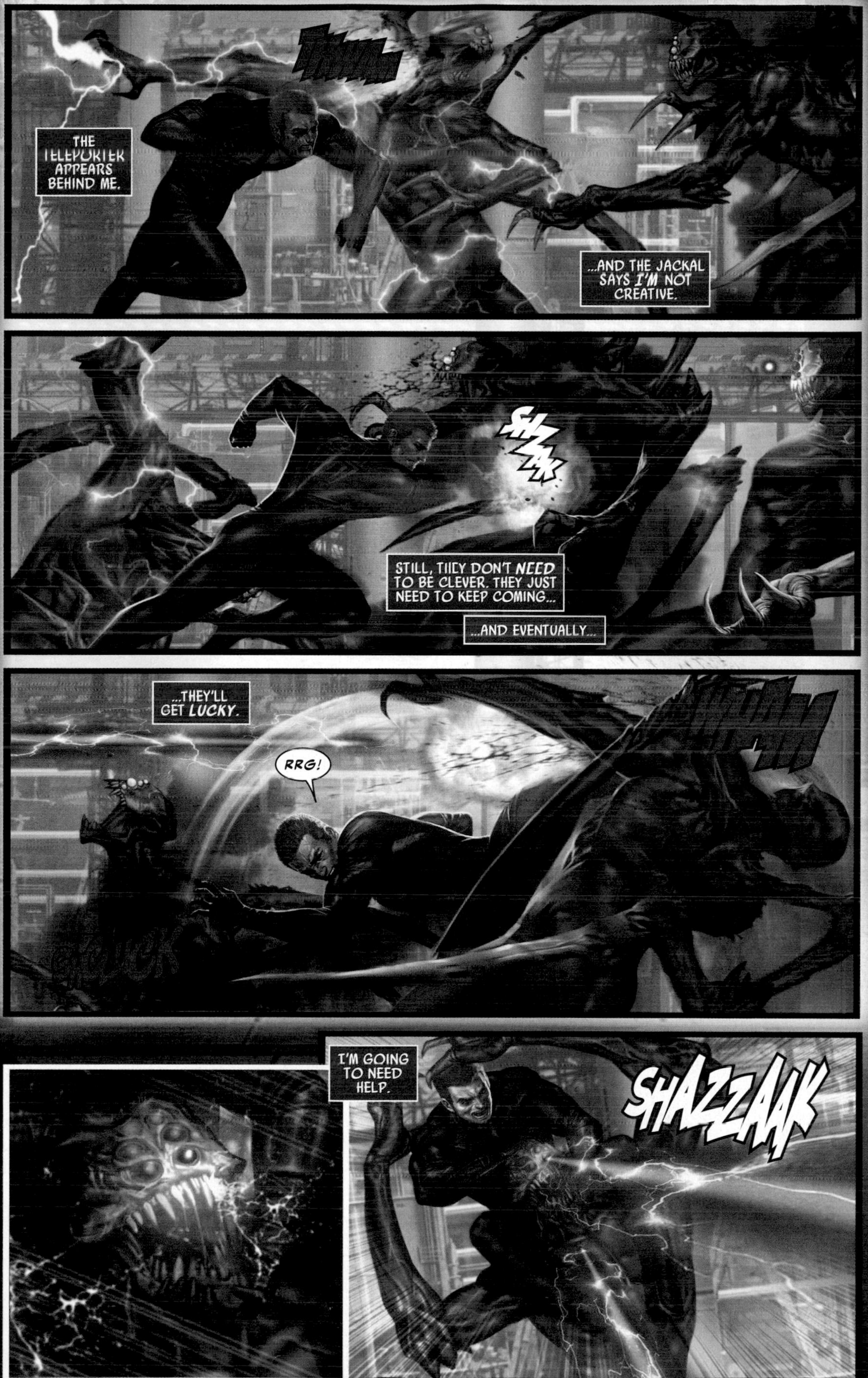

THE TELEPORTER APPEARS BEHIND ME.
...AND THE JACKAL SAYS I'M NOT CREATIVE.
SHZAK
STILL, THEY DON'T NEED TO BE CLEVER. THEY JUST NEED TO KEEP COMING...
...AND EVENTUALLY...
...THEY'LL GET LUCKY.
RRG!
I'M GOING TO NEED HELP.
SHAZZAAK

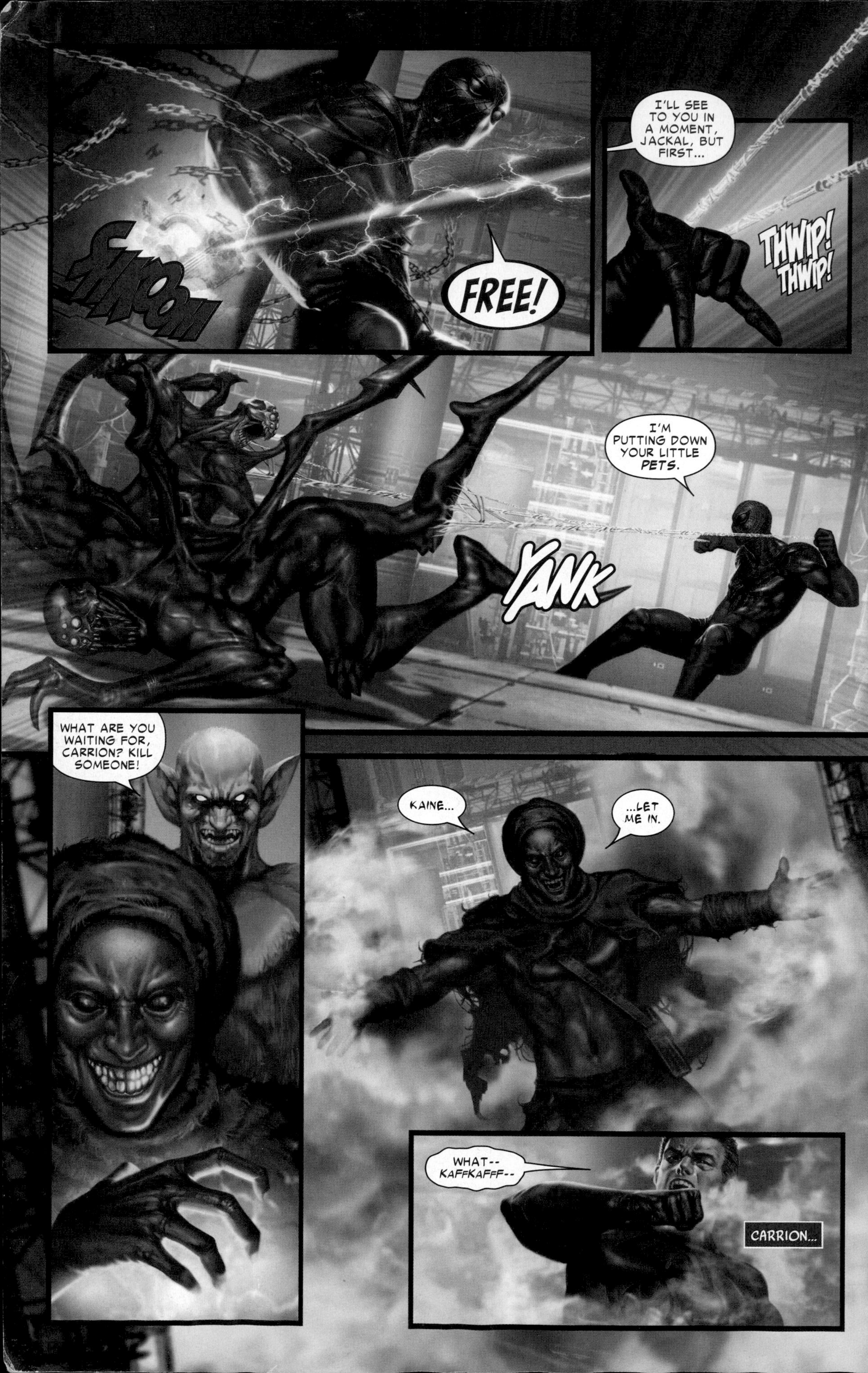
SHOOM
FREE!
I'LL SEE TO YOU IN A MOMENT, JACKAL, BUT FIRST...
THWIP! THWIP!
I'M PUTTING DOWN YOUR LITTLE PETS.
YANK
WHAT ARE YOU WAITING FOR, CARRION? KILL SOMEONE!
KAINE...
...LET ME IN.
WHAT-- KAFFKAFFF--
CARRION...

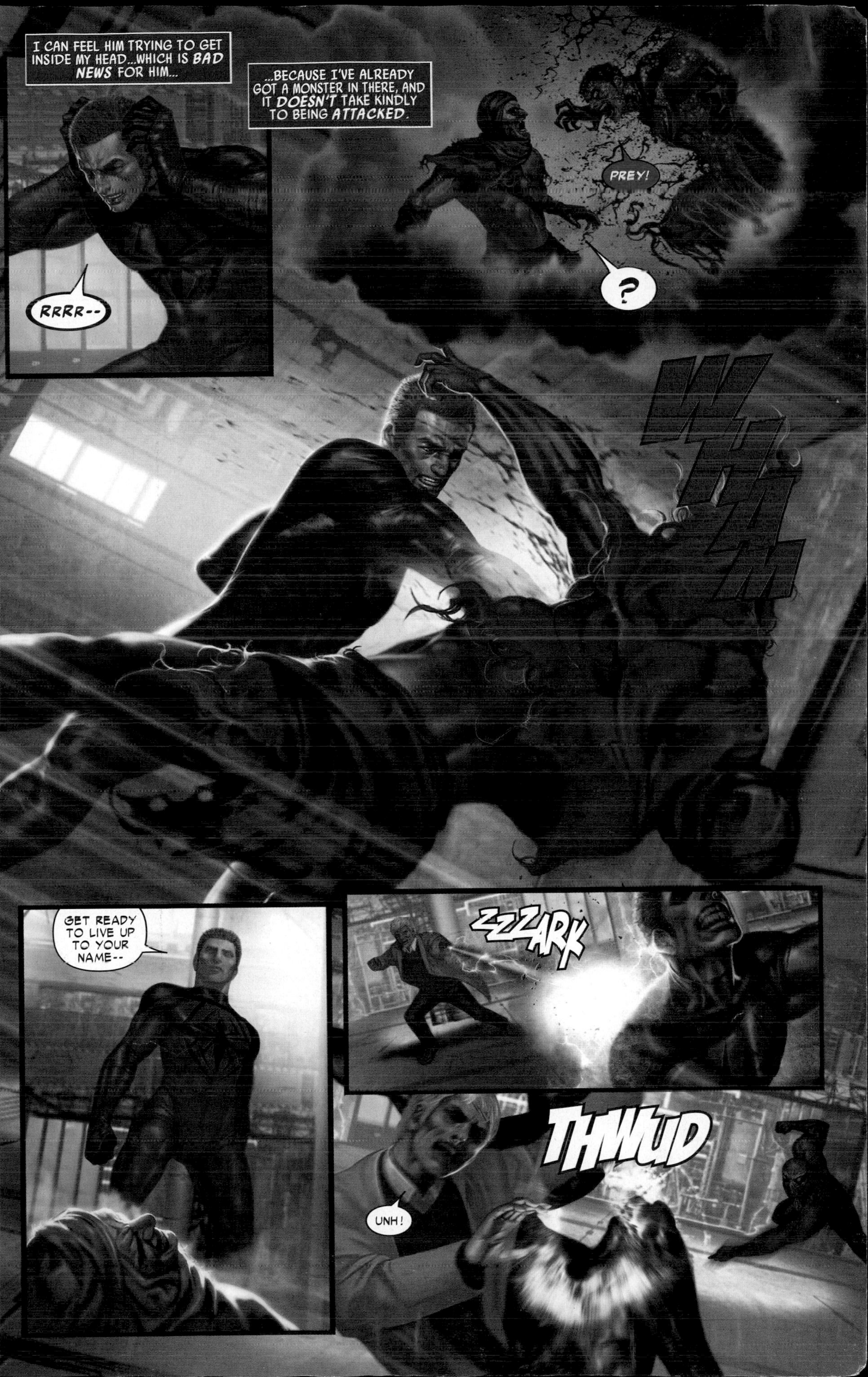
I CAN FEEL HIM TRYING TO GET INSIDE MY HEAD...WHICH IS BAD NEWS FOR HIM...
RRRR--
...BECAUSE I'VE ALREADY GOT A MONSTER IN THERE, AND IT DOESN'T TAKE KINDLY TO BEING ATTACKED.
PREY!
?
WHAM
GET READY TO LIVE UP TO YOUR NAME--
ZZZARK
THWUD
UNH!

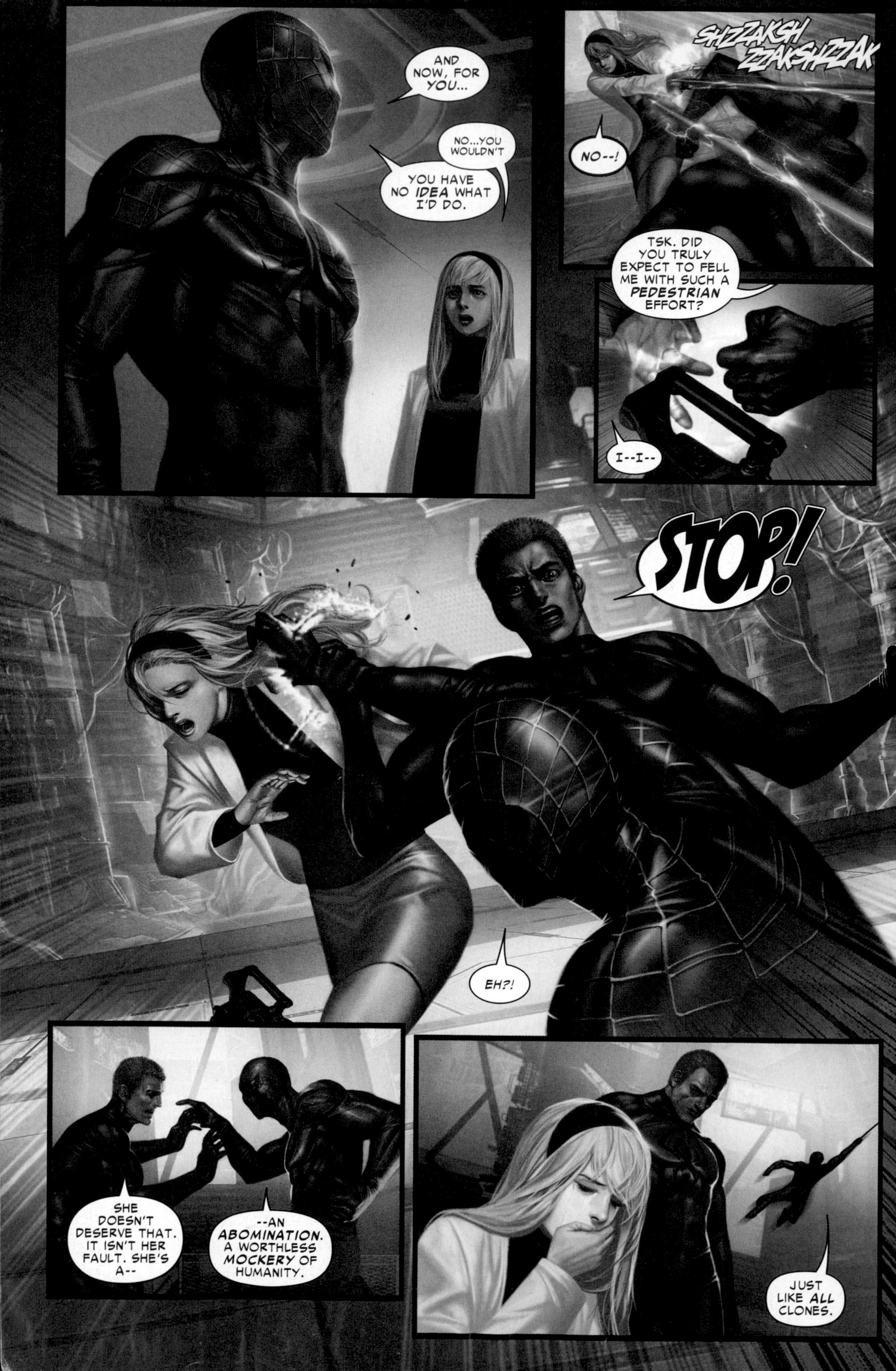
AND NOW, FOR YOU...
NO...YOU WOULDN'T
YOU HAVE NO IDEA WHAT I'D DO.
SHZZAKSH ZZAKSHZZAK
NO--!
TSK. DID YOU TRULY EXPECT TO FELL ME WITH SUCH A PEDESTRIAN EFFORT?
I--I--
STOP!
EH?!
SHE DOESN'T DESERVE THAT. IT ISN'T HER FAULT. SHE'S A--
--AN ABOMINATION. A WORTHLESS MOCKERY OF HUMANITY.
JUST LIKE ALL CLONES.

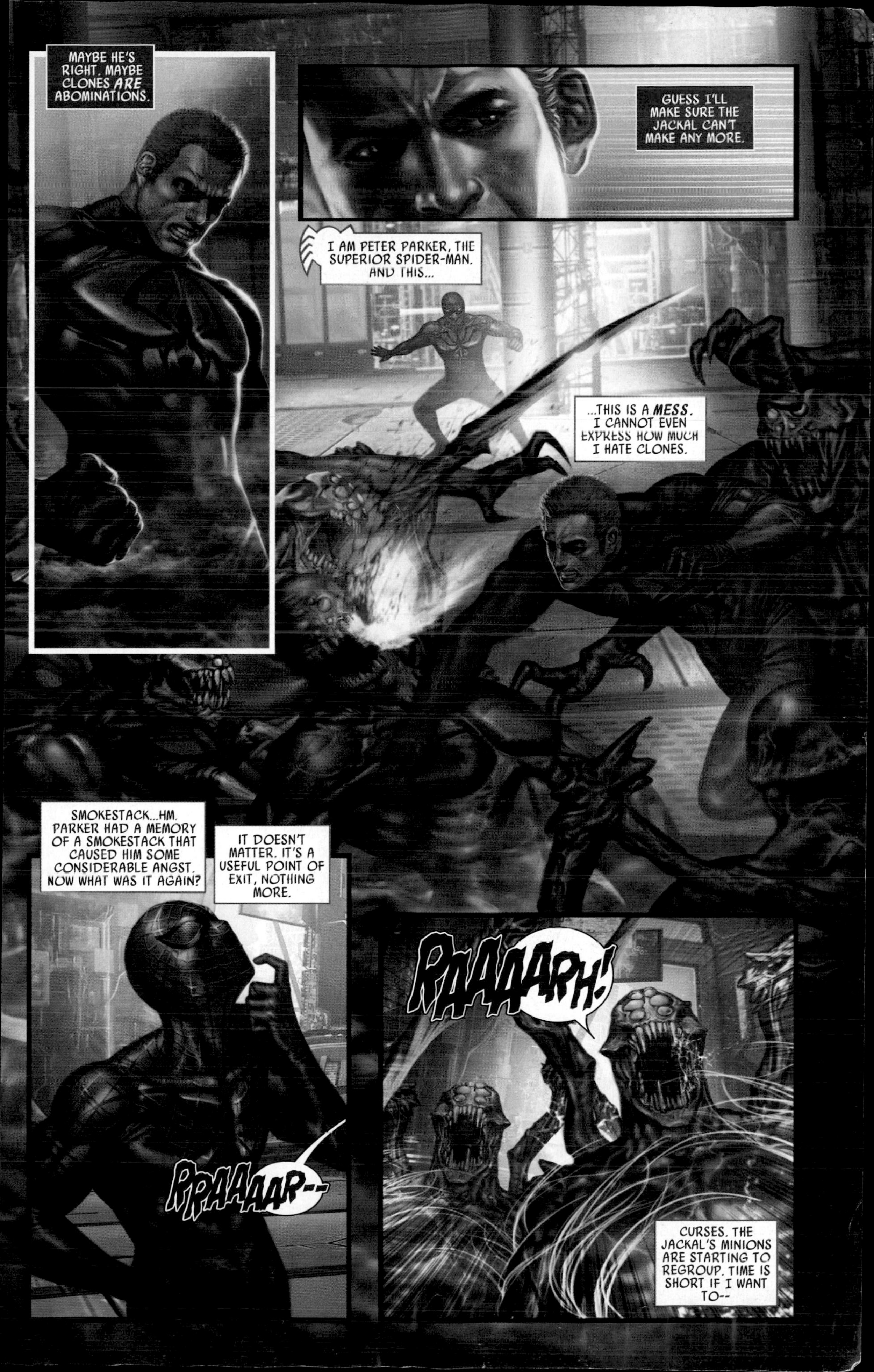
MAYBE HE'S RIGHT. MAYBE CLONES *ARE* ABOMINATIONS.
GUESS I'LL MAKE SURE THE JACKAL CAN'T MAKE ANY MORE.
I AM PETER PARKER, THE SUPERIOR SPIDER-MAN. AND THIS...
...THIS IS A **MESS.** I CANNOT EVEN EXPRESS HOW MUCH I HATE CLONES.
SMOKESTACK...HM. PARKER HAD A MEMORY OF A SMOKESTACK THAT CAUSED HIM SOME CONSIDERABLE ANGST. NOW WHAT WAS IT AGAIN?
IT DOESN'T MATTER. IT'S A USEFUL POINT OF EXIT, NOTHING MORE.
RRAAAAR--
RAAAAARH!
CURSES. THE JACKAL'S MINIONS ARE STARTING TO REGROUP. TIME IS SHORT IF I WANT TO--

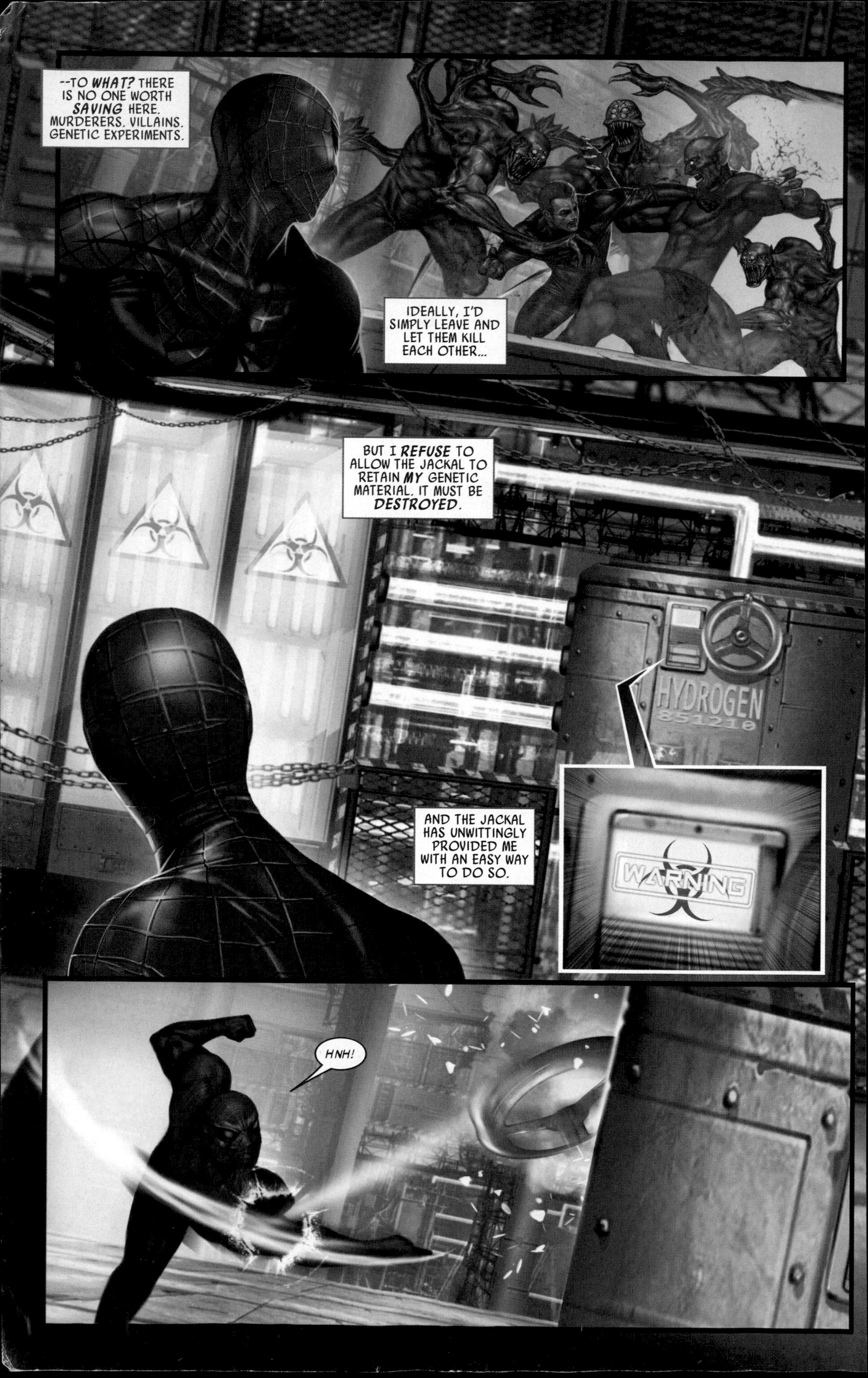
--TO *WHAT?* THERE IS NO ONE WORTH *SAVING* HERE. MURDERERS. VILLAINS. GENETIC EXPERIMENTS.
IDEALLY, I'D SIMPLY LEAVE AND LET THEM KILL EACH OTHER...
BUT I *REFUSE* TO ALLOW THE JACKAL TO RETAIN *MY* GENETIC MATERIAL. IT MUST BE *DESTROYED*.
HYDROGEN
851210
AND THE JACKAL HAS UNWITTINGLY PROVIDED ME WITH AN EASY WAY TO DO SO.
WARNING
HNH!

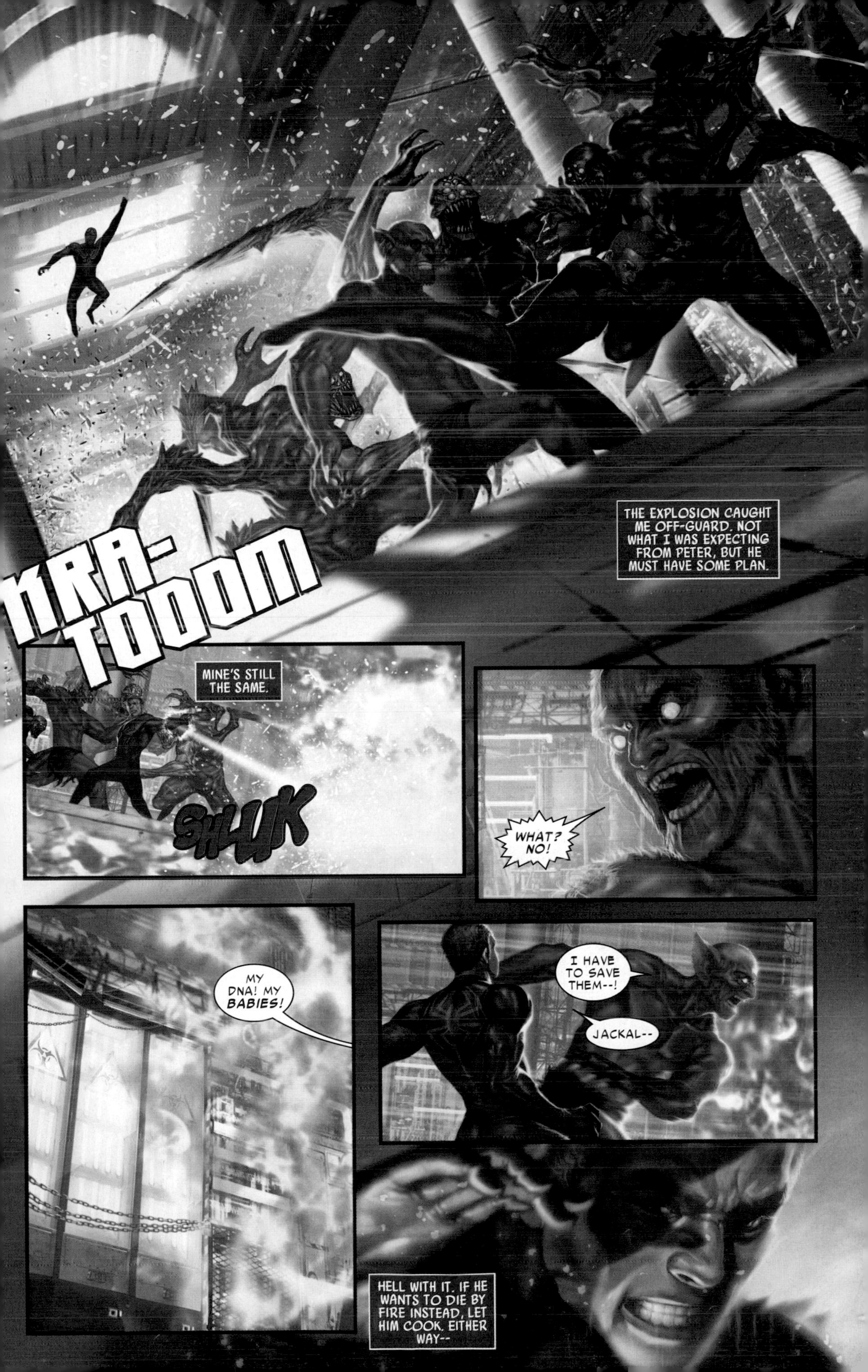
THE EXPLOSION CAUGHT ME OFF-GUARD. NOT WHAT I WAS EXPECTING FROM PETER, BUT HE MUST HAVE SOME PLAN.
KRA-TOOOM
MINE'S STILL THE SAME.
SHLUK
WHAT? NO!
MY DNA! MY BABIES!
I HAVE TO SAVE THEM--!
JACKAL--
HELL WITH IT. IF HE WANTS TO DIE BY FIRE INSTEAD, LET HIM COOK. EITHER WAY--

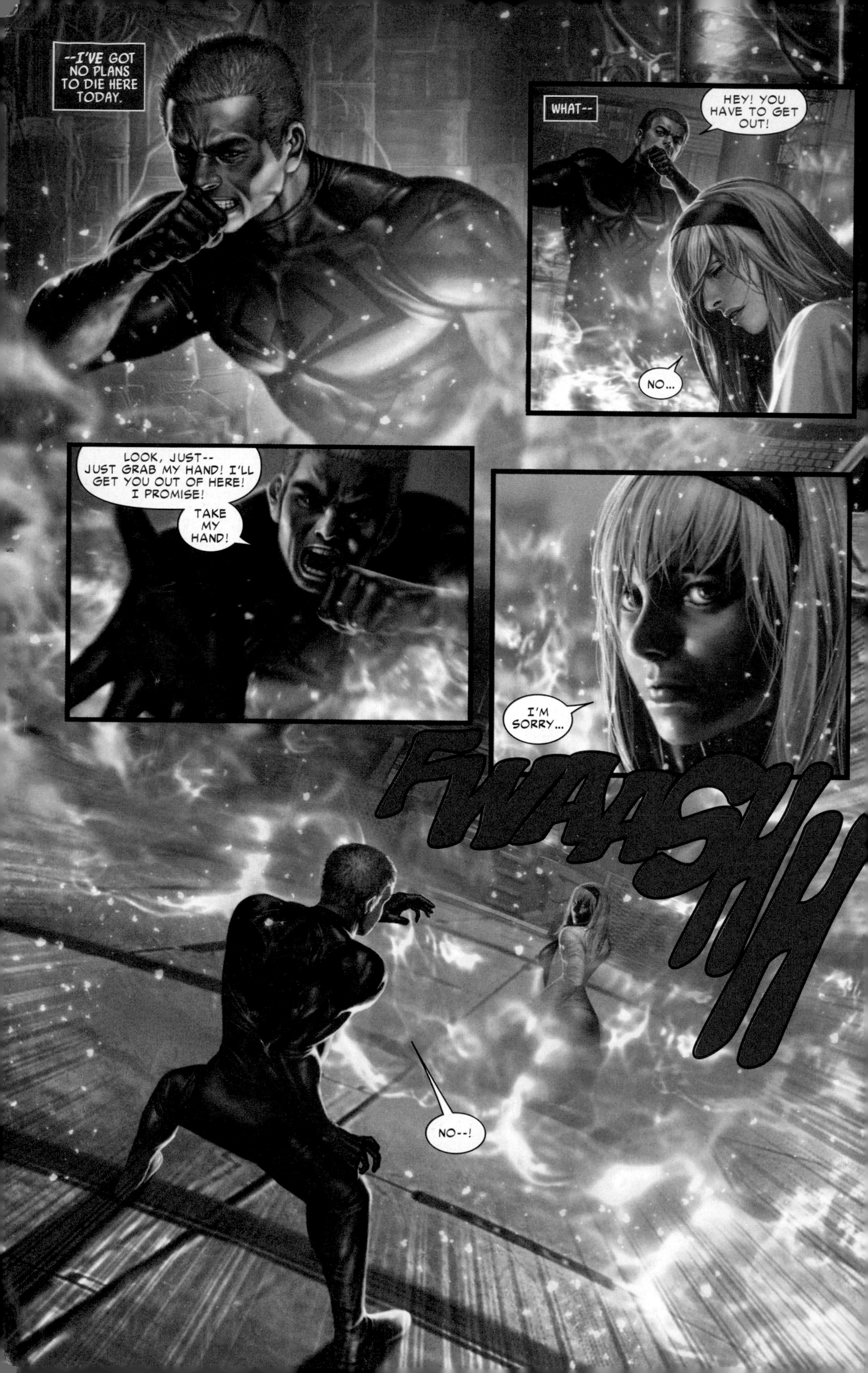
--I'VE GOT NO PLANS TO DIE HERE TODAY.
WHAT--
HEY! YOU HAVE TO GET OUT!
NO...
LOOK, JUST-- JUST GRAB MY HAND! I'LL GET YOU OUT OF HERE! I PROMISE!
TAKE MY HAND!
I'M SORRY...
FWAASHH
NO--!

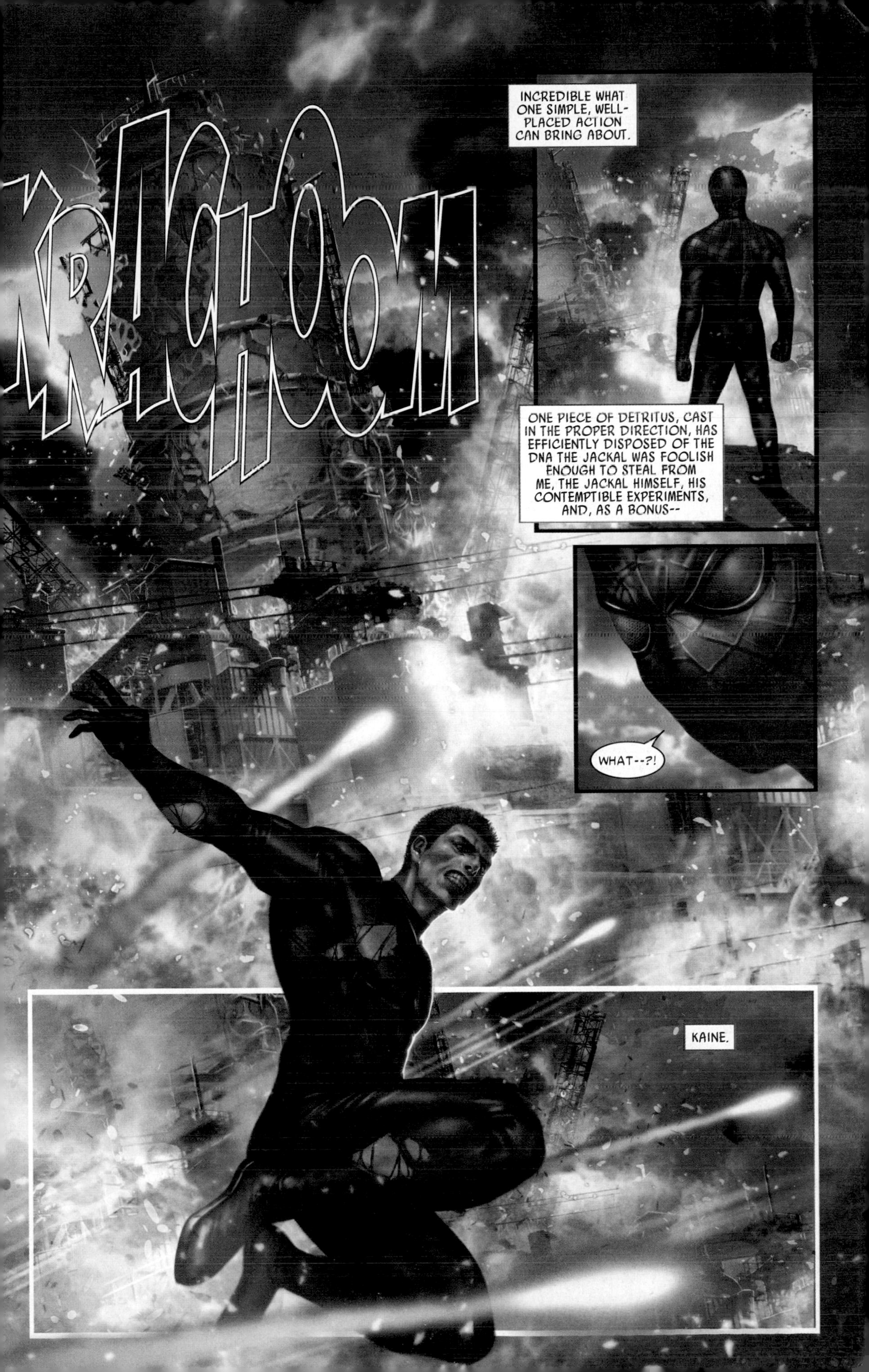
KRAKOOM
INCREDIBLE WHAT ONE SIMPLE, WELL-PLACED ACTION CAN BRING ABOUT.
ONE PIECE OF DETRITUS, CAST IN THE PROPER DIRECTION, HAS EFFICIENTLY DISPOSED OF THE DNA THE JACKAL WAS FOOLISH ENOUGH TO STEAL FROM ME, THE JACKAL HIMSELF, HIS CONTEMPTIBLE EXPERIMENTS, AND, AS A BONUS--
WHAT--?!
KAINE.

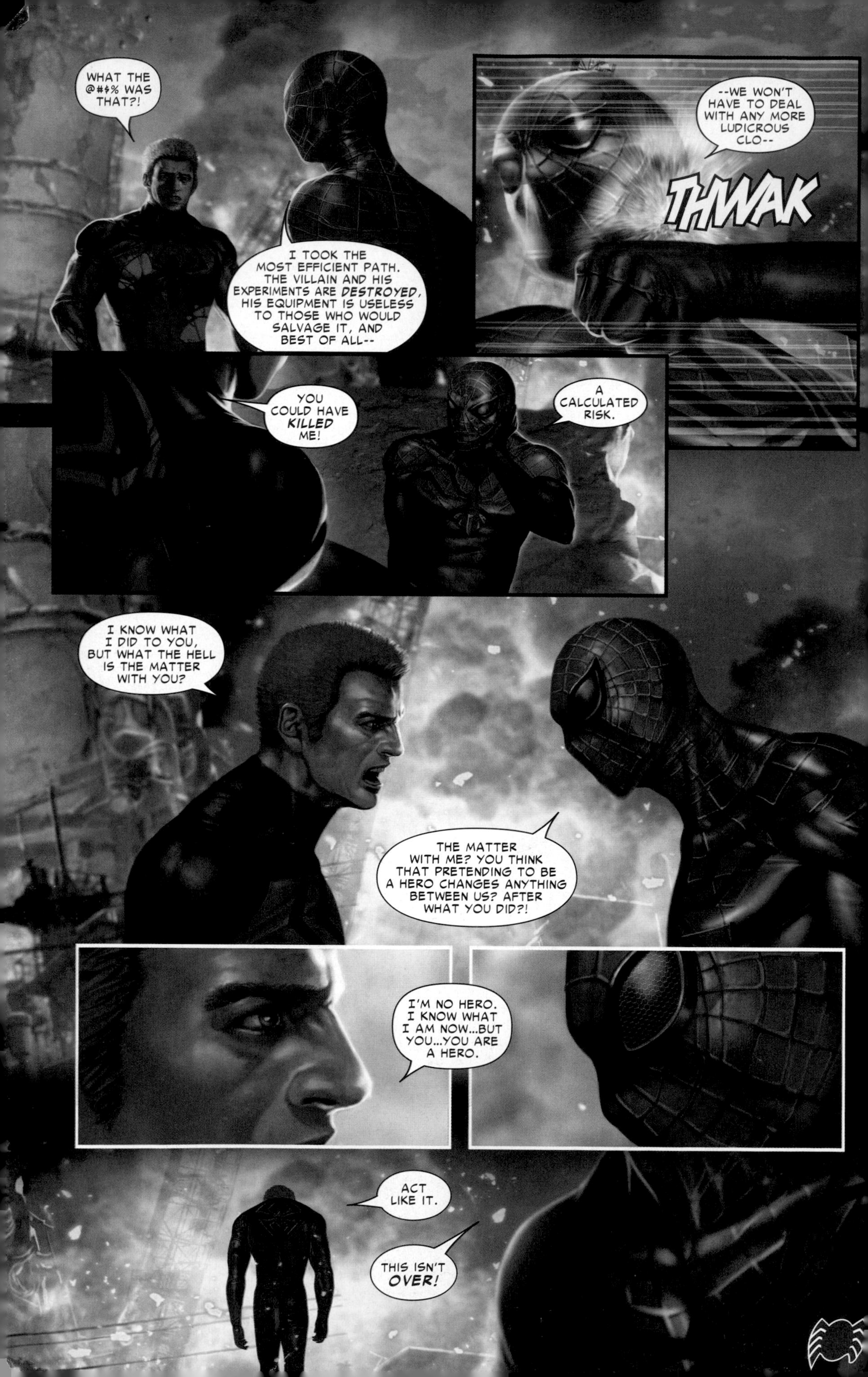
WHAT THE @#$% WAS THAT?!
I TOOK THE MOST EFFICIENT PATH. THE VILLAIN AND HIS EXPERIMENTS ARE DESTROYED, HIS EQUIPMENT IS USELESS TO THOSE WHO WOULD SALVAGE IT, AND BEST OF ALL--
--WE WON'T HAVE TO DEAL WITH ANY MORE LUDICROUS CLO--
THWAK
YOU COULD HAVE KILLED ME!
A CALCULATED RISK.
I KNOW WHAT I DID TO YOU, BUT WHAT THE HELL IS THE MATTER WITH YOU?
THE MATTER WITH ME? YOU THINK THAT PRETENDING TO BE A HERO CHANGES ANYTHING BETWEEN US? AFTER WHAT YOU DID?!
I'M NO HERO. I KNOW WHAT I AM NOW...BUT YOU...YOU ARE A HERO.
ACT LIKE IT.
THIS ISN'T OVER!

Epilogue.

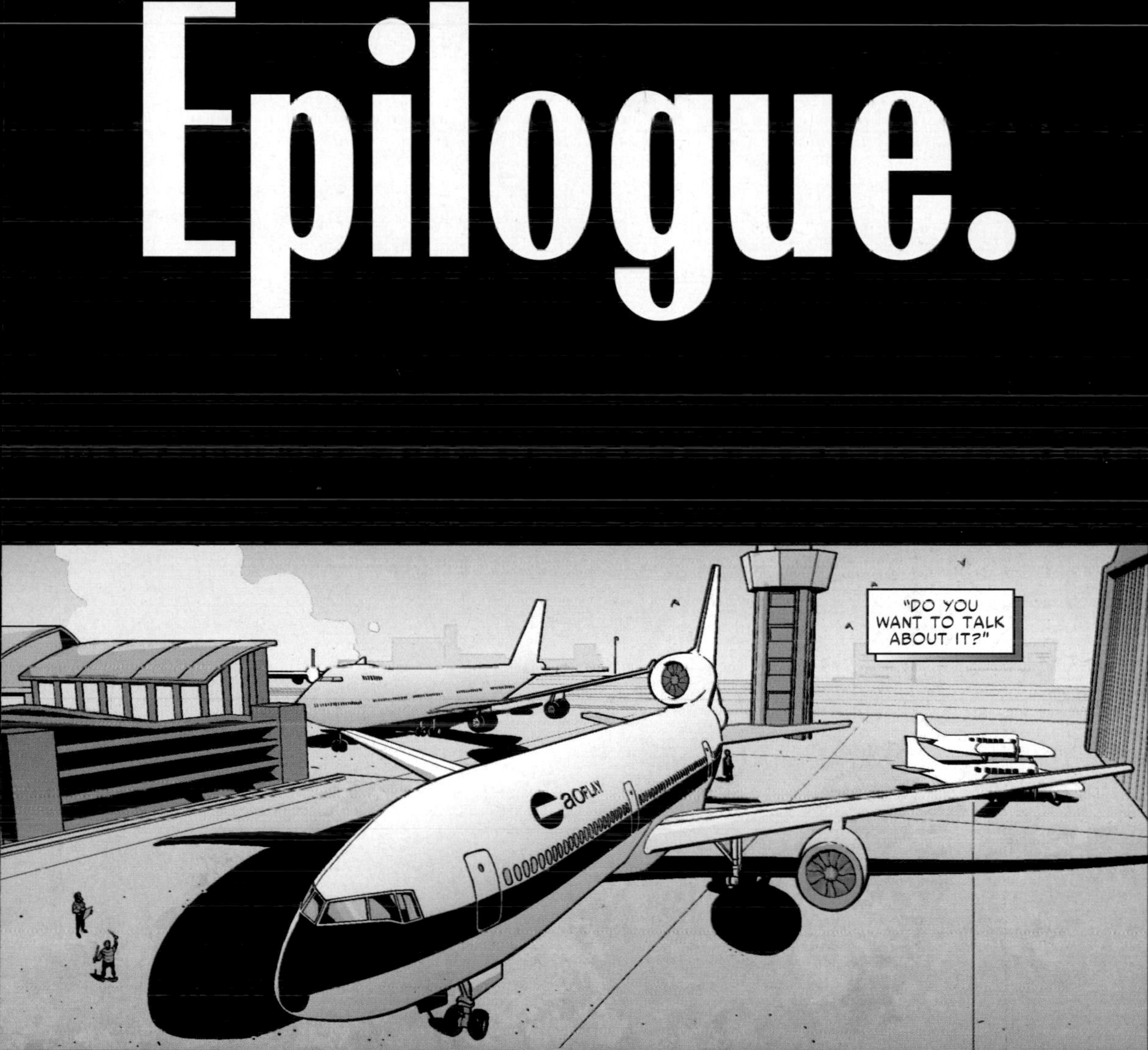
"DO YOU WANT TO TALK ABOUT IT?"

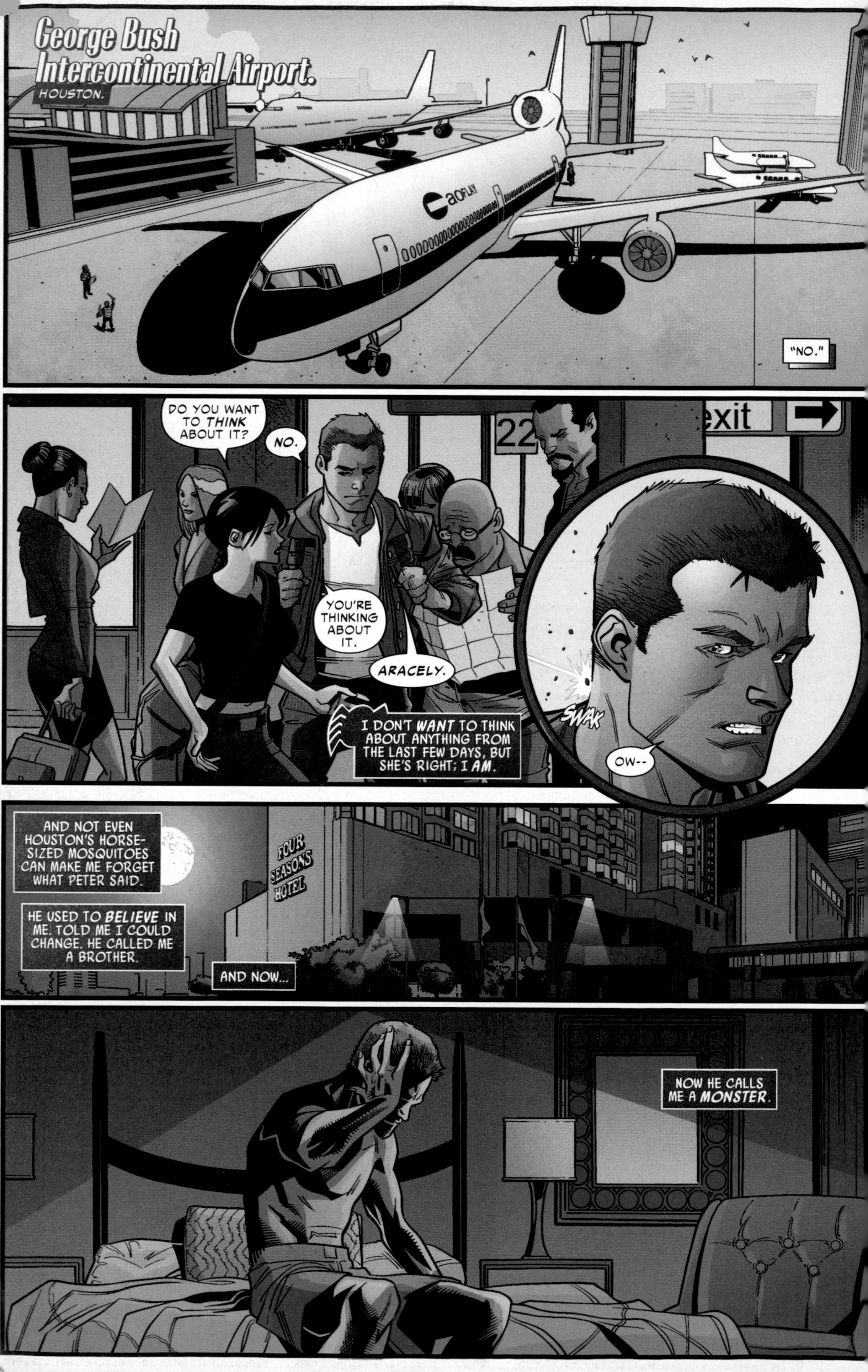
George Bush Intercontinental Airport.
HOUSTON.
"NO."
DO YOU WANT TO THINK ABOUT IT?
NO.
exit
22
YOU'RE THINKING ABOUT IT.
ARACELY.
I DON'T WANT TO THINK ABOUT ANYTHING FROM THE LAST FEW DAYS, BUT SHE'S RIGHT; I AM.
SWAK
OW--
AND NOT EVEN HOUSTON'S HORSE-SIZED MOSQUITOES CAN MAKE ME FORGET WHAT PETER SAID.
FOUR SEASONS HOTEL
HE USED TO BELIEVE IN ME. TOLD ME I COULD CHANGE. HE CALLED ME A BROTHER.
AND NOW...
NOW HE CALLS ME A MONSTER.

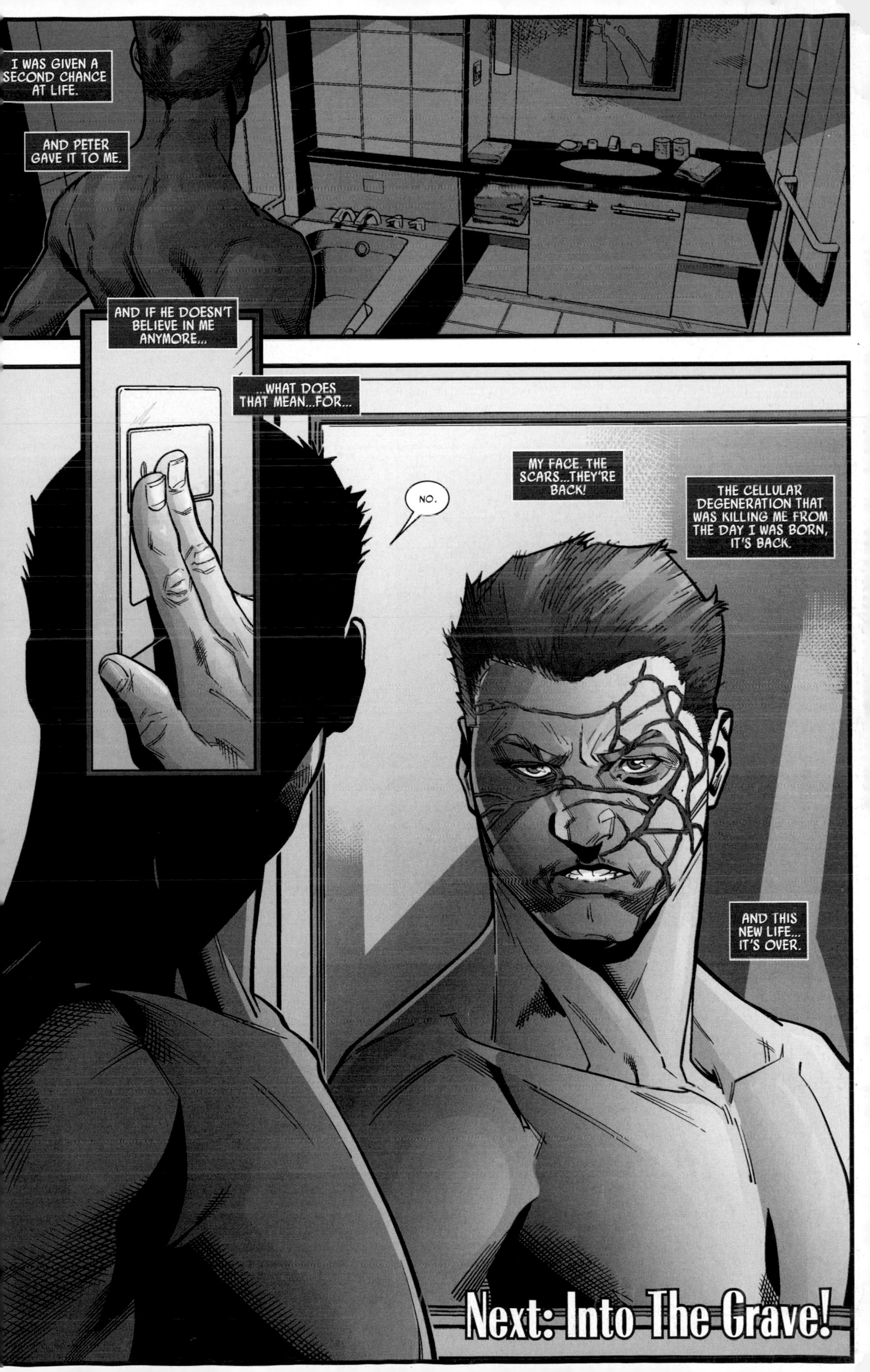

I WAS GIVEN A SECOND CHANCE AT LIFE.
AND PETER GAVE IT TO ME.
AND IF HE DOESN'T BELIEVE IN ME ANYMORE...
...WHAT DOES THAT MEAN...FOR...
NO.
MY FACE. THE SCARS...THEY'RE BACK!
THE CELLULAR DEGENERATION THAT WAS KILLING ME FROM THE DAY I WAS BORN, IT'S BACK.
AND THIS NEW LIFE... IT'S OVER.
Next: Into The Grave!

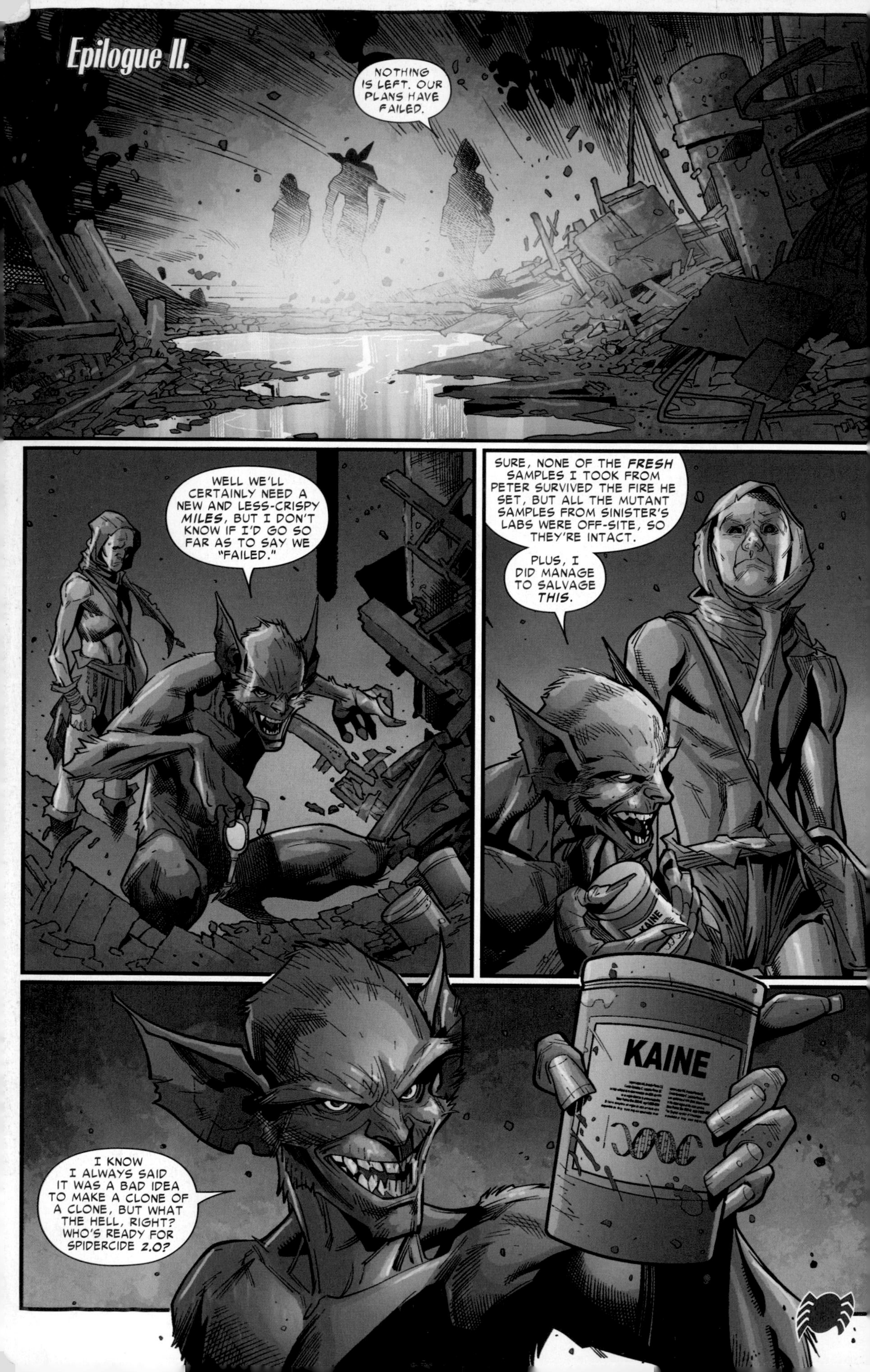
Epilogue II.
NOTHING IS LEFT. OUR PLANS HAVE FAILED.
WELL WE'LL CERTAINLY NEED A NEW AND LESS-CRISPY MILES, BUT I DON'T KNOW IF I'D GO SO FAR AS TO SAY WE "FAILED."
SURE, NONE OF THE FRESH SAMPLES I TOOK FROM PETER SURVIVED THE FIRE HE SET, BUT ALL THE MUTANT SAMPLES FROM SINISTER'S LABS WERE OFF-SITE, SO THEY'RE INTACT.
PLUS, I DID MANAGE TO SALVAGE THIS.
KAINE
I KNOW I ALWAYS SAID IT WAS A BAD IDEA TO MAKE A CLONE OF A CLONE, BUT WHAT THE HELL, RIGHT? WHO'S READY FOR SPIDERCIDE 2.0?

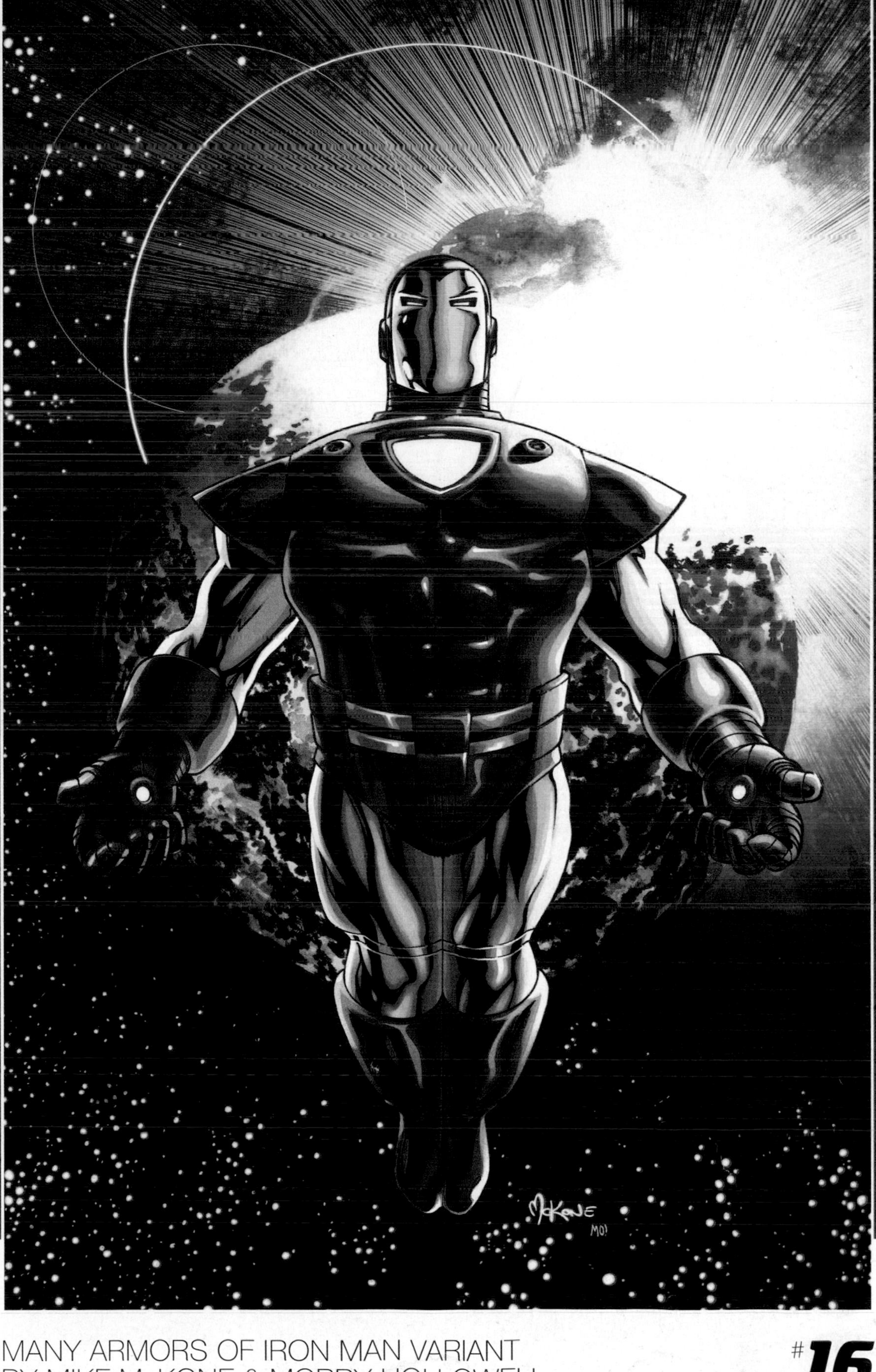

MANY ARMORS OF IRON MAN VARIANT
BY MIKE McKONE & MORRY HOLLOWELL

#16

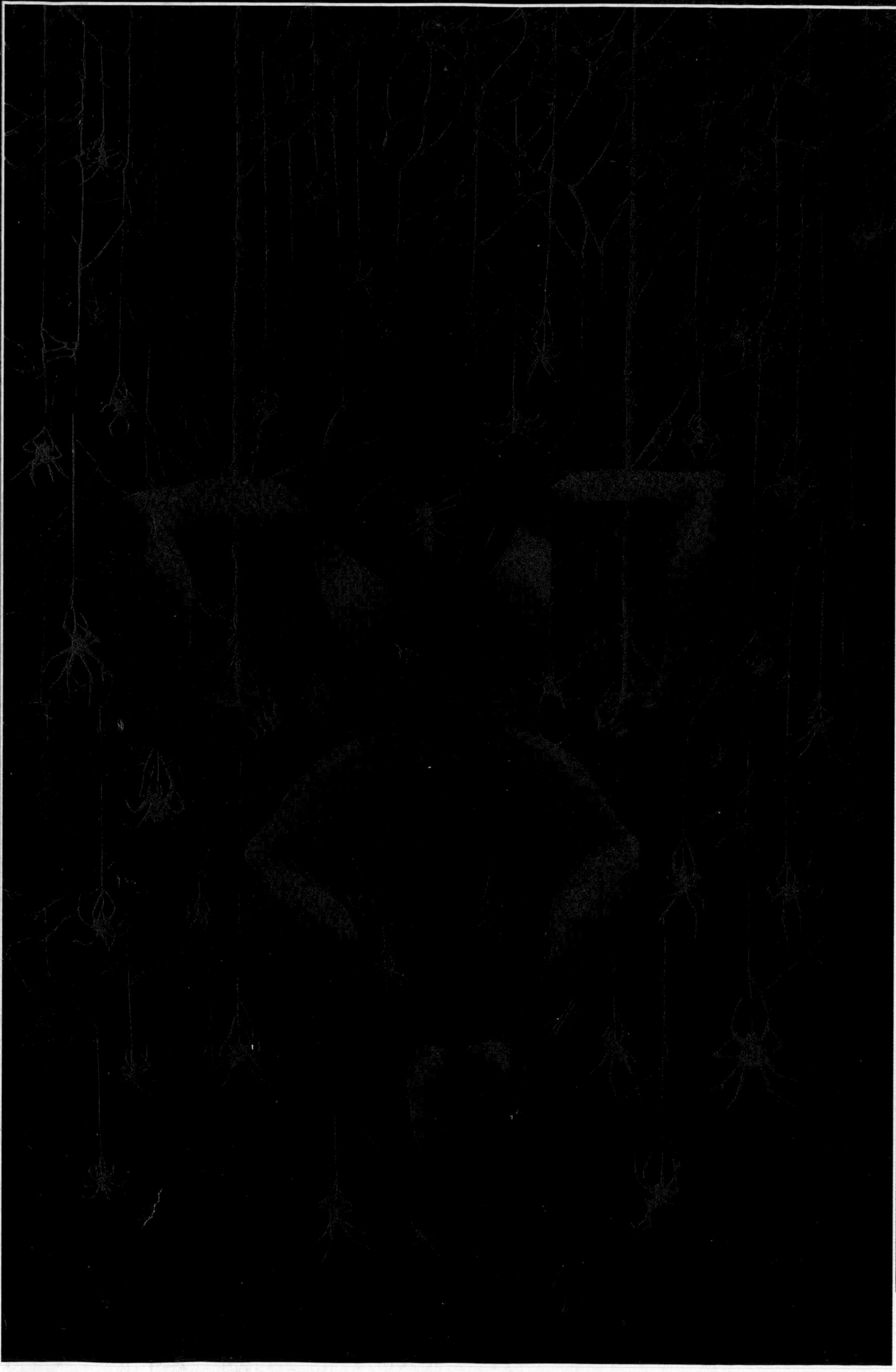

#17

VARIANT BY GABRIELE DELL'OTTO

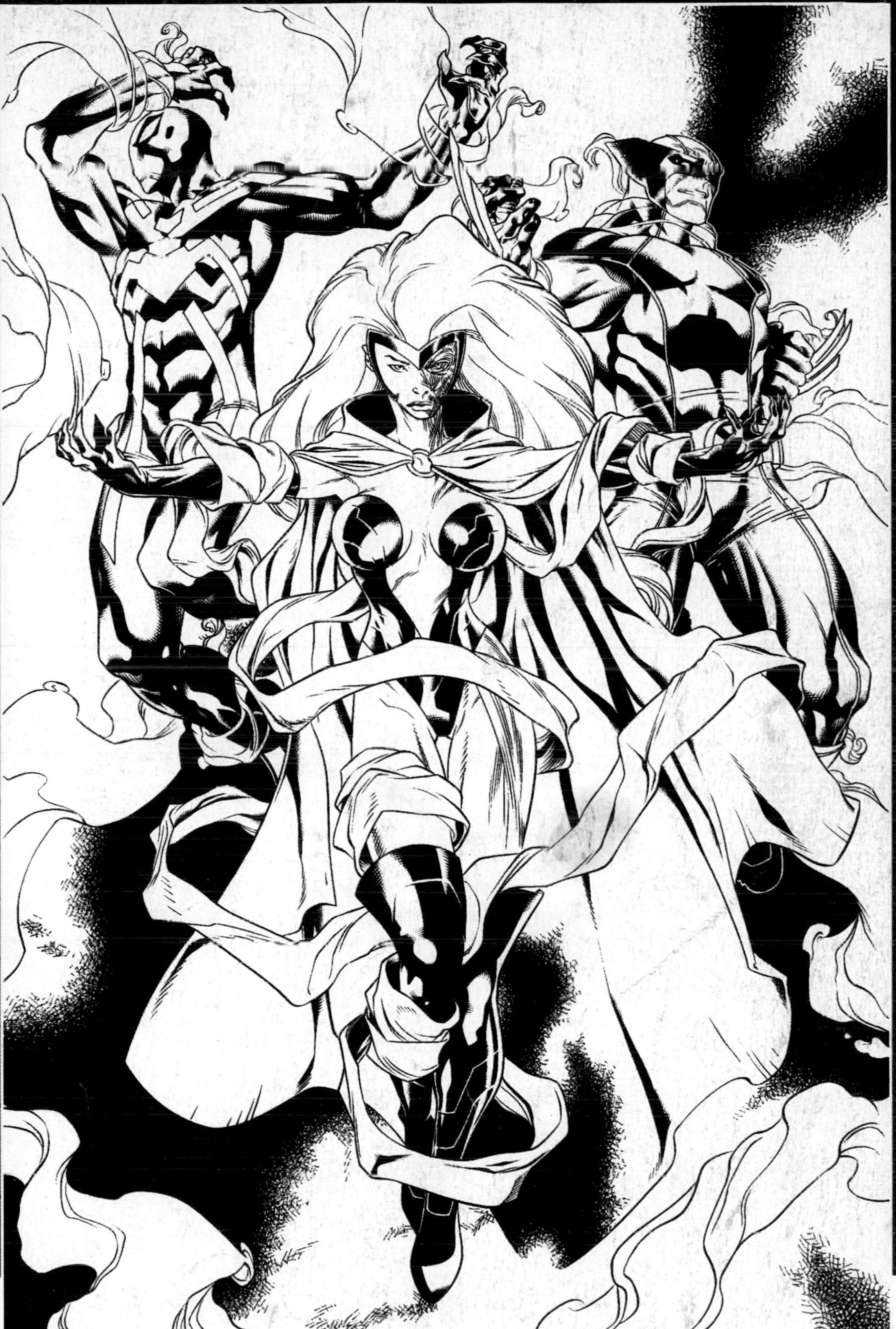

PAGE 2 ART BY CARLO BARBERI & WALDEN WONG

#19

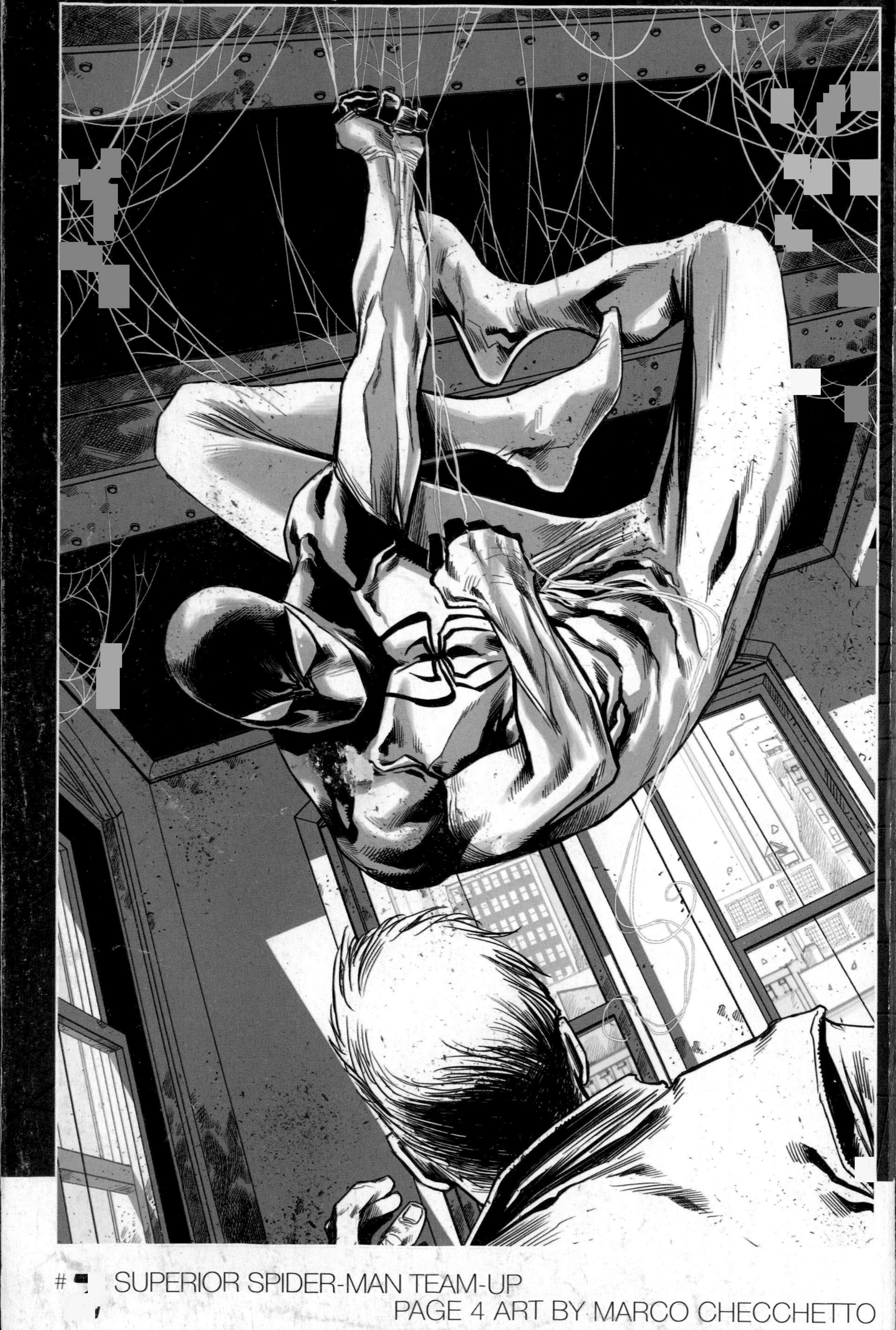

SUPERIOR SPIDER-MAN TEAM-UP

PAGE 4 ART BY MARCO CHECCHETTO